ACTOR
MOVEMENT

ACTOR MOVEMENT:

Expression of the Physical Being

A Movement Handbook for Actors

VANESSA EWAN AND DEBBIE GREEN

Bloomsbury Methuen Drama
An imprint of Bloomsbury Publishing Plc

B L O O M S B U R Y
LONDON • NEW DELHI • NEW YORK • SYDNEY

Bloomsbury Methuen Drama
An imprint of Bloomsbury Publishing Plc

50 Bedford Square	1385 Broadway
London	New York
WC1B 3DP	NY 10018
UK	USA

www.bloomsbury.com

**BLOOMSBURY, METHUEN DRAMA and the Diana logo are
trademarks of Bloomsbury Publishing Plc**

First published 2015

British Library Cataloguing-in-Publication Data
A catalogue record for this book is available from the British Library.

ISBN: PB: 978-1-4081-3441-2
ePDF: 978-1-4081-6612-3
ePUB: 978-1-4081-6613-0

Library of Congress Cataloging-in-Publication Data
A catalog record for this book is available from the Library of Congress.

Typeset by Fakenham Prepress Solutions, Fakenham, Norfolk NR21 8NN
Printed and bound in India

To all actors

CONTENTS

ACKNOWLEDGEMENTS

We would like to thank the many people who have supported the work on this book both directly and indirectly, including the following:

All the actors with whom we have worked and had the privilege to teach, including all those on the 3-Year Acting Course at The Royal Central School of Speech and Drama 1989 –to date.

Jenny Ridout and John O'Donovan at Bloomsbury Methuen Drama, for their ongoing support and belief in the book and Kim Storry and the team at Fakenham Prepress for their calm and utterly professional handling of the final stage.

All at Central, in particular the Research Department, the 3-Year Acting Course and MA Movement teams, including Peter McAllister and Claudette Williams of the BA and both Nick Moseley of the BA and Ayse Tashkiran of the MA for their patience and support through sabbatical and teaching cover.

All those who supported the development of the writing of the book itself: Jake Harders and Kate Sagovsky for their respective editing work during the developmental process – Jake for giving vital detailed feedback from an actor's perspective as the book progressed; and Kate who offered such intelligence and heart in her contributions. Also Jane Dickson, for her steady and skilful way with words just at the right time, alleviating a panic attack. Lorna Marshall for her invaluable feedback as a reader and astute advice in the early stages of writing. Roanna Mitchell and Sue Mythen for their contributions to the research process, including collation of Ewan's material that informed the writing on Neutral Mask and Laban Efforts work respectively. Richard Whelan and Bret Yount for the material on specific professional guidelines for Chapter 9.

All who acted as readers and contributed their thoughts on the writing of the work, namely Abby Eletz, Peter Elliott, Nina Fog, Jenny Frankel, Sarah Henderson, Alexander Neal, Jenny Ogilvie, Sinéad O'Keeffe, Dominic Rouse, Debbie Seymour, Milly Thomas and Sue Weston.

To all the actors involved in the imagery for the book and video content, with particular thanks to Vivienne Bell; Nina Fog; Lynsey Murrell; Luke Norris; Sinéad O'Keeffe and Matt Tait. Also Taylor Frost; Reece Richardson; Reice Weathers and Rob Wilkinson; and all those involved in creating the imagery,

Patrick Baldwin, Pavel Dousek, Toby Elwes, Todd Padwick and Richard Williams.

With special thanks to Ken Mizutani (video content editor) and everyone else who made the video content possible: thank you Peter Elliott; Peter Todd (camera work); Kyle Horne and Todd Padwick (additional camera work).

And lastly, the greatest thanks of all to the essential network of support that has made the book possible, the friends, particularly Christopher Marlowe, and family members Buz, Harry, Jemima, Matilda, Peter, Phoebe, Rowan, Simone and Todd who have all given their unconditional love and support during the process of writing and editing.

INTRODUCTION

Who the Book is For

This book is for the actor who realizes that using 'movement' for expression in acting is not something he was born knowing how to do, but who wants to offer it in performance, in all its complexity and range, *as* if it were something he was born knowing how to do.

Actor Movement is for the student, the working actor and all those who lead and witness the work of movement for the actor including movement tutors, choreographers, movement directors and directors.

How the Book is Structured

Each chapter is constructed in three parts in increasing detail: the first part gives a brief overview of the chapter; the second part gives an explanation of the underpinning philosophy of the work; the third part then offers detailed practical exercises and explorations. These are for the actor working alone unless otherwise stated.

Throughout the book and particularly within the practical sections there are 'In Context' insert boxes which offer suggestions for direct application of the particular work for the professional actor in rehearsal or performance context.

The video content offers readers a visual insight into the experience of an exercise or a process outlined in the text – the symbol ▶ appears next to sections where there is relevant video content. All videos can be seen at https://vimeo.com/channels/actormovement/. Links to the individual videos are printed at the back of the book.

Themes in the Book

Actor Movement as a subject works from the principle that each actor is unique, and has a unique way of seeing and being in the world, and aims to develop the individual actor's body and expressive potential. To this end, *Actor Movement* does not focus on what the actor is able to 'do' *per se*, for example, learning the foxtrot, the skill of which is generally applicable to all actors regardless of their individuality. Rather, the intention is to offer ways of thinking and working for actors and movement practitioners – ways that enable precision and ease in a full range of physical activity for each individual. The book works on the premise that the actor has to own, embody and believe in his own choices. It offers the tools and the crafting through exercises that can be used by the actor on his own or under the guidance of a teacher to develop and fine-tune his intuitive physical responses.

The reader is encouraged to begin and maintain an ongoing process where he responds to movement every day via observation, practical experience and reflection. Such a process can then in theory be applied to any potential acting work. Some chapters do include group work and although the book does not offer development of a company or of a rehearsal group, groups can work together on individual exercises which cumulatively can assist their ensemble work. Its eye, however, is principally on an individual's journey and the unique nature of that journey.

For the trained actor, the exercises, processes and journeys in the book can be personally adapted for specific acting tasks or, indeed, for any general movement class. It is easy to lose what was learned at the beginning of actor training – all actors must move forward and some lessons are inevitably left behind. However, that knowledge can easily be reaccessed or reinterpreted and potentially enhanced through additional processes. This book provides that possibility for the actor who wishes to engage with his craft in an ongoing process.

The writing reflects the philosophy of the movement curriculum experienced by actors on the 3-Year Acting course at The Royal Central School of Speech and Drama. For those who work in other programme structures, or even have no programme structure at all, *Actor Movement* provides elements of the thinking and practice of a live example of a three-year progression of movement for acting.

Although the book is organized in chapters, this is not a purely linear journey. All of the subjects up to Chapter 5 are designed to work in parallel in practice and can be read as such.

Notes on Gender/Third Person

The actor is referred to in the third person, except within the practical sections[1] when he is addressed directly. This approach allows the actor the space to connect personally, but deliberately also remains open as an invitation to other practitioners to share in exploring the work.

This book is gendered throughout as 'he' for consistency, but speaks equally to both the male and female actor.

About the Authors

Vanessa Ewan and Debbie Green have worked for over 20 years with the actors on the 3-year Acting Course at Central. Working with actors over those two decades has further inspired their work and their respect for its heritage, leading to the development of Actor Movement as a subject, to initiating the creation of the MA in Movement: directing and teaching at Central and most recently to this book.

---

[1] If work is done following the practical sections, movement health and safety regulations should be followed.

1
ACTOR MOVEMENT

OVERVIEW

The actor comes to acting with a personal physical history which includes skills gained through life. It is likely that some of these will be as a result of different sports or dance activities. Recognizing what is of value to him as an actor, and what is not, enables him to make full use of his physical heritage.

For the actor, the study, interrogation and practice of movement is a lifelong commitment, a deepening process of discovery. Awareness of our moving self operates on many levels and so it is important for the actor to explore each level thoroughly.

Traditional Western actor training is generally broken down into Acting, Voice and Movement. Acting and Voice function easily as distinct fields of study and have been amply documented in writing by their leading practitioners. Movement, however, perhaps precisely because it is not of the written word is not as easily captured and so remains under-represented as a field of study. It is scarcely surprising the actor is confused when:

- movement practices, such as yoga or Pilates, are often used exactly the same way for acting as they are for self-improvement or for therapy;
- movement for actors is often perceived as Physical Theatre – creative movement as a performance style for theatre;
- movement work for the actor is often seen as 'acting through movement' rather than 'movement for acting';
- there is such ambiguity surrounding ethical practice within movement work for the actor both in education and in the profession.

In an effort to gain 'movement skills', some actors – possibly at the expense of their acting instincts – give themselves over to a fully systemized movement practice such as martial art, sport or dance. Others take the decision to do no movement work at all.

An Actor Is; An Actor Does

Actor Movement sees the actor as someone who is open-hearted, receptive and naive in a positive (that is, childlike) sense. This is underpinned by an extraordinarily strong determination. The actor is always learning and has a zest for new things, 'collecting' at the same time as moving on and seeing things with a fresh eye, constantly gaining insight from other actors and directors. He is comfortable with the responsibility of a starring role but – simultaneously and equally – relishes being part of a company and an ensemble player. In short, the actor loves, and feels the lure of, being an actor.

Movement is different from dance and different from acting. It is an element of acting. Great actors are not simply great interpreters of text. They are also great interpreters of movement, able to 'embody' all aspects of a character's life. Movement work assists with physical characterization but is also fundamental to an actor's understanding and presentation of personality. The analysing mind lives in the body. It affects and is affected by the body, as are the voice, the spirit, the senses and the dreams of a character.

The Human Condition

Movement relates to the human condition and it is of paramount importance for the actor to understand this relationship. Humans evolve. Behaviour, knowledge and understanding, developed over millions of years, are the actor's currency. Movement, as the human's original and inherent mechanism of communication, speaks eloquently when the actor understands its possibilities and makes it his specialism.

He can be a vehicle for the expression of human nature within all forms and styles of theatre. He is an investigator and storyteller of the human condition.

What then is Actor Movement?

Actor Movement is the name the authors use for the process given to the study of the physical expression of the imagination and body of an actor.

The body communicates whether a person wants to say something or not. Sometimes it contradicts what he says; sometimes it backs him up. It interrupts him, surprises him and makes plain what he feels, even when he is convinced he is offering what he thinks. In short, the body never shuts up. None of us knows completely what our own bodies are saying. Yet an actor has to know.

The body and his imagination are his instruments. In his work he is expected to become many bodies, each behaving differently from his own. He has to construct, inhabit and offer each character's body, with its multiplicity of known and unknown physical expression.

When Actor Movement works it does not show. It looks instinctive because embodiment is accurate within its specific context; the action is in keeping with the character and with the 'world of the play'.[1]

The Body Retains Knowledge

The actor must reach a stage where he can work from instinct, and trust that his body holds any learning.

The actor should remember that while conforming is an important part of community and survival, it is also an obstacle to his acting potential. One of the first tasks of Actor Movement is to guide the actor-in-training away from mediocrity and towards an understanding of what makes him unique. Oscar Wilde's attributed quip 'be yourself, everyone else is already taken' is funny because it is true.

The actor-in-training needs to be shown the routes to self-sufficiency and self-confidence, so that he can continue to develop his bespoke physical process throughout his career. The spirit of work done in training can stay with him.

---

[1] 'World of the play' is a common term which refers to the imagined reality of the play, the world in which a play is set. It is also used here to describe the actual world as observed and seen through the actor's eyes – the actor is encouraged to see the world 'as a play' – as he collects observations.

Basic Philosophy

The action is the story. The story is not the actor doing the expressive movement. The expressive movement is in the body of the actor. The excitement in a performance comes from the character, not the actor. Actor Movement's focus is on the actor as a vehicle to transport the audience.

The actor must aim for a completely 'alive' body which is sensitive to outside stimuli and which can learn to treat the imaginary situation as real. Then he can get on and live in the world of the play.

Acknowledging His Own Physical Heritage

Any actor with a trained body has work ahead of him to access the untrained, natural side of himself. He also possesses much that, once interrogated, can serve his acting. While he may not, for example, have considered his once-weekly ballet class encountered from the age of four to 13 as a specialist movement training, it amounts to 370 hours of accumulated body knowledge.

Most dance and sports in the UK are taught within the school club or Saturday morning ethos, which is grade-, competition- or show-oriented. The focus, for instance, of modern/stage dance is predominantly geared to the commercial market and is 'out front' as entertainment; the dancer moves around the stage, often in spite of the body – its size, shape, quality and aptitude. As a result, there is a desensitizing of the fine moves, of the breath of the movement and of the dancer's personal way of moving.

Changing Perspective

If an actor learned tap aged seven because, for instance, he liked the shoes, tap for him is a pastime not a vocation, and will be remembered as such. However, by revisiting and understanding the resonance, depth and cultural heritage of a technique learned in the past, the actor can change his perspective of it and derive enhanced access to it.

Traces are left in the body from any 'forgotten' practice and the actor can now become aware of these and bring them up to date. Each specialist activity – dance, yoga, Pilates, rugby – leaves a 'mark of design'. For example, tap offers rhythm, flexibility, performance confidence; it has a relationship with 'off balance' and easy movement that is in constant connection to the legs and feet.

The actor who takes skills from his past seriously can recognize what is of value to him as an actor and what is not (the show persona emphatically is not). The childhood perspective has to go. The things the actor liked and disliked about his former pastime can be reassessed.

The Body Remembers it Differently

Specialist development in some areas of movement will mean underdevelopment in other areas. For example, Tae Kwon Do demands strong dynamics, straight lines and a heightened awareness of centre of gravity. Consequently, the playfulness and 'off balance' required by the actor will be compromised or completely repressed.

Complete physical technique is an extraordinary thing for anyone to experience. The practitioner understands a moment of total engagement right through the body, every particle exactingly employed. Although this is good experience for the actor to learn from, he must be able to release himself from total body commitment when necessary. This is hard to do. Each practice has its own 'style' and it is style that keeps dynamics and posture within a limited range. The actor must be able to see beyond the external style and find the essential inner – the essence[2] – of a given movement vocabulary. For example, a ballet dancer walking down the street is not actively engaging his ballet muscles, but they are nevertheless being employed and his walk is influenced, quite radically, by 'turn out' and strong flexion of the feet. If an actor can peel away the external form of the ballet moves and retain the inner motivating sense of uprightness, then he has something useful. It would help him, for example, if he had to play an upper-class character in a period drama.

Look Beyond His Own Improving Actor Body

If he is still fully involved in a physical practice while he is training to be an actor, he may struggle to do anything other than follow his impulse to respond from within technique. This makes transformation particularly challenging until he has learnt to reimagine his existing practice as an actor. An actor's job is to empathize with many ways of being in the world and to transform to any body, fit or unfit. To do this he must look beyond his own, improving actor body.

---

[2] Finding the core, the fundamental nature, real meaning and so on of movement/action is the actor's constant search within his expression.

Examples

Sensitivity

Rugby and football, as teamsports, offer coordination, teamwork, strength, and so on. Warm-up practice includes dexterity of legs and lightness on the feet, reflex physicality and, in the case of rugby, contact work – all useful for acting. Injury is not uncommon: pulled and damaged knees as well as back problems and broken bones and cartilage (nose) breakage. Injuries can become ongoing obstacles to work with. However there is a much less obvious but no less invasive obstacle. Of necessity, over time, team sports players become desensitized to pain and feelings in play. Actors, on the other hand, have to be highly sensitive. This needs to be acknowledged separately in order for the change to happen without losing the other qualities of the rugby player.

Control

It can be that the strengths of certain practices that are normally celebrated need to be unpicked and worked on. The martial artist has, for instance, a practised and strong sense of both self-discipline and existing in a disciplined world. This is an obvious advantage. However, it can mean that there has been a handover of control and therefore a lack of practice in owning decision-making. This has to then be consciously exercised to readdress the balance.

Expression

In ballet, a popular childhood practice, the meaning of each 'gesture' is often not lived, as it is so constantly practised as a technique. The vocabulary is so dense that only the very accomplished have any chance of speaking the language with their bodies at the speed required. For instance, the pirouette is an example of a rich and complex expression of which turning is only a small part. The pirouette is a turn and yet the experience is one of going up, 'spotting' a fixed point and working on a still axis. This has the effect of a turn as a fantastical illusion against all odds. However, an actor must experience the turn and the physical conflict, and not focus on the technique to achieve the illusion. (See Chapter 4, Practical: *Turns Across the Room*.)

These examples illustrate just three of the issues that an actor can become aware of to maximize any past practice. They are offered as guidance; the actor can decide what to reflect on and look out for in his life, in his own time. He can go through this book with his past practice in mind. The practice belongs to him to unpick, and it is perfectly possible to do this whether his background includes Irish or classical Indian dance, tennis or sailing. (See Appendices: *Acknowledging Your Own Physical Past*.)

2
CONNECTING WITH
THE BODY

OVERVIEW

This chapter looks at the fundamentals of movement. The actor learns through 'doing'. He develops an inner relationship with movement, either through group oriented work or by listening, in silence, to his body breathing and moving. This starts with the interior of the body – the skeleton and the breath – and moves onto the connection the actor makes with his body. The aim is to deepen his connection to himself and to other actors.

The human has at his disposal a basic repertoire of movements (walking, running, leaping, skipping, sitting, lying down, and so on); seemingly simple, but endlessly expressive. In order to attain the essential skill of each action, the actor must work on the specialized mechanics within these basic movements (swinging, spiralling, extending, shrinking, and so on).

Gradually, with the introduction of specific movement language, the actor develops a sophisticated level of understanding, coordination, dynamic contrast and physical accuracy. This prepares him for the complex demands of acrobatic, stylized or choreographic movement. The actor's challenge is to develop the grace and fluency of an athlete without acquiring the look of an athlete.

The following are key elements of Movement Fundamentals[1] practice. The journey of this learning[2] can be understood through the practicals following this section, since it is through the experiential that the journey is discovered.

---

[1] Movement Fundamentals is experiential: the actor practises allowing himself to be dictated to by the movement and so with time he discovers the deeper meaning of the movement.
[2] Green's process of work in the studio with the actors.

The Key Elements of Movement Fundamental Practice

Body Work

Body work is the practice of grounding, centring and alignment. The emphasis is on how the whole body is connected – through the breath – from head to toe to fingertip. Bodywork also includes exploration of key points of focus for the actor: feet, pelvis, spine, neck and head.

The actor may believe he needs a mirror for body work. In fact, a mirror is detrimental to this process as it can lead to looking rather than experiencing.

Silence

While movement, like dance, may be perceived as going hand in hand with music, silence brings space for the actor to listen to his body. With no external stimuli to 'tell him' how to move, he is thrown back on his own resources.

Working with music is often an extraordinary experience and can open up extended possibilities of movement. However, it may influence and control the response of the body to the extent that the actor is simply 'moving to the music'. The actor needs to spend a substantial amount of time moving in silence. He meets music only when he can appreciate its power without being carried along by it. (See Chapter 4: Relationship with Music)

Experiential Work

Experiential work offers a space free from analysis. It is an approach that facilitates experience without judgement or censorship and which allows the actor to remain 'open' to physical response.

To be open to things is to be willing to receive. Working experientially requires the actor to be available, curious and patient. The learning becomes clear through an accumulation of present-tense movement experiences. This takes time. Experiential work is exacting; it has purpose and a clear trajectory.

Form

Actors work within a form (the play, the speech, the poem, and so on). Exercises, for the actor-in-training, are an initial encounter with form. Repeating the exercise feeds the imagination through accumulation of detail and awareness. Form offers exploration of personal limits, and repetition expands these boundaries. Each exercise is a journey, enabling rigour and ownership.

Form is, in effect, a limitation, yet in its limitation lies its potency. If, in practice, the form is embellished – even just through overworking – this is an (inadvertent) signpost that form is considered less important than the actor himself. In a form designed to emphasize precision, it is the form that holds the quality. It is not the actor acting 'precise'. Control develops with the advance of technique.

Focus

A strong inner focus needs to be developed right at the start of any experiential process. By envisaging his kinesphere[3] as an imaginary bubble whose boundary he can touch at arm or foot length, the actor has the conditions in which to develop his relationship with personal space undisturbed.

Inner focus means engagement in and awareness of the task at a deep level. The actor learns through his body and must stay on task even when the work is the embodiment of abandon.

Working with eyes shut is not a means to an end. It is one part of the journey. It solves an immediate focus problem but can make the longer journey more difficult. The same is true of zoning out with eyes open. There must be a point at which the focus opens outwards.

A Place to Start

Experiencing the Skeleton

See Practical: *Experiencing the Skeleton* (p. 26)
See Practical: *Visualizing the Skeleton* (p. 27)

By observing a life-size skeleton in the movement studio, the actor learns to associate movement with the structure of the body. This is an opportunity for the actor to become aware of the extraordinary nature of the human frame and its mechanics. He may, for example, be surprised by the amount of space between ribs and pelvis, or by the strong curves of the spine (when there is so much talk of 'standing up straight'). (See Appendices: *Finding a Visceral Language*.)

---

[3]Established movement terminology, but originally a concept from Laban referring to the sphere of space the body takes up as it reaches to its extremities; the actor envisages being at the centre of this imaginary geometrical form created by his reach through the space.

Floor Work

See Practical: *Fluid, Muscular, Flexible You* (p. 28)

The floor offers a personal workspace. Lying down, the actor is less concerned with what is going on around him and therefore more able to immerse himself in the breath of the movement. Being on the floor also shifts the responsibility of weight bearing and balancing from the feet to other areas of the body. Transferring body weight opens up areas of physicality which are denied when the upper body is carrying too much tension or stress. This enables more freedom in movement response.

Working on the floor provides an experience the actor may not have had since early childhood. This association and response is further enhanced by working in 'free-form'. Free-form, as the term suggests, opens up possibilities for physical articulation in a spontaneous way. It liberates the body for movement, physical exaggeration and boldness (which may have been inhibited by the learning of form). At first, floor work may be uncomfortable: the actor may feel his bones 'crunching' on the floor. If this is the case, he can exploit imagery that enables a different response. In exploring how movement quality can be fluid/fleshy/muscular/bony, he can discover how to be compliant with the floor, rather than at odds with it. (See Appendices: *Curl-up*.)

Moving from Floor Work to Standing

See Practical: *Creep to Crawl to Stand to Rise* (p. 30)

By being on the floor, the actor begins to explore being grounded. After a time, however, the floor becomes too compelling; the horizontal is a place of sleep and relaxation, not a place to act. This work moves on; it follows the developmental pattern of supine baby to walking child. It takes the actor from the floor to crouching, kneeling, sitting, going on all fours, lunging on one leg to stand and – finally – to standing and walking.[4] Implicit in the work is the understanding of the progressive nature of the process: crawling, for instance, is a necessary precursor to walking. It also removes any sense that the actor is simply indulging in rolling around on the floor. The actor learns that the pelvis is the source of momentum needed for this progression. It has the capacity to initiate movement and propel the body, first along the floor and, once upright, into the space. (See Appendices: *Stroking up the Spine*; *Rolling down the Spine*.)

---

[4] Source text: Bartenieff Fundamentals in I. Bartenieff and D. Lewis, *Body Movement – Coping with the Environment*, Philadelphia: Gordon and Breach, 1980.

Centring

The concept of centring developed through this work is linked to an under-standing of the power of the pelvis. To be 'centred', or in balance, is to know how to work from the core of the being. The pelvis is the 'centre', the junction between the lower and upper body and it is through the pelvis that the two halves of the body relate to one another. The core comprises the muscles that link the pelvis/hips to the legs and the muscles that run the entire length of the back and the abdomen. The centre can therefore be seen as the power-pack of energy that enables clear physical intention. For the actor, being centred indicates the presence of core strength and self-awareness. (See Practical: *Fluid, Muscular Flexible You*; Appendices: *All Fours to Walking*; *Partner Assisted: All Fours to Walking*.)

The Breathing Body

Actions, emotions and psyche all affect breathing, and the breath has an effect on the psyche, emotions and actions. Self-awareness of breathing is the key to understanding these relationships. (See Appendices: *Leg Slide with Sound*.)

Integrated Gesture and Breath

See Practical: *Action on the Breath* (p. 35)

Working effectively with breath facilitates an integrated sense of the body, lower half and upper half. Learning comes from structured breathing through the exercise, allowing the breath to move the actor, rather than him working the breath. At first, attention can be focused solely on the out-breath.

Although breathing is a reflex action, it takes conscious exploration. Placing action on the in-breath requires awareness. Hearing the length of the out-breath can be surprising. Anatomical knowledge in connection to breath may help with the form and quality of movement. (See Appendices: *Curl-up*; *Rising and Rocking*.)

Flow

See Practical: *Diagonal Sit-up* (p. 37)

'Flow' denotes the movement of energy in the body. 'Free flow', as the term suggests, is unimpeded energy. Practising it encourages an ability to release

Figure 2.1 Acrobatic biplane with smoke trail. © SindreEllingsen/Getty Images.

tension and 'holds' in the body and so to move more easily on the breath. (See Chapter 8.)

Free flow energy depends on 'yield' in the body. The actor feels the movement change tempo and dynamic as energy shifts: fast, racing energy slows down, and narrow-feeling states expand to a sense of overwhelming breadth. Each shift leads to another, so that a virtual trail of movement flows through the space.

'Going with the flow' relies on the actor allowing himself to be swept along by the body, moving at a pace that prevents introspection or over-sensing. This can be uncomfortable in some exercises, where the actor wishes to honour every movement of the work.

Stillness

The actor has experienced being still in daily life: it may be something that he is largely unaware of; it may be something that he finds alien if it is his habit to be always on the go; or it may be that he is practised in being still because of a particular sport, hobby or way of life. Through bodywork, stillness is given dedicated attention and explored as a container of action and impulse.

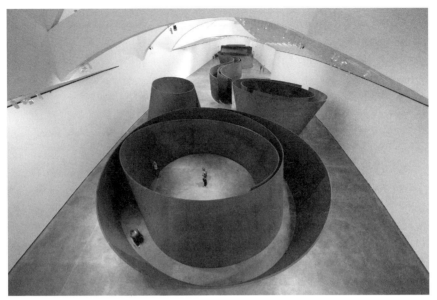

Figure 2.2   The Matter of Time, Richard Serra. ©RAFA RIVAS/AFP/Getty Images

The experience of stillness is highlighted, and can be heightened by, movement. The key to isolation work, for example, is the stillness of the non-moving body parts. A small, separated movement can be highly expressive. For instance, a conscious stilling of the body and a raising of the eyebrows clearly denotes 'thinking' in the performing space. (See Appendices: *Isolations*.)

The actor must discover the difference between stillness and stasis (being stuck or inert) and begin to understand stillness as central to movement. When he is still, awareness is heightened; looking becomes 'seeing' and hearing becomes 'listening'. Within stillness is breath, readiness and the actor's anticipation of the future. Stillness contains the potential for any movement.

Kinesphere

See Practical: *Personal Space Exploration* (p. 39)

The actor has looked at the frame within himself (the structure of the body). Now he looks at the frame around him and within which he works (the space around the body). (See Appendices: *Marking the Kinesphere*)

Laban's 'Dimensional Scale'

See Practical: *Dimensional Scale* (p. 40)
See Practical: *Walking Backwards* (p. 43)

The actor must seek to work with a willing openness that radiates outward. The 'bubble' or kinesphere can also become a cube, a frame for his work. The use of these imagined spatial structures[5] brings clarity to the actor's perception of three-dimensional space in a way that the sphere cannot (the minute a mind conjures a cube, the actor becomes aware of himself in three dimensions).

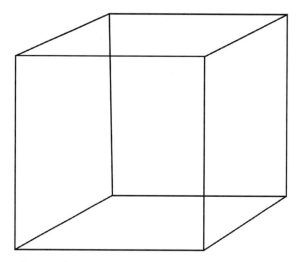

Figure 2.3   Personal space cube.

The Dimensional Scale takes the actor through a 'pure' physical experience of three-dimensional geometry. It allows the actor to inhabit the space which relates to the imagined qualities of vertical, lateral and sagittal.[6] The actor, placing himself at the centre of his defined personal space, is ready to move anywhere. The concept of a line being pre-existent and infinite means that the actor just 'joins' it – finds the sensation of it and becomes one with it.

---

[5] If accessible, see Laban's *A Vision of Dynamic Space*, Abingdon: Routledge Falmer, 1984. See Valerie Preston-Dunlop and Lesley Ann-Sayers (eds), *The Dynamic Body in Space, Exploring and Developing Rudolf Laban's Ideas for the 21st Century*, Southwold: Dance Books Ltd, 2010.
[6] Sagittal – medical term. Here used as the plane that is situated at the vertical mid-line of the body and defines the forward and back direction lineally (other terms for the planes: median/sagittal, coronal/frontal and transverse planes). Also arrow-like, which is a useful image. Sagittal is related to the wheel plane.

The body experiences upwards and downwards, sideways, backwards and forwards. This provokes pure movement devoid of literal explanation. The idea of the lines can remove inaccuracy and excess movement, as the actor is either in-line or not.

Heightened awareness of the back of the body adds to the perception of the space behind it. This re-emphasizes the fact that the body is three-dimensional and the world is happening all around it. Insight can be gained from any of these directions, not just from straight ahead. Being at the centre of the up, down, side to side and forwards and backwards results in stability and in possession of control in the space.

Within the scope of the scale, other aspects that define use of space also offer themselves. The lateral experience of space invokes 'near-reach' and 'far-reach' space, with 'mid-reach' placed along the movement journey from one extreme to the other. Once the sagittal experience is finally added, 'near' space wraps closely around the actor, and 'far' space is wherever the actor can touch at full extension of limbs.

Joining a line that is already there gives a sense of lengthening and widening as opposed to stretching, or indeed pushing or pulling. Over exertion – being physically over intense – often occurs. There is an extreme to reach and therefore it can seem as though the movement needs to feel and be extreme. Tension, however, will overwhelm the expression: it is the released body that is committed to the moment that is expressive.

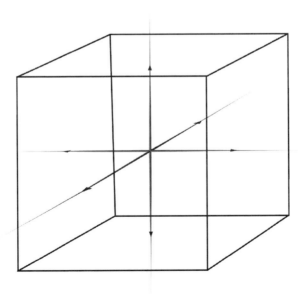

Figure 2.4   Dimensional Scale within the space cube.

Physicality defined by the spatial planes[7] is inherent in the work. The alternative terminology for the spatial planes (door/vertical, wheel/sagittal and table/horizontal) offers a choice of how each is to be conceived by the actor. He explores movement in each of these planes to understand them equally. Over time, he can discern which he prefers to use in action, finding his natural affinity to movement in one spatial plane or another. (See Appendices: *Additional to the Dimensional Scale*).

Having taken his attention beyond his own space and on into general space, the actor can create a balanced composition not only of his own body but with others in the space. He develops an understanding of the connection between focal points, including the space between bodies.

Posture and Alignment

The ultimate aim in exploring alignment is to find a state of total 'availability'. This requires both internal relaxation and precise realignment of the body, working towards an entirely free diaphragm. Visualization when lying on the floor provides the experience of spinal length. When crawling, attention can be drawn to the energetic intention, from the crown of the head along the spine to the tail bone. Similarly, once he is standing, the actor may be led through imagery that highlights the sensation of ascent and descent of the spine, the length of the spine, and the breadth of the back.

Actor Movement uses a 'neutral stance' for bodywork that consists of standing with straight legs, hip-width apart with parallel feet. If the actor understands the reason behind this starting point, he can recognize that the tiniest of changes represents a choice to step out of neutral and make an expressive movement. (See Appendices: *Alignment of Feet*; *Stroking up the Spine*.)

Feet

See Practical: *T'ai Chi Slow Walk* (p. 44)

Being physically present means standing at the centre of personal space, ready to move in any direction. When standing, the actor has to develop a relationship with his feet as the body parts that not only support the rest of his upright body but move him about.

---

[7] See Laban for spatial planes within his Choreutic work. J. Newlove, *Laban For All*, London: Nick Hern Books, 2004; P. Hackney, *Making Connections: Total Body Integration through Bartenieff Fundamentals*, Philadelphia: Gordon and Breach Science Publishers, 1998.

Knowing what the feet are doing when they are so far away from the head – our place of immediate thought – can be challenging at first. Testing this ability is reason enough to use parallel position. This clear-cut position means that the ability for basic physical awareness can be worked on daily.

Footwork comes alive when the actor consciously acknowledges his past and present experiences of his feet: how they move him normally, how they move him through dance, sport, hiking, and so on. Observational and experiential anatomy and use of imagery add to this awareness. Areas of the feet can be discovered through identification and naming: for example, T'ai Chi's 'bubbling well point' at the centre of the sole, and use of the terms 'ankle foot' and 'heel foot' for the outside and inside sections of the feet.

Through attentiveness, the actor begins to be able to meet the floor softly with the heel when walking and to stand his ground when both feet are planted. The understanding of the articulation enables greater pliancy within whole-body movement. Connection with the sensation of the feet on the ground is cultivated gradually. By making the feet work with precision – standing, walking, running, jumping, skipping and leaping – they will of necessity develop the ability to work more efficiently. The feet will then more effectively support and propel the body through the space. (See Appendices: *Jumping off the Wall*.)

Swings

See Practical: *T'ai Chi Side-to-Side Turning* (p. 46)

The actor can relate to swings in movement work because of their existence in daily life. To swing is to use free weight and momentum. By experiencing the rhythm when he drops into his weight, the actor relinquishes control from the intellect and finds a 'natural' use of the swing to enable movement and the release of any pent-up energy. The whole body can 'get behind' exercises using swings. (See Appendices: *Swings – Some Examples*.)

Grounding of Weight

The more grounded the actor is the greater his support, balance and orientation. Being physically 'grounded' leads to the idea of a centre of gravity within the body. Imagining a plumb-line may help the actor envisage a centre of gravity which can at times even be outside the body. Grounding allows the body weight to be fully experienced; it sinks the weight into the lower body and feet so that not only does the weight descend but – simultaneously – the feet are pushed into the ground and draw energy up from it. By releasing shallow breath, the actor has the opportunity to feel his weight give in to the ground.

Rhythm and Tempo

The actor explores the rhythm of the body in its interface with the world. A human being can immediately understand and produce complex, universal rhythms (think of an army marching). All action, all life-force has rhythm. The actor might see rhythm in energy flow or in the accents of changing tensions in the body, or as a combination of dynamics that have a particular pattern of timing.

This exploration is not about imposing rhythm on the actor. It is about the actor discovering how rhythm works, even if initially he finds it hard to match the rhythm of the exercise. If something has a fast rhythm, he needs to work out what he has to relinquish in his body movement to keep up. This calls for a mental and physical renegotiation of tension. This can be experienced clearly in an exercise that accelerates and decelerates.

Observing form gives insight to the actor's own predominant rhythm and, ultimately, the rhythmic pattern of body movement for a character. This can only be produced if body and mind are 'in tune'. Matching the 'natural' is to understand that rhythm follows a pattern that has ebb and flow and shape. Different stresses and phrasing create the pattern and dynamics of the rhythm. These include breath within the form, contrast and change within the movement, arcs and phases of the movement and use of different body parts.

Movement work can be done to culturally familiar tempos (e.g. 4/4), so that the actor works within a time frame and thinks of time in a form.

Working with a slow tempo offers experience of stillness and spaciousness. The mind does not cease working, but provides space for consciousness of breath-flow and for visualization. There is time to discover any physical manoeuvring that is occurring – in the T'ai Chi Slow Walk this would include being in or out of balance while aiming for continuously flowing movement and focused core energy. Ultimately, maintaining this connection between mind and body enables a freely flowing quality, whatever the tempo.

Stamina

Building fitness for acting is about matching agility of thought with agility of action. It also requires the development of stamina and a practical understanding of the differing purposes of 'fitness'. The actor body needs to be 'fit' while remaining flexible, adaptable and sensitive without inhibiting freedom of movement or the ability to transform. (See Appendices: *Speed Skipping*; See also, additional online resources – *Circuit Training*.)

Balance

The actor needs to work on balance in relation to alignment. In this way he understands that change or correction in one part of the body affects every other part. There is no quick fix here.

To balance is to be in a constant state of flux. In order to facilitate this, the body must be allowed to release the muscular hold of the neck and head and experience postural release. Any work that requires moving off-centre demands that the head–spine line is broken. The minute the line is broken, the actor can shift from the concept of balance as control. If an actor truly physically surrenders, releases the neck and head and follows the movement of the head, he can reach off-balance and balance in extraordinary ways. To maintain equilibrium is to create movement through the play of opposing forces and directions. (See Appendices: *Finding Flow from the Head*.)

Working within the dimensions as explored in Laban's Dimensional Scale is a stable way of being in the world. Following the diagonal will cause instability – an off-balance way of being in the world. The diagonal is wonderfully dynamic; it is about change, it is about going with the momentum and potential fall, as opposed to being in control.

Laban's Diagonal Scale

See Practical: *Diagonal Scale* (p. 48)

The Diagonal Scale is structured on the four diagonals of the cube. The form of the scale follows the natural impulse to 'fall' from high to low but the body has to move fast using the necessary impulse to pull into a moment of balance. Although the actor remains sufficiently in balance to perform the scale, the effect is dynamic and chaotic.

Falling

See Practical: *Falling* (p. 50)
See Practical: *Rolling* (p. 51)

An actor cannot allow himself to let go and experience a fall until he knows he has a safe outcome. The mind demands that the body protects itself which is likely to mean the body tenses up. Rugby players are necessarily desensitized to falling and have knowledge of the mechanics of falling and landing; as introduced in Chapter 1, these falls are not dramatic and the viewers can keep their minds on the game itself. The actor, however, has to learn to fall safely but with full meaning and drama.

Falling offers a different experience from collapsing. The dance world has vocabulary from which the actor can draw, but it is important that the falls are not stylized or contrived but are real falling even if accompanied by music. With time, the actor may come to relish falling.

Roth Rhythms

See Practical: *Finding Free Flow on Your Feet* (p. 51)

When the actor reaches a stage when he can take the work further for himself alone in the space, work such as Roth's 5 Rhythms can offer an experience of dance that is also not concerned about how it looks and is not watched by an audience expecting a performance. Roth's 5 Rhythms offers the actor a chance to move with abandon. He learns to identify the contrasting times when he does and does not allow himself to find freedom in movement.

The 5 Rhythms can offer the actor an opportunity to take the courage to explore and to let go to spontaneous movement; committing to the risk of letting go to the body. The result can be joy and a real 'feel good' factor; being taken over by dance and music (where used) may well be cathartic. What it offers, though, is an experiential grasp of the scope of different rhythms as movement qualities that he can embody.

Developing the Self through Partner Work

Trust and Risk

See Practical: *Sticking* (p. 52)
See Practical: *Falling* (p. 55)

An effective learning environment is one in which the actor feels safe and secure. Trust is often perceived as trusting in someone else when actually it also means 'trusting yourself': initiating and being receptive, giving and taking, directing and responding. Physical confidence is a by-product of growing trust, as is physical sensitivity. When trusted, the actor experiences and understands the responsibility of never betraying that trust. (See Appendices: *Additional to the Diagonal Scale*.)

Trust exercises offer a realization of courage. Trust is not taught; it is expected and manifested through exercises such as the physical practice of weight-bearing (that is, giving personal body weight to someone else) or falling and being caught. It is important for an actor to be able to receive the body and the weight of another actor falling and to admit the resultant sense of vulnerability and openness. A group can feel elated at the end of a session by the sensation of mutual trust and courage. (See Appendices: *Finding Flow from the Head*; *Throw Head Backwards*; *Partner Falling*.)

Physical Risk-taking

Incorporated in physical risk-taking work are 'light touch' experiences of either momentary fear, experienced little and often, or sustained chunks of fun-fear (such as clowning). The actor can become accustomed to a practice of facing and dealing with fear in physical tasks such as falling or tumbling and recognizes this as different from justifiable real fear.

Partnered Work

The fundamentals of work with contact can be experienced in paired posture work, for example stroking up the spine, and in exercises on personal space, such as 'Sticking'. In these, the contact, though inherent, is one amongst several focuses and not the main subject of the work. It can become the specific focus in partnered physical/dance improvisation work as Contact Improvisation (CI).[8]

Contact Improvisation

See Practical: *Draping* (p. 56)
See Practical: *Counterweight Exercise* (p. 58)
See Practical: *Checking in with Partner Work* (p. 60)

CI is physical improvisation from the contact of a surface of a body part with a surface of support. The actor presses into the supporting surface in order to move away and on from that moment of contact. This can provide an accessible and challenging experiential frame. By whole-heartedly committing to this physical work and actively listening to his body, the actor learns to appreciate his own imprint. It is through working with the partner that his own influence or

---

[8]CI was developed by Steve Paxton, dance maker, in the early 1970s. Emerging from the New York experimental arts and performance scene of the 1960s and 1970s, it is a form that offered Western dance a new sense of partner work. It is about the use of weight and is improvised through points of contact (touch) in duets. It developed out of an exploration of the human body and it draws on elements from martial arts, social dance, sports and child's play. See also B. Bainbridge Cohen, *Sensing, Feeling, Action*, Northampton, MA: Contact Editions, 1993.

lack of influence can be understood. This physical dialogue does not work to a plan; neither partner plans for the other, and the improvisation evolves from mutual negotiation. It involves bouncing off from or struggling through another's agenda, with moments of conflict as well as synchronicity. His listening becomes attuned through practice with different partners and, gradually, sensitivity to movement stimuli develops. The connection with the partner can be as slight as fingertips on a wrist (as in 'Sticking'), but the smallest reaction reads. It is an example of cause and effect and it may surprise the actor that what seems so slight a physical response is in fact sufficient to generate dynamic reaction in his partner.

It is important to change partners regularly. Seeing the partner's body objectively as 'support' and the work as 'dance' creates a safe context in which to explore close physical contact in any given partnership. It challenges actors' notions such as female 'frailty' or embarrassment at letting someone else bear his 'heaviness'. Using the pelvic girdle and lumbar spine to bear weight safely means the student is confident in offering sturdy support.

The practice can become highly acrobatic. Contact improvisation as partner work helps the actor understand that he is in possession of a body that exceeds any limit the mind may have imposed on it. It offers freedom through movement (it doesn't matter how it looks – and it is not performance oriented) and the experience of both abandon and responsibility.

CI uses many of the same improvisation rules as acting improvisation: an active offer is made and taken up. This partner work allows the actor to explore whether he is able to be spontaneous through use of touch, weight-giving, weight-bearing and commitment to the ongoing contact. It highlights where and when he is holding onto a previous moment, whether he can commit to a movement impulse, or is bold even when in doubt. The aim is to reach a sense of timelessness when involved in an improvisation. (See Appendices: *Experiencing Light Touch*.)

The key to CI is that the actor works with a 'psychologically non-attached' relationship to touch and to physical closeness. The contact has no significance in itself and has no meaning expression-wise. Yet the result is a meaningful experience that involves listening to both the actor's and his partner's bodies. The actor always learns something from the partnership. It is an important practice that the partners always say 'thank you' to each other after every exercise.

This 'psychologically non-attached' physical closeness fosters confidence with intimacy. Each partnership offers the actor not only his partner's strength and weight, but also a physical sense of that person. An actor may find physical improvisation with one partner exciting and energetically charged. With another, he may discover a nurturing impulse, or the partnership may feel incompatible.

IN CONTEXT: INTIMACY

A touch that feels passionate, but is delivered dispassionately, helps the actor to see that he can develop a professional take on intimacy-as-quality-of-movement. His CI encounters remain in his body-memory and can be 'called up' when working on an intimate scene in a play. (See Chapter 8: Personal Safety in Movement.)

Returning to Self

Reflection

Work on Movement Fundamentals develops a self that has gained understanding of:

- Simple connection to breath
- Strong commitment
- Openness and engagement
- Free-weight and momentum
- Spinal alignment
- Pliability
- Moving from centre
- Whole body movement
- Connection to the ground
- Inhabitation of personal space
- Physical accuracy
- Coordination
- Contrasts of quality and dynamic contrast

The experience of Movement Fundamentals nurtures openness towards movement and generosity within it. It leads to acceptance of momentum and 'letting go'. The actor learns to relinquish exaggerated physical endeavour, resulting in physical fluency. He is able to identify overworked reaction or response in himself and in others. He is flexible enough to inhabit each moment in an environment of shifts and dynamic changes.

Connecting with the Body: Practicals

Experiencing the Skeleton

This is described within a group setting, but also works for the individual. This work is about the framework of your body – the bones.

- Observe a full-sized skeleton in the movement space.

- What are surprising features to you?

- Handle the bones and compare structures with your own.

- Look at the shapes of the bones: long, slender, curved, round, triangular, bulbous, and so on, or shapes that remind you of other objects.

- Ascribe memorable descriptions to the bones, for example, the roundness of the heels; the tininess of the individual bones of the fingers; the 'S' bends of the spine, and so on.

- Notice the quality of the bones: for example, arms hanging from the shoulder girdle; kneecaps resting or perched on the legs, and so on.

- Look for the textures and sizes of the bones; note also the sizes of the skeletal areas, for example the size and length of the feet in comparison with the skull. Note also the gaps and spaces, such as the space between the lower ribs and the pelvis.

- Look for sculptural or delicate features, such as the bows of the clavicles at the top of the chest connecting to the scapulae at the back of the body.

- Look at the mechanics, such as the way the ribs encircle the upper body.

Feet, pelvis, spine, head and neck are all areas you will focus on as you begin body work, but take the opportunity here to:

- Look at the whole of 'you'.

- Look at anatomy books (including *Gray's Anatomy*) to highlight various body parts. This will of course also take you to anatomy beyond the skeletal. You may have associations with the skeleton (Halloween, for example), or it may make you feel uncomfortable (e.g. from associations with hospital visits, death, and so on). You will have to move beyond these associations.

Visualizing the Skeleton

Once this observation period is over:

- Lie down supine;[9] allow the legs to roll outwards comfortably and aim to maintain this posture; but if real discomfort starts to take over you can move to semi-supine.[10]

- Allow yourself to travel round your body in your mind's eye, starting with your head. Envisage the roundness and the smoothness of the skull. Work down through your body: from your head to your shoulder girdle, arms, elbows, fingers, ribcage, pelvis, legs, knees, feet, toes and, finally, the sense of your whole skeleton from toe to head and head to toe. You may be guided by a tutor's words as you visualize your skeleton within you. If you are doing this alone, take yourself on a journey round your body as mapped above.

- Pay attention to any imaginative and sensorial associations with specific parts of your skeleton or bones.

- If it helps to actually 'move your bones', allow yourself to roll and stretch now and then and listen to the body as it does so. You may find though that the focus you bring to the visualization is all-consuming and you do not want to move.

Animating through breath

- Visualize[11] and experience the outside of yourself being moved by the breath from the inside of your body. Bring your attention to each individual body part and feel your breath filling it completely.

- Once you have worked your way around the body, then feel the whole length of your body malleable to your breath – try breathing in from the soles of your feet, letting that breath travel up your torso and breathing out through the crown of your head.

Key points

This work is not about having to stay still, statue-like; allow yourself to move if the visualization provokes this. If you find your mind wandering, bring it back

---

[9]Supine: Lying full length on the back, face up, arms resting on the floor slightly away from body.
[10]Semi-supine: Lying on the back with knees bent and feet hip-width apart, feet sufficiently close to buttocks to feel grounded, arms resting on the floor slightly away from body.
[11]For further inspiration see M. Tufnell and C. Crickmay, *Body, Space, Image*, Southwold: Dance Books, 1993.

to the task in hand; if you get left behind on the journey round the skeleton, move the mind gently to the body part being focused upon.

Working In and Out of the Floor: Shifting Sensibilities – One

Fluid, Muscular and Flexible You

Fluid

- Lie on your back, legs outstretched.

- Move one foot on the floor all around you. It must stay in contact with the floor as it moves and may cross your other leg. Let your leg follow the moving foot – its extremity – easily as if it was liquid or cooked spaghetti. Let the leg move easily in your hip and let your knee and ankle feel free and easy. Continue this for a while.

- Let this foot rest and then repeat the exercise with your other foot.

- Repeat with both feet at the same time, knowing that each foot possesses its own mind. Each limb follows each foot and travels independently of the other wherever it will on the floor.

- Repeat the exercise again, but this time using your hands. Move one hand on every surface on the floor. It must always be in contact with the floor. Ensure that the hand and arm feel free and easy, just as you did with your foot before. All the same principles apply.

- Repeat with the other hand and arm.

- Repeat with both hands and arms simultaneously.

- Repeat with both hands and both feet simultaneously.

- Allow yourself to truly follow the extremities in contact with the floor. Breathe.

- Roll and twist and turn, and gradually find yourself able to rise out of the floor even though your hands and feet remain in contact with it. Imagine yourself to be boiling mud that bubbles up and then drops softly back to the surface.

- Allow your hands and your feet to take you back again to the floor; elongating through your limbs. Soften every body part that comes into contact with the floor. Follow the extremities; they are the furthest point or limit of yourself and, therefore the extremity of your reach.

- Spot if you can feel yourself 'doing' a movement, that is, making it muscular, say on a lift out of the floor or a return to the floor. Let that working go and see if you can let your hands and feet really lead you and therefore move you. Imagine being sucked up out of the floor and poured back into it.

Muscular

- Move keeping just your hands and feet – and nothing else – in contact with the floor. Obviously you will need to lift each hand or foot off the floor in order to 'step'.

- Do this for a while, knowing that this is weight-bearing, uses muscle strength endurance and is cardiovascular.

- Continue moving on your hands and feet and interact with a partner in the space: you might move closer, far apart, alongside, faster or slower but, whatever you do, keep a physical dialogue going between you and your attention on both your partner and yourself. If in a group context where numbers are uneven, this can be done with three.

Flexible

- Now move on the floor making sure that your extremities are not in contact with the floor. Listen to how your torso can move you, how you can move absolutely from your core, your pelvis and spine. Allow yourself to relish the possibility of hugeness as you move in this way over the floor still keeping ease as well as dynamic.

- Notice if your arms and legs are tightly bent as you manoeuvre yourself: as you twist, turn, roll, curl, uncurl, open, close, and so on. If you find that they are bent and tense, try to open the limbs out into the space remembering the release of the limbs you experienced in the fluid phase of this experience. Why should they now be gripped and held to the body?

- If you find yourself making moves ('walking' on your knees, for example), relinquish this kind of heaving yourself around.

Relationship with the floor

- Go back to the first part of the exercise (extremities in contact with the floor all the time) with all this experience. This time allow yourself to rise up out of the floor to sitting, or onto your knees, and then sink back into it. Follow the extremities without using muscular effort to do this. Let the gathering and scattering action from the centre of your torso mobilize you.

- Improvise with fluid, muscular and flexible, making sure all three are clear.
- Reflect on this experience and also in relation to your work with form.

Key points

The gathering movement offers momentum and movement possibility when the limbs and extremities are off the floor as well as in the usual on-floor positioning. Note how the body has both a yielding and a vibrant quality as it develops a close relationship with the floor. This work offers a chunk of time entirely on the floor to provide you with a taste of freedom and opportunity to experience different qualities in movement with the floor as the sole environment; keep a sense of play.

Working In and Out of the Floor: Shifting Sensibilities – Two

▶ Creep to Crawl to Stand to Rise.

Creep to Crawl to Stand to Rise

This is a form that instils a sense of progressive journey and of flow, moving from the ground to vertical and back down again to the ground.

How to crawl in a movement context

The term 'crawling' may evoke many images for you, of babies, for example, but in a movement context it is defined by the instructions below. These terms are precise, in order to offer the experience of suspension and propulsion.

- Move onto all fours.
- Move in opposition: opposite thigh to arm.
- Find the power in the legs to propel you with free flow along the floor. The thighs initiate the crawl and the arm follows. The thighs move into forward space in a direct line under your hips. You can slide the knees lightly on the floor from the movement of the thighs.
- Release your limbs, your arms particularly. Have a sense of the arms

being free flowing and mobile in response to impulse: able to move independently and yet always in connection with your intention.

- Let the shoulder girdle rest on your arms.

- Meet the floor with your hand sequentially from the fingertips down to the heel of the hand. Then lift away from it after weight-bearing by peeling off the heel of the hand first.

- Make sure that the elbows are not hyper-extended (over straightened at the elbow joint): hyperextension prevents you experiencing the sense of the length and freedom of your arms, or mobility in their support of the crawling. If this happens then unlock the elbows and lightly bend them.

Beginning to crawl

- Focus on your arms and keep the flow of energy moving through the channel of the joints, as each arm moves ready for the weight to be transferred into the hand.

- Crawl backwards maintaining the length of your spine from head to tail bone, keeping the same flow and intention out of the top of your head.

- It might help you to find the flow of this if you envisage a cheetah's head as it runs: its head stays still as its torso and legs power its incredible speed.

Now for the full exercise

- Start on the floor in a semi-supine position with your arms on the floor above your head, shoulder-width apart, hands above and in line with your shoulder joints.

- Breathe in and on the outbreath gather yourself into your centre and then into the foetal position on one side of your body. Let the crown of your head and knees draw towards your centre like a sea anemone closing.

- Continue this gathering movement to bring you over to face the floor in a 'creep' position: knees, elbows, hands close to the shoulders and top of the head on the floor. The position is about curving inwards towards the navel with your bottom on your heels. Draw your tail bone down towards the ground, keeping close to the floor.

- Lift up and out onto all fours, anticipating the crawl forwards.

- Crawl forwards for about four crawls. Think of being propelled forwards.

- Crawl backwards for three or four crawls, still with the intention out of the crown of the head.

- On the third or fourth crawl backward, draw your head in towards your navel and bring your thighs in line under your hips, as you curl your toes under your feet.

- Bring the weight from your hands into your feet, lowering your heels down to the ground – so that you are hanging over the hips, stood with bent legs and pelvis up in the air (rather than crouching near to the floor).

- Curl around and over your centre as you round the 'outer' spine – the outer back. Then roll up through the spine, to stand upright with straight legs. Feel the unfurling of the body upwards.

- Imagine that in getting up out of the floor and standing, you are upright on your feet for the first time.

- It is your first time with a horizontal eyeline and you are therefore looking out at the world from a new vantage point. You have joined the pre-existing vertical, which possesses infinite upwardness.

- Continue the sense of moving vertically upwards, of rising, and let this sensation take you onto the balls of your feet, still keeping an ongoing sense of rising. In your mind's eye, see the landscape and horizon ahead of you. Experience the sense of uplift and inner expansion.

- Feel the suspension and imagine that you are being pulled back down to earth before lowering your heels. Imagine yourself keeping your height but allow your feet to sink once more into the ground.

- Reverse the unfurling process, going with gravity and sinking back towards the ground: curl your head down, keeping the sense of connection between the top of the head and the navel as you round the back of the neck and upper body closing around your centre and rolling down through the spine.

- Bend the knees until your fingertips sweep the floor out in front of you to take you into forward crawling.

- Crawl forwards for about three crawls. Again, experience the sense of opening and then anticipate closing and …

- Crawl backwards a couple of times, allowing this to take you back into the creep position, tops of the feet on the floor. Imagine as you do this that your tail bone is being pulled downwards into the ground so that it stays close to your heels.

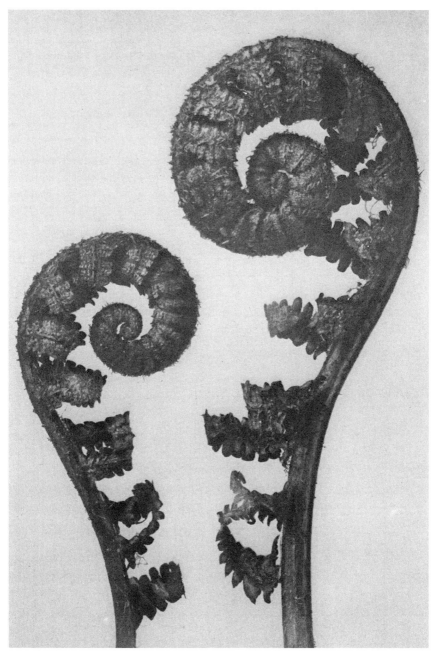

Figure 2.5   Common fern. From Karl Blossfeldt, *Art Forms in Nature* (Munich: Schirmer/Mosel, 1999). © Karl Blossfeldt / Archiv Ann and Jürgen Wilde, Zülpich, 2014.

- Descend into the floor further into the foetal position (on the same side as you started).

- Open up, moving from the tail bone and sacrum to pour the back into the floor, returning to the starting position (semi-supine with the arms aligned above the shoulders on the floor).

- Repeat the exercise, curling into the foetal position on the other side of your body.

However many times you repeat the form, each time is like a new beginning and a new end – as if each rising is the first time you have ever come to standing and faced outwards.

Key points

'Gathering to centre' has a sense of closing – drawing both the top of the head and the tail bone towards your navel/centre. Develop the compulsion and rhythm of opening and closing. Keep a sense of spinal alignment on the vertical. Maintain intention. Curl the top of the body over on the descent. Use the gather to intensify the straight line direction through the spine of the subsequent 'all fours' position when crawling, and then up into standing.

Additional: Free Flow Exercise

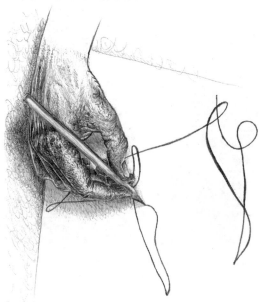

Figure 2.6 Flow trail. Illustration by Toby Elwes.

The essence of the movement of the *Creep to Crawl to Rise* exercise (or *Diagonal Sit-up*) can be drawn. When the exercise is watched and followed with pen on paper, its flowing nature is both felt and seen.

Capture with a pencil on paper the free flow uncurling and arrival at verticality, and then its reverse: simply follow the lines of the movement 'trail' in the space. This drawing has nothing to do with whether or not you possess any drawing or painting skills; it is about translating the flow of the movement that you are watching and seeing onto the paper.

Action on the Breath

- Lie on the floor in a semi-supine position.

- Gently rock your pelvis back onto the tip of the tail bone. Notice how this exaggerates the curve of your lumbar spine, arching your lower back away from the floor.

- Now gently rock your pelvis forward. Notice how this movement softly pastes the top and back of your pelvic girdle onto the floor.

In-breath

- Now match the in-breath with the backward pelvic tilt: breathe in, listen and experience the sensation of expansion inside yourself,

- Include your upper back and ribs as well as, the subtle lengthening of the spine and the dropping of the tail bone into the floor.

- Think of this movement as being a way to elongate the lumbar spine, letting the tail bone lengthen away from the crown of your head and along the floor. It will also help to fill your ribs sideways when you breathe in. Try not to allow your belly to spill upwards, or dome, to the ceiling.

Out-breath

- Match the out-breath with the forward pelvic tilt.

- Soften the chest and ribs as you breathe out and curl the tail bone towards your navel which pastes the back of your waist into the floor. Do this with ease.

- Imagine doing this without muscles, just moving the bones – the girdle. Notice that the more you begin to recruit the abdominal muscles the greater the curl-up of the pelvis is.

- Increase the muscular squeeze a little if you wish and if you want to take this into more abdominal core strengthening work.

Integrated breath

- Continue rocking the pelvis on the breath.
- Let the movement surf on the breath and keep the movement free.

Key points

Pay conscious attention to the breath and to the corresponding gestures that occur.

Working In and Out of the Floor: Shifting Sensibilities – Three

▶ Diagonal Sit-up.

Diagonal Sit-up[12]

- Lie in a semi-supine position, arms spread out to the sides at shoulder level on the floor, palms down: T-shape. Work to find accuracy in this position so that you know where you are returning to.

- Breathe out and move your right arm up to top-right diagonal on the floor, rotating the arm in the shoulder socket and turning the palm to the ceiling, as both your knees fall to the left. Your gaze moves along the diagonal of the arm (eyes looking to right hand and beyond). Feel the pull of the diagonal through your body from right fingertip to knees.

- Circle the right arm over the top of the head, drawing an arc with the fingers on the floor. Keep the gaze of the eyes, following the hand as far as possible, so that the head rolls across from right to left on the floor.

- Continue to draw the ongoing sweep of the circle on the floor with your fingers, which draws the torso onto the left side.

- Continue the circle of the right arm beyond and past the knees which

---

[12] 'Diagonal Sit-up' here is distinct from a fitness sit-up exercise and is a Bartenieff Fundamentals term (see I. Bartenieff and D. Lewis, *Body Movement – Coping with the Environment*, Philadelphia: Gordon and Breach, 1980).

begins to lift you out of the floor. Use the left hand to assist you and support you by drawing the elbow in towards the torso and letting the hand take some of your weight. Concertina at the waist.

- Continue circling the right arm and sit up with your weight on your left hip and both legs bent to the side on the floor. This manoeuvre has taken you from a gathering into your centre to an opening up to sitting upright.

- Continue the circle of the fingers on floor, creating an arc beyond the feet and back across to the right-hand side of the body. Notice how this allows the right side of the pelvis to return to the floor. Pull the right hip back so that the thigh comes back into the groin so you are 'sitting on both hips' and even-weighted across both sitting bones. You are now sitting with the knees perpendicular and the upright torso close to the thighs.

- Breathe in, with the right arm still circling (fingers on the floor to your right-hand side).

- Breathe out, twisting the upper body, and find the original diagonal with the right arm, keeping the elbow joint soft so that the arm can give and bend into the floor rather than push away from it, keeping you at arm's-length from the floor. In the mind's eye, the floor can be 'allowed' to come up and meet your descending body and take its weight, as you simultaneously lower yourself down to it. Sink down into floor along the diagonal of the arm, with the gaze following the diagonal, pouring the back, bit by bit, into the floor, maintaining stability and centring of the pelvis. Land the whole back so that the knees remain upright as your diagonal emerges, and lengthen the arm away from the stable pelvis, with an ease of movement at the waist and ribs.

- You are in semi-supine, but renegotiate the position of the arms to where they started in the T-shape.

When this action of touching the edges of your kinesphere at low level becomes more familiar, you can ask yourself imaginative questions:

- What is and where is the circle you are creating with your arm?
- What are you touching?

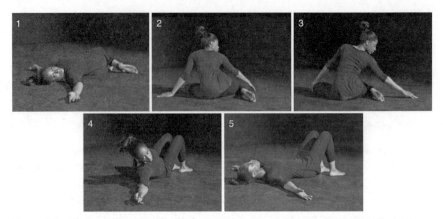

Figure 2.7 'Diagonal Sit-up' storyboard. Actor, Lynsey Murrell. Photographs by Todd Padwick.

Key points

Remember to make the circle huge; allow yourself to work with the natural give in the body following the pattern of the in- and out-breath; allow yourself to be taken along the diagonal to the floor, with the breath and give of the body. Find triggers that can inspire or compel you to let go of the careful approach and 'go for it'. Once you know where the blocks to the flow of energy through your body habitually reside – in the shoulders, or hips, for example – you can work to release these areas.

You can continue to practise allowing a free flow of energy and discovering a sense of ease and release using the diagonal sit-up, with the following:

- Attempt the whole action of the diagonal sit-up on the out-breath.

- Commit to flow, as opposed to any holding of energy that may originally have been present in the exercise when you did it on several breaths.

- Breathe out as you drop the knees and find the diagonal and come up out of the floor, following the circle, and find the diagonal and land back in the floor on this one breath.

- Try it with one out-breath on the fall, an in-breath somewhere circling past your knees when sitting, and let the out-breath take you back to the floor, finding the diagonal behind you.

- Then try the exercise with an in-breath as you descend to the floor to find out the different experience this gives you. Then when you go back to the rising and falling breath that makes sense for you, you will get the most out of the free flowing descent to the floor on the out-breath.

Personal Space Exploration

Near space

- See this as a mobile cylindrical space formed by closeness to the outline of your body from head to toe; closeness to your skin – the outermost part of the tangible you.

- Start with one foot grounded and work the other one around it, trying to get as close as possible to the supporting foot and the rest of your body. Work for extreme physicality with your body, contorting as it twists and turns within very narrow boundaries.

- Change feet after a while.

- Use both feet now and move through the working space in your near space. Let your imagination conjure this limited space and its boundary: for example, shrink your body in gathering movements, wrap around your skin or even imagine a silky flow of movement of the skin. Explore movement of differing qualities, dynamics and sensations, whilst maintaining the release in the body to allow these. Know that the cylinder is 'bendy', so it surrounds the body whether you bend forward, backwards or sideways – it is not just an upright tube into which you fit. You could of course just respond by feeling trapped and tied up, but this is a choice that prevents you being available and receptive physically.

Far space

See this as the opposite of your near space.

- Ground one foot. Lengthen outwards from that foot and your core with the other leg. This can be on the ground or in the air and all around this pivotal point.

- Ground this foot and repeat with the other leg lengthening outwards.

- Ground both feet.

- Allow your arms to extend to the furthermost reaches.

- Release the feet and move through the general space with your movement generated by your far space. Move so that your limbs elongate out through the space and move you through it. Release the energy through the clear channels of your limbs. Expand your length. Move freely in this expansive and 'huge' manner through the space.

- Move cleanly from near space to far space and then improvise with both.

Medium space

See this as in-between the two opposites.

- It is as if you are contained within a space in which you don't extend the arms or limbs fully — so the arms are bent, the legs are bent if lifted, as if you were in a swimming cubicle, old-fashioned phone box, photo booth, and so on.
- Check if this space feels familiar, in which case be vigilant that you are aware of the precision of this quality of movement which is unextended yet maintains space away from the body.

Experience of Each in Proximity to Others

- Move cleanly from one spatial reach to the other and then improvise.
- Simply walk. Feel the quality of each of the spatial reaches as you walk through the general space and amongst others in it.
- Do the same in stillness.

Key points

Work for accuracy.

Dimensional Scale[13]

 Dimensional Scale.

- Make a cube for yourself – kids' model connecting straws are useful for this.
- You can then place the dimensional lines in it: up and down, side to side and forward and back and all meeting at the centre. This is the model[14] for what you are about to do physically.

---

[13] Green's interpretation of Laban's Dimensional Scale.
[14] The 3D shape that in fact is made when the end points of the dimensional cross (dimensional lines intersecting at the centre of the kinesphere) are connected is an octahedron (one of the five Platonic solids). This fits nicely within the cube, however, the faces of which make for a clearer frame for the actor to work accurately within.

- Keeping the model in mind, stand in the space at the centre of an imaginary cube, which is the height, width and depth of you and your reach.

- Stand with your feet together: big toe joints together, ankles and inner knees touching (slightly rotating the knees outwards if necessary).

- Feel the heightened sense of the vertical mid-line up from ankles, inner thighs, crotch, up through your torso and out of the top of the head. This narrow posture creates a focused sense of energy – like a laser beam of light.

The scale that you are about to do fits within the imaginary boundary of the cube, but you can also imagine the lines as infinite and the directions intersecting at and radiating out from your centre.[15] You may prefer to imagine being at the centre of a sphere. Use whichever works best for you, but the image of the cube is offered here.

- The idea of working within a cube can help to maintain facing front in the postures. As it is geometrical work, hold in the mind's eye that the body stays true to the form: keep your shoulders and hips square to the front face of the cube. If they are not, it means you have changed your front, so the scale is no longer true to form.

The scale

- Step up onto the ball of the right foot and lengthen vertically with the right arm as if joining an infinite line that already exists. You will step forward of the central space at the middle of the cube but as you do so, you simply bring your cube forward into alignment with your manoeuvre.

- Transfer the weight to the left foot, with the ball of the right foot slightly behind this, and sink down on a vertical line you imagine as infinite – simply recreate this centre of the universe. Think of the body as a tube or channel: so the rising up to your full height and beyond, and sinking down and into the ground, is all within this tube. As you sink downward, feel the pull down of your right fingertips also joining into the downward verticality.

- Come back to centre, then take the right leg sideways across the left.

- Feel yourself closing and narrowing as you also take your right arm across your body and the left behind your body on the same lateral line.

---

[15] For further information, see Laban's Dimensional Cross in J. Newlove, *Laban For All*. London: Nick Hern, 2004.

All the time imagine that your arms and hands are being pulled along this infinite line. Keep square to your front to keep in line.

- Step to the right side with the right foot and open your right arm out on the lateral. This is a wide position; have a sense of your heart and lungs being open. Keep the left arm down. Be careful neither to retreat nor advance. Maintain vertical as you fill the space sideways. Open across the clavicle and upper chest and lengthen the arm out from the shoulder blade. Feel the space this produces for the in-breath, as well as for sending the breath out beyond the fingertips. Try tipping sideways with one leg lifted on that line, lengthening along the lateral line in an oppositional pull to the leg.

- Bring yourself back to centre.

- Step behind with the right leg and feel the backwards pull from the back of your head. At the same time, cross your right arm in front of your body with your hand under your left armpit and your fingertips also pulling you backwards from the waist. As much as you can, physically join the backward pulling line. The left leg can be lifted up to the front so that you feel the oppositional pull forward at the same time. Feel yourself drawn along by the sagittal.

- Be compelled to join the forward direction of the line and step onto the left and then the right leg, with torso and right arm along that forward pulling line and the left leg lifting to the back in opposition. Each direction is ongoing through your body. Feel your body imbued with the opposing pulls and find the balance between them as a result. Find an image that creates the imperative of each direction for you.

- Repeat this with the left arm and leg leading.

- Repeat using both arms, first with right leg leading and then left leg.

- When working the lateral as you step across the supporting leg, move both arms across the front of the body, pulling in opposite directions and imagine the movement continuing with the effect of closing the torso: tightening your legs, inner thighs, the groin, the chest and shoulders, heart and lungs. Feel the narrowing and straitjacketing of the whole body whilst at the same time sending energy out in the opposite directions through your fingers on that line.

- Open the arms out on the same lateral line as you step outwards to the side.

Key points

Try to keep yourself square to the front without distorting. Find the breath of each direction. Keep the movement going inside the body even once the postures have been reached. Go for the extremity of the movements whilst still staying true to form. Make sure you are not over stretching the arms – perhaps you are hyper-extending the elbows, locking the joints and bracing the arms rather than allowing the channel of the joints to remain open so that the energy can pass through.

Walking Backwards

- Create a corridor, or a lane, in the space.
- Walk normally backwards along this lane. This can be slow to start with so that you feel each moment as fully as you can.
- Then play with changing tempo but being aware that the exercise offers most when it is breathed and lived at a pace that allows total awareness of each moment.

How does walking backwards affect your sense of the spine?

- Notice the toes bending to meet the floor. As the heel reaches the floor, notice the lengthening of the back of the leg; the opening of the back of the knee; the lengthening up the spine to the crown of the head; the opening of the back of the neck – even feeling the hairs on the back of your neck; noting the uprightness of the spine and sense of verticality out of the top of the head as that heel descends.
- Walk forwards, seeing if you can use that residual sensation of the length of the spine.
- Walk back once more; focus on the widening of the back of your neck; the expansion and opening of the middle of your back which counteracts any pushing forward or flexing up of your rib cage; and the opening of the lower back. (See Practical: *T'ai Chi Slow Walk*; Chapter 3, 'Seeking Neutral': *The Walk*.)

T'ai Chi Slow Walk[16]

A basic exercise that demands physical release: you keep walking as slowly as you can, dropping the weight down so the knees remain bent throughout while maintaining an even flow of movement and breath.

For the individual; for the individual within a group

If in a group, create a circle and stand facing in the direction of the circle – anticlockwise. If working alone, work within a circle or in the most appropriate direction for the space in which you are working.

- Bring the heels together and turn the feet out (five to one on a clock face), with arms hanging by your sides. Sink the weight and bend the knees.

- Transfer your weight onto the left leg and release the right foot from the floor, with the right leg loose and 'empty' (non-muscular).

- Move the leg forward to take a step, keeping the leg travelling under and in-line with the hip – square to the belly[17] as the pelvis (and shoulder girdle) faces to 'the front'. Keep the hip joint released and allow the leg to move unimpeded in the hip with a spacious and mobile feeling (rather than the leg moving as one solid unit with the hip).

- Let the right heel softly meet the floor.

- Feel the strength and pliability of the foot and how sensitive it can be to the body weight and the floor.

- The rest of the foot articulates, meeting the ground through to the toes to take the weight. The right, therefore, becomes the supporting foot/leg. The toes are directed straight ahead (12 o'clock), square to the hips – with the hips 'yielding' to the movement of the leg as it is released from the floor at the back and carried under the hip to step forward.

- As the weight is transferred onto the right foot, peel the left (back) foot off the floor, with the toes leaving the ground last. The leg is loose and 'empty'.

- It lifts in order to take the step without any sense of muscularity.

---

[16]This, and others like it, is a T'ai Chi warm-up/preparatory exercise. It is used here separately from the practice of T'ai Chi and described from an Actor Movement perspective of its ultimate nature as a martial art and self-defence form.

[17]Belly is the term used for abdomen in this work.

- Move the leg forward under the left hip, with the relaxed foot low to the ground. The foot skims over the surface of the ground as if sensing it: as if it were a metal detector. It moves forward to find its step onto the floor, being placed down ahead of the body with the hips square to it. The heel meets the floor in such a way that if the floor were water it would not cause a ripple. The foot softly spreads as the weight descends into it, as if the floor now were sand or mud which you are moulding. Pay attention at the same time to the back foot so that you do not allow yourself to get 'stuck in the mud'. Within the practice of T'ai Chi, the footwork is done at times with the idea of moving on ice.

- This gives real lightness although always connected to the belly for rootedness.

- The rest of the foot articulates to the toes as it lands and takes the weight of the body, and so the walk continues. Imagine as you walk that the body is hanging from the ceiling from the crown of head with the spine dropping down under it ('braid to rafters'); or that your spine is hanging like a 'string of pearls'. Be aware of the need to feel the 'dropping down' of the tail bone towards the ground.

- Notice how moving slowly from one leg to the other tests your balance and how inattention may uproot you. Come into balance: 'sink the weight' down into the ankles and feet, which need to be released; release the hip, knee and ankle joints of the supporting side.

- Do not sag into or collapse on your feet. Quite the reverse: aim for a sense of upwardness. This is gained from the way in which you draw energy from the ground through your feet – so you are both rooted and poised.

- If the work remains too much 'in the head', the body will be unable to sink and let go into the slow speed. If focused down into the feet, the walk can become stuck and placed too stolidly into the ground. When it is connected to centre, the walk has the potential always to change and to shift speed or direction. Think about this slow walk as possessing physical 'economy': efficiency, fluency and ease.

- Make sure that the hips do not get left behind the feet, but that the foot and belly are always in relationship – where the foot goes the belly goes (and vice versa).

- Imagine that the movement is on a continuum. The walk is being drawn on by a pull beyond and in front of you, in a line from your centre. Imagine that you are simply following the line or thread that is already drawn, or is continuously being spun.

- Experience the quietness and spaciousness of the form. Just because you are working so slowly, your mind does not cease working or take on the mindset of slow motion. Instead, use the slowness to give you space to be aware of your breathing, and for the inner dialogue about the work that is going on all the time. Avoid literal connotations or associations with the walk: these will lead you into doing the walk for a purpose outside of and other than the embodiment of it. Pay attention to the different things that are happening: emptying the gesturing leg, for example, and feeling the thigh and knee move through the space. Walk a little faster or even slower, but keep the quality of the movement as you breathe fully.

Key points

Note each moment of movement, whether of the moving leg or of the supporting leg. Work with ease and no sense of panic: the doing of it is the learning of it, at whatever stage you are. Let go of any of the over intensity that occurs in the process of learning how to do it. Avoid zoning out with the eyes glazed over because of the endeavour or the slow pace. Keep the attention on the movement; the body; the breath. Find the rhythm. Keep a sense of ease and release.

T'ai Chi Side-to-Side Turning[18]

This is a good exercise for group work as everyone works to the same rhythm and in the same direction, but it can also be used in a solo context.

- Stand in neutral stance with your arms by your side and bend your knees. The legs remain bent throughout the whole exercise.
- Focus on your belly.
- Put your focus about three centimetres below your navel (the *dan tien*).[19] For this exercise, the *dan tien* can be imagined as an eye or camera lens, and the belly as a beacon of light that creates the impulse of the movement. The belly is the originator and leader of the movement: its focus and intention derive from the energy at the *dan tien*.
- Allow the belly to turn to the right. As you scan the horizon or

[18]See note 16.
[19]The *dan tien* of martial arts practice is the centre of life-force energy. It is located about three centimetres below the navel and slightly to the left. It is the foundation of rooted standing, breathing and body awareness.

landscape on the journey to the right, take in the whole view with the *dan tien.*

- Find the point when your pelvis cannot turn any further without distortion of the neutral stance.

- Then scan the horizon to the left.

- Continue turning from side to side with this level of attention throughout the horizontal arcs of the movement.

- Let the movement from the belly be the impetus for turning the torso to the side, back to centre and then to the other side. Remember to release any hold or squeeze of the abdominal muscles.

- Maintain hips over knees and knees over ankles by also making sure that each little toe joint, as well as the big toe joints, stay on the floor as you move. Also be aware of your heels manoeuvring. Allow the impetus from the feet in the floor to help galvanize the movement along with the belly. (Maintain an imaginative connection to the three points of weight distribution under your feet – head of metatarsal 1 and 5 (big toe and little toe) and the centre of the calcaneum (your heel). Notice how these points form a triangle under your feet.)

- Now speed this movement up to a comfortable rhythm without losing the idea of the belly leading and the sense of moving in a unified way. You may prefer to think of the movement initiating from the pelvis and lower back as the speed gathers momentum.

- Think about the waist easily and lightly twisting around the spine as though this were a greasy pole at the centre of the movement.

- Let the eyes stay 'in the head' (perhaps think of the point of your belly 3cm below your navel; or even your navel as your eye or lens through which you are seeing the world).

- The head remains aligned rather than twisting around further in the direction of the turn. Keep the gaze of your eyes soft and far-reaching – find peripheral vision.

- You may find that turning from the lower body is easier if you think of yourself hanging from the ceiling from the crown of your head (use the image of 'braid to rafters' if helpful).

- As you turn, let the foot on that side take a little more of the weight and, therefore, become the front foot. This is only a subtle weight shift. Stay aware of triangles under your feet.

- Let your arms follow the impetus of the belly as it turns your torso. The arms will swing, wrapping around the torso as the belly and pelvis reach the furthermost point of their turn. The arms swing low through the air around the body no higher than your navel. The forearm of the outside arm (opposite arm to the direction in which you are twisting) bangs the middle of the belly. The other forearm and back of the hand tap the lower back at the end of the hip twist, just before the pelvis initiates the movement to the other side. Think of this as keeping in touch with yourself. Make sure that the swinging remains compact – flinging or flailing the arms through the space denotes tension in the arms as opposed to moving from the belly. The swing is the result of releasing tension and responding to movement of the pelvis. The arms are heavy and released enough to swing.

- Continue for any length of time in a settled rhythm. Later you can change the tempo, slowing down and then speeding up but without the swings ever becoming frantic. Find out what you need to do physically to accommodate the changes of tempo.

Key points

The impetus for the movement is from the *dan tien*. The movement is rooted throughout.

Diagonal Scale[20]

- As with the Dimensional Scale, it is worth making a cube for yourself – the same cube serves both exercises and may prove useful.
- Stand at the centre of your imagined cube, feet together and toes facing forward so you start in a focused position.

These directions are embodied first with the right foot and arm, and then with the left.

Each diagonal moves from high to deep. When starting with the right arm, the direction of the scale is anticlockwise. When starting with the left arm, the direction of the scale is clockwise. Find your way to embody the diagonals, while simultaneously staying true to the geometry of the cube, keeping the shoulders and hips square to the front.

- *High right forward* – step up onto the ball of the right foot, right arm lifted along the diagonal. The left foot joins the downward diagonal.

---

[20] Green's interpretation of Laban's Diagonal Scale.

- *Deep*[21] *left back* – take the right foot behind the left along the diagonal and allow the right arm to cross the front of the torso along the downward pull of the diagonal. This will bend your legs and torso as they keep square to the cube whilst still embodying the diagonal.

- Rebalance moving through the centre to *high left forward* – step across the body onto the ball of the right foot, taking the right arm up and along the high diagonal. The left foot takes care of itself, defining the downward oppositional pull.

- *Deep right back* – take the right leg and foot back along the downward pulling diagonal and the right arm back along the diagonal.

- The left leg may be able to lift to the opposite upward diagonal but it may not be physically possible for you in which case it needs to do so imaginatively.

- Rebalance, moving through the centre to *high left back* – step onto the ball of the right foot, crossing it behind the left onto the diagonal, and cross the right arm across the front of the torso along the upward pulling diagonal.

- The torso joins in without losing the physical integrity of being at the centre of the cube.

- *Deep right forward* – take the right foot and leg forward into a lunge along the downward pulling diagonal. The left leg again finds its connection with the high back diagonal while the right arm lengthens along the downward pulling diagonal.

- Rebalance, moving through centre to *high right back* – step onto the ball of the right foot back onto the high pulling diagonal. The right arm lifts along this diagonal with the left leg pulling downward in opposition.

- *Deep left forward* – take the right foot and leg in a lunge across the body onto the downward pulling diagonal with the right arm lengthening along this same diagonal. The left leg finds a way to express the opposite direction.

- Rebalance, moving to centre in alive stillness, ready to repeat with the left leg and arm.

- Find that moment of movement potential at the end of the scale. This is when you gather yourself right into the centre of the cube; once more you are ready to continue to the next high on the other side.

---

[21] 'Deep' is exchangeable with the words 'low', 'down' or 'downward', but is commonly the favoured term for this scale.

Key points

Find the rhythm – this needs to be quite fast because of the nature of the scale's physical instability. You have to wrest yourself back from falling in one direction by moving to the opposite direction. That then takes you back to centre for the next high position, and so on. You need to do this with energy and stamina as it is robust and demanding, relentlessly taking you out of balance again and again. Find the breath of the rising and falling rhythm of the scale.

Falling

Find a place in the room and stand in neutral stance.

- Let the weight of the body sink bit by bit, falling under itself not away from you, perhaps an inward curling and outer body rounding as the legs 'buckle' underneath the torso, without the use of the hands to save or to assist you with the fall.

- Do this slowly and then, once you feel confident, do it fast. Now imagine your whole body dropping like a stone in one simultaneous fall.

- Move around the room and suddenly fall. Think of some images that may also be helpful, such as: being sucked down into the floor; a gap appears in the floor so that you disappear in a moment; egg-timer sand falling; a waterfall, and so on.

- Allow the body to experience the undiluted sensation of the out of balance, and falling, as the inevitable outcome of out of balance, downwards to the floor, along the floor and at diagonals to it, but always ending up on it.

- Now from standing still, spiral down to the floor and up again, fall forwards, sideways and backwards – starting low and then from standing.

- Make sure that you stand back up again from out of the floor too. You get up to fall down.

Sequential

This is a pathway of continuous movement; a sequence of movement from body part to body part, each following the last and triggering the next.

- Stand or lie in the space and visualize a pinball somewhere in your body.

- As it shifts it sends a ripple through your body. Imagine it travelling systematically round your whole body including your limbs and extremities.

- Every time you move, the movement sends the pinball on a further journey through your joints.

Rolling

 Rolling; Free Roll.

In this roll you are practising the ability to land every part of you in the ground, really allowing release and sequential movement through your torso.

- Lie supine – fully outstretched with your arms above your head. Cross your outer leg diagonally across your inner leg in the direction you are going to roll, as if it was being pulled gently away from you diagonally along the floor. Feel the pull across your hips and ribs and follow this leg so that it turns you sequentially – pelvis, waist, ribs, shoulder, head – each initiated by its predecessor moving onto your front.

- Feel your torso turning over. Twist bit by bit, so that the twist reaches your head last: feel the connection of the crown of your head to your tail bone as the head pulls up and back as the hip lands on the floor.

- Feel as though you are leaving something of yourself behind – a sort of surrender – as you softly 'fall' onto your front and are received body part by body part into the floor.

- Let the circling of the shoulder girdle and the underside shoulder turn you from your front to your back. Allow the shoulder, then the waist and then the hip to twist sequentially as you roll over onto your back with the floor again receiving you firmly body part by body part. Let the movement dictate the timing/rhythm.

- Engage with the sense of the diagonal through your body.

- Find the sense of spaciousness, timelessness and possibility.

- Find the continuum, the spiral. Keep moving into new territory without undoing a move.

- Finally roll onto your front and roll up the spine to your feet and notice how you are at the top.

Partner Work

Sticking[22]

The task is to 'stick' to your partner's wrist with your fingertips, eyes closed, and stay in contact as your partner moves.

Use the ward-off posture:[23] a posture to ward off your opponent's attack. This ward-off protects the heart and defines the psychological space in front of you.

- Delineate this space with a 'circle' of your arms: hold them in front of you at chest height with fingertips a couple of inches apart and palms facing inwards towards your heart. The circle is as large as it should be for your person – length of arms, breadth, height, and so on. Hold your arms from your back, resting in and supported as it were by the latissimus dorsi.[24] Keep a sense of space under your armpits and with your elbows dropping down with gravity. This is not the ballet first position with the elbows lifted, though its placement in front of the chest is the same.

- Seek a sense of a 'liquid' or 'airy' personal space, demarcating this space with a malleable and moveable boundary. Wrist, elbow and shoulder joints are relaxed; imagine them filled with fluid or air, whichever works best for you. Use this space lightly and easily.

For the purposes of this exercise you use just one arm for the sticking, whether you are the partner with your eyes shut or open. It is, however, important to know and own the true ward-off posture for yourself before embarking on this exercise.

- Visualize, maintain and stay connected to the circle in front of you from the fingertips of the working arm to the opposite shoulder: visualize the imaginary semicircle from that shoulder tip to the fingertips of your lifted arm, so your arm stays square to your chest. If it helps, think of the hand being in front of the heart.

---

[22] See note 16.
[23] Ward-off is key to the martial art – the attack is seen, accepted with the ward-off and yielded to, with the result that the opponent's energy and intention are deflected or diffused. Actor Movement works with this exercise to enhance the actor's understanding of the demarcation of his personal space and the interrelation with a partner whilst remaining aware of his own state, listening to self and the other, being alert and responding with physical ease and fluidity. For further reading on the practice, see Cheng Man-Ch'ing, *Cheng Tzu's Thirteen Treatises on T'ai Chi Ch'uan*, Berkeley, CA: Frog Ltd, 2008; Angus Clark, *Elements of T'ai Chi*, Shaftesbury: Element, 2002.
[24] Latissimus dorsi – broad flat triangular muscles on either side of the back that swing the arms backwards and rotate them inwards.

- Keep 'your opponent' in front of you. If you open this circle up, you have lost your defence; you are vulnerable; you have allowed your opponent into your space.

- Keep the connection of your arm to your spine and initiate the movement from your belly (and/or the *dan tien*).

Partners A and B

- Stand opposite each other.

- Decide who is going to start in which role: the person with eyes open (Partner A), or the person with eyes shut (Partner B).

Partner A

- Present your right arm.

Partner B

- Use your left arm so that the position between you is open. Rest your left fingertips and thumb on the top of A's right wrist, lightly but clearly. You can also rest the middle of your hand beneath your middle finger on the wrist if you can keep the image of your hand being as light as a butterfly landing on a delicate flower.

- Shut your eyes.

- Once A starts to move, try to stick onto the wrist as A moves through the space, anticipating A's next move. Respond; yield to the journey, 'knowing' where you are, because of your ward-off. Keep listening to yourself in the present, as well as listening to A, paying attention and doing all this with the least amount of effort for most effect. Keep in touch through the physical contact and in your mind's eye.

Partner A

- Keep the palm open and facing the body more or less opposite the chest.

- Walk through the space once B has settled with his fingertips on your wrist. There is actually nowhere specific to go: you can go anywhere in the space so there is no need to pull or push B around. Are you moving in all directions and not just backwards?

- Try staying in one place for a short while. There is no need to keep walking round the space. 'Sticking' can be done on the spot, if the arm is released and malleable and your personal space flexible and defined lightly.

- Work out how to use the body softly. Find that sense of being rooted and light at the same time. Pay attention if you feel yourself becoming ungrounded, tense or busy. If this happens, quietly remain still. Wait until you refind the form. Notice if you are tensing your arms, having lost the fluidity and softness you find when your eyes are shut. Are you taking responsibility for B and concentrating and gripping with the body?
- Shut your eyes for a short while to see if you can again find that fluid, listening quality, so both of you have your eyes shut whilst staying in role, as long as someone/the rest of the group keeps you safe.

Partner B

- Release and drop the wrist down; drop your elbow; relax the ankles and feet, keeping them pliant; notice if you are shuffling.
- Keep the circle of the ward-off, staying upright and moving from your *dan tien*.
- Notice if and where you are physically holding on now that your eyes are shut. Keep your fluidity and ease. Don't panic!
- Keep checking where you need to be to maintain this personal space. Keep alert to your partner so that you can change direction instantly, working with whatever presents itself – it is an improvisation – but never leaving yourself exposed by opening the arm out of the ward-off.

Partner A

- After a while, stop moving, reach for B's other wrist with your left wrist and lift it up to your ward-off and only then gently release B's left wrist.
- Give yourself time as you change to this other side to listen to the different sensations of working with the other half ward-off. This is still a whole-bodied activity but just by working with the other arm the sensation may surprise you.
- Start moving when you are ready. Notice any differences working with the right and left arms in ward-off.

Partner B

- Let A lift your right hand and move it onto his wrist. Then let your left arm drop down to your side as A releases it.

- Repeat the sticking with the right arm in ward-off. You are 'sticking' with the other arm but still in whole bodied ward-off.
- Notice if there are any differences working on the right and left sides.

Partner A and B

- Change roles.
- Within an ongoing class situation, keep changing partners. In this way you will be exposed to a different experience of sticking each time.
- As a later experience you can do this without contact and with eyes open, with energy in the spine, and explore the spatial tension between you and your partner.

Key points

This exercise can be misconstrued as a blindfold leading exercise, but leading someone round the room with a blindfold is a different experience. Sticking is not a leadership exercise and the words leading or leader are not included in its explanation. Within sticking you make a choice to keep your eyes closed. Keep it playful. You can talk together about light things as you 'stick' should the work start becoming over precious. You can then go back to being silent with a lighter feel to the work.

Falling (for the individual in a group)

- Move around and through the space, walking at differing speeds, with a sense of your three-dimensional nature rather than just walking forward.
- When you are touched on the shoulder by the hand of someone else in the space, respond to this and fall with the sense of your body falling directly underneath itself and land and spread yourself on the floor, give yourself a moment of 'being' on the floor and then gather yourself and get up sequentially through the body, head coming upright last, and continue walking through the space.
- As you move through the space, touch someone on the shoulder so that he falls.

Partner A

Continue moving through the space, and at regular intervals select a partner.

- Touch the shoulder of Partner B.

- Wait until B falls, and as B starts to get up, use your body weight to give him a resistance to push against as he gets up from the floor to standing and walking once again.
- As B rises from the floor, give a gentle pressure to B's head so this is the last body part to arrive upright.
- Once upright, gently push B into the space.
- Continue walking through the space as either A or B.

Partner A

- Allow yourself to fall into partner B's body.

Partner B

- Catch and potentially fall with A to the floor.

A and B

- Rise once more from the floor.
- Move round the space and continue an improvisation of falling into and supporting one another.

Key note

The touch on the shoulder is a soft pressure downwards and then a release rather than any kind of shove or pat – it follows the principles of CI (Contact Improvisation). There is no sense of dominance or competition in this touch and fall sequence.

Draping

Work in partners

This is about draping your body, or part of your body, over the surface of support that is your partner. The quality of 'draping' enables the posture of surrender.

Partner A: 'Supporting' partner

Go onto all fours and remain in that posture. You take responsibility for how long you wish to remain in this position and when you wish to end being the support, indicate this by starting the return to sitting which will prompt B to move. If comfortable, come out of the posture as you feel B start to move off.

Partner B: 'Working' partner

- Lie across your partner's back – this can be cross-wise over the midriff and lumbar spine or along the length of the back for more support. Make sure you meet your partner's body with the lower back or centre of your weight so that both halves of your body can fold open from that point.
- Allow yourself to remain draped – this does mean allowing yourself to 'let go' and physically drape over the surface of the support – and then 'pour' yourself off the support.
- Change roles.

Stage One: Exploring draping and supporting

Partner A

- Find a position of support.

Partner B

- Drape yourself over A, as if you were pouring yourself over his body.
- After really being draped over the support for a while, pour off again.

Partner A

- Continue with your role as support with four other firm positions, for example: strong lunge position with the torso upright and hands on the thigh of the leg in front or with the chest and hands on the knee; lying down; standing with wide feet and bending forwards with hands on thighs, and so on.

Partner B

- Let the positions of support influence your movement and dynamic.
- Notice if you are mentally deciding what to do or allowing the draping to happen.
- Swap roles.

Stage Two: Alternate roles of draping and supporting

- Allow the draping and the supporting to divulge what the next move will be.

Stage Three: Support now moves in response to the drape and vice versa

- Stay in contact as you both move in response to each other.

- Improvise with draping, sometimes draping and sometimes being the support. Each role affects and moves the other.

- Surrender to the release of your body. Find how you might allow moments of stillness and surrender of body weight.

- The head may be back with the throat exposed as your body weight is draped over your partner's supporting body. You can relinquish all responsibility in this posture as your partner, like you, is taking responsibility for himself.

Key points

Keep the word 'drape', and all this evokes for you, in mind and body; let your body listen to the movement. Be honest with yourself with giving your weight – either you are or you are not.

Counterweight Exercise

Partner work

Height and weight differences and similarities may both be used for partner selection. Some exercises can be more accessible and encouraging at the beginning if the height or weight of the partners is similar.

Find the counterweight to your partner. Your partner's height and weight might be very different from you own. This exercise is a tester of how your weights balance.

- Stand opposite each other in a slightly over hip-width, wide-legged position. Use both arms and grasp each other's wrists.

- Bend your knees, and start to pull away from each other so that your backs round. Feel how your lower back opens as a result, creating a C-curve.

- Allow yourself to gently control the descent and rise through giving your weight as you take your partner's.

Begin again, but this time Partner A lies down while B stands with his feet on the outside of A's feet: A and B link wrists.

Partner B

- As you breathe out, allow your body weight to take you towards the floor – bending your knees and C-curving your back.
- Allow yourself to sink to the floor, first sitting and then lying.
- Pull away to bring A upright.

Partner A

- As B lies down, continue holding his wrists, which means that you are bent over his legs to keep the hand hold.

Partner B

- As you feel A pulling back, breathe in, keep your arms long and allow yourself to be drawn up in counterweight to A's descent.
- You will come arcing upright, allowing A to sit and lie down.
- Bend over his legs to keep the hand-hold when he lies down.

Partners A and B

- Continue see-sawing, listening to the breath – the rising and falling pattern between you. As you move downwards, you breathe out; as you rise, you breathe in.
- Take this practice of listening into other partnerships.
- Mould your body into the shape it needs to be to sink into the floor as well as rise from it.
- Give yourself time to allow your body to form the curves.
- Wait for the momentum, rather than use your bent arms to muscularly heave your partner up, or to manoeuver yourself down to the floor.

Key points

Make sure that you release the arms and are not holding your partner's weight by bending your arms and using muscular power. It might be that you nearly reach the floor before the partner stands; allow the possibility of this – just wait for the see-saw to work.

Checking in with Partner Work

- Find the drive to go through the barriers you may be putting up. These could be planning the moves; inhibiting yourself because you are taking responsibility for your partner; not allowing yourself fully to commit your weight to your partner; or holding back out of self-consciousness.

- If your body weight is actively reciprocated you can know that you are working with your full weight. This offers the improvisation true dynamism.

- Offering yourself as support to your partner may seem to be an easier role: when your partner's weight is given to you, you have no choice but to be the support. You may prefer being receptive as opposed to initiating through giving your own weight and following through with the momentum of this. Either way, this involves yielding and responding through careful reading of the contact situation.

- Are you on the way to finding the evidence within CI that actors' different weights are not an issue?

- Go back to the rules: take responsibility for yourself, listen and have respect for yourself and your partner.

- Keep in your mind that the point of contact in CI is simply a surface of support into which you press. This is the same whether you are using your full body weight or just a light touch.

- If you find yourself giggling, calculate for yourself when this is happening and from that you can locate why it is occurring.

- Seek ever greater intention within your work. This means that the movement is dynamic and energized, which leads to a fuller experience. Take, for instance, the experience of preparation trust work into the dance partnerwork you are encountering.

Back to Self

Finding Free Flow[25] on Your Feet

- Start by lying on the floor and moving just to establish the quality of free flow.

- Bring yourself onto your feet.

- Find a space in the room to stand.

- Begin flowing freely around the space.

- Follow through any swing of the limbs and every movement (not just doing what happened with the right arm with the left, for example).

- The movement of the torso, arms and legs create imaginary trace patterns or vapour trails in the space.

- Whatever your imagery, be compelled onwards in your movement. Perhaps have an image of not being able easily to brake when cycling down a hill, or when skiing; envisage water streaming down a hill, or a river in flood. Can you remember what it was like to have to keep on running down a hill once you had started, knowing that to stop would hurt you and that sometimes it's just best to keep going?

- Move in curves, circles, spirals, undulations, waves, arcs, and so on. Use sequential movement. Release any holding in the joints. For those with travel sickness, do this for only a short while (and be aware if you are tightening either your stomach or belly and consciously aim to drop your weight into your feet).

Key points

Imagine the joints as channels and keep them open so that the energy is able to course through the body. Distinguish between using the right amount of energy just to do the job and 'pushing' the energy/force in a way that feels powerful but would be untenable to carry on for any length of time. Do not do this for too long and allow lulls in the flow. Listen to your body.

---

[25] Green's interpretation of Laban's Free Flow.

3
SEEKING NEUTRAL

OVERVIEW

The exploration of Neutral is the search for an alert state of embodiment,
a way of being which holds no particular persuasion and yet contains
all possibilities. The actor may undergo significant personal change. The
movements that have accumulated to hide and protect him in everyday life
are exposed as he is made aware of his body in a performance context. The
process reveals what he is offering each time he gets up to perform.

The word 'neutral' is often associated with blandness, nothingness, an idea of
brightness dulled. In the context of movement, however, it is a tremendously
liberating concept.

The concept and practice of Neutral is explored in this chapter through a
combination of two seminal movement studies: the philosophy of the Neutral
Mask as formulated by Jacques Lecoq[1] and Jacques Copeau; and the
Movement Analysis of Rudolph Laban.[2] Bringing together core aspects of
these disciplines allows the actor to reach a deep understanding of the habitual
movement patterns, body stories and inherent physical expressiveness that
make up the 'self'.

The process outlined here[3] focuses on developing the actor's instinct. It
begins by building an awareness of innate human behaviour (the ability to read

---

[1] For further reading see, J. Lecoq, *The Moving Body* [*Le Corps Poétique*]: *Teaching Creative Theatre*,
London: Methuen Drama (Performance Books), 2009; J. Lecoq, *Theatre of Movement and Gesture*,
new edn, Abingdon: Routledge, 2006; S. Murray, *Jacques Lecoq*, Abingdon: Routledge Performance
Practitioners, 2003.
[2] For further reading, see R. Laban, *Mastery of Movement*, Tavistock: Northcote House, 1980.
[3] Ewan's process of work in the studio with the actors.

body language, for instance). Close observation and precise articulation of movement function together to broaden the actor's expressive scope.

Both the Neutral Mask and the concept of Neutral are established teaching tools and the exercises are designed to be worked on in a group, generally led by a tutor. This is because the Neutral is dependent on, and always aware of, an audience. However, this chapter can offer thought-provoking stimuli for the lone actor or one who is undertaking a process of led workshops on the Neutral or the Neutral Mask.

Neutral and the Epic

See Practical: *Colour as a Shared Abstract Physical Language* (p. 74)

The first stage of working on Neutral is to build an understanding of the concept. Neutral is a place of potential: within it there is no doubt and no opinion. There is only purity, economy and appropriateness.

Neutral accesses the Universal Elemental Nature that Lecoq called the Epic. 'The Epic', in the context of Actor Movement, should not be taken to mean 'heroic' or 'grand'. It is a heightened way of being. The Neutral accepts the miraculous; it has an extraordinary connection with life and the world. Yet it is grounded in everyday existence and must translate to mundane activity (for instance, getting on the bus). If the actor only ever makes the landscape of the Neutral a magnificent space, where does that put the bus journey? The actor must learn to locate the Epic in the everyday. Children understand the Epic: my name is Joe, I live on Acacia Avenue, London, England, United Kingdom, Europe, the World, the Galaxy, the Universe. They understand their place in the world. When an actor has that same understanding he is in contact with the audience in the right way.

Do Less

See Practical: *Becoming Someone as You Talk about Him or Her* (p. 76)
See Practical: *Outer Stillness on Text* (p. 79)

Whilst working on Neutral, unconscious and subjective qualities are deliberately brought to the actor's attention. These qualities may be altered permanently or even stigmatized. It is, for example, difficult for the actor to retain a relaxed posture if he has been made aware that his posture is not well aligned or that it 'reads' in a particular way during performance. Work on the Neutral has a responsibility not to destroy such qualities, which may one day be viewed as a specialism. For example, a habitual wandering focus may seem 'woolly' or vague, yet when accurately and consciously embodied, it can also be poetic, sensual and compelling.

Neutral Action

This process articulates Neutral Action as 'pure' action: action that is free of adverb just as the Neutral is free of adjective. 'A person walking' is exactly and only that, not 'the "confident" person "happily" walking'.

The Mask Reveals More than it Hides

In the process of exploring Neutral, the actor may be introduced to the 'Neutral Mask'.

The Mask works by hiding the face and shifting attention to the physicality of the actor's body. A paper bag would do the same job, but it would totally exclude the face. The Neutral Mask, with its symmetry, defines basic facial outlines, which appear to take on expression (such as a smile or a frown) from the actor's 'body story'. Of course, the body tells a story with or without a mask, but this story is usually obscured by the overall impression of the body, facial expression and words. The Mask reveals more than it hides.

For the actor-as-observer, the Mask is a masterly analytical tool. However, if it is introduced too early in the process, the actor can feel blind without it. This process offers exercises which allow the actor to engage with the principles of observation and Physical Action before the Mask is introduced. The actor is subsequently – and gradually – provided with the necessary tools to understand what is observed when he finally comes to work with the Mask.

Structuring a Neutral Process

The process here is divided into three stages. The first stage bridges work in the studio with the wider world. Its starting point is the actor's everyday body and its engagement with familiar Physical Action. An initial exercise concentrating on the specific action of walking develops a general understanding of Neutral. The process is a simultaneous opening up of perception and unearthing of the concept. The actor practises switching between these worlds, maintaining his authenticity while exploring the Neutral.

The second stage, concentrating on unfamiliar Physical Action, opens up the concept of the Epic. Concentrating on the simple fact of the action, it allows the actor space to make each moment matter.

The third stage is the practice of the Neutral through a range of learned and repeatable tasks. This process gradually reveals the possibilities of the Neutral Mask. Acknowledging the actor's personal body story – and the body stories of others – it works on the subtle shifts between reality and theatre-reality. The actor builds the relationship between self-analysis and silent acceptance of audience response.

Stage One: Pedestrian (Everyday) Action

See Practical: *The Walk* (p. 76)

Neutral is not a problem to be solved. There is no single answer to any question that might be asked. The actor observes the world from his own vantage points. His understanding is personal and particular. Connection to the movement is achieved by relating to – and empathizing with – observational experiences from his own life.

Living with a Question

This stage in the process of seeking Neutral offers the practice of 'living with a question'. It plants just one question about an action and asks it repeatedly over a period of time.

The question is large enough to warrant contemplation and small enough to be carried through the actor's daily life as he engages in a familiar action, for instance, walking. In other words, it is both Epic (e.g. 'What is *the* Walk?') and everyday ('What is *a* walk?'). The question can be asked as the actor walks to and from work; as he walks along a beach or through some vast and spectacular landscape; as he walks alone or in a crowd. The exercise includes observing others' walks and other animals walking, reading about walking, looking at walking in art or poetry, learning the mechanics of walking, all without seeming like tasks to the actor.

IN CONTEXT: LIVING WITH A QUESTION

The questions an actor carries with him when involved in a play and a film must get 'into his bones'. His body, imagination, senses and experience are all equally engaged. The actor is curious about the world he finds himself in and thinks with his whole being.

Saying What He Sees

The actor can engage in an exercise designed to move the actor-as-observer away from his usual, considered classroom response and encourage him to say what he sees. This is to get as near to hearing his own thoughts as he can. Taking place in the studio, it involves the actor performing 'the Walk' along a pathway created by other actors who, as an audience, offer imaginary 'film titles', for example 'On the Way to Work', 'To the Headmaster's Office' or 'Leering Elf'.

Capturing the Impression

Imaginary film titles are self-generated responses from a personally understood pool of reference. As an imaginative articulation of the actor's observations this is a valuable tool and one that he can also practice as he observes people in the outside world. However, in order to be truly useful it requires a constantly widening pool of reference and ever more precise observation. The practice in the studio offers this.

Information in the Film Title

Details about the body in action are contained in the film title. The story implicit in the title suggests physical idiosyncrasies which can be mined for meaning later in the process. An actor homing in on someone else's habit of leading with a specific body part, or focusing on the fact that a person's shoulders are not the same height would, at this stage undermine his process. (Anatomical details can always be examined at any points in the future). When watching other actors, some actors mistakenly see and think like a tutor, and this process redirects them to see and think like an actor.

The film title offers a lot of information, some directly articulated and some implied. For instance, the title, 'To the Headmaster's Office' places the performer at school age. Why school age? Is it because he moves with lightness and small steps? The body stories are a combination of habitual embodiment and in-the-moment behaviour. For example, the observed 'narrowness' in the body that led to the perception of a corridor to the headmaster's office, might not be habitual for the actor. It might be his way of dealing with group feedback or an attempt to close it out. Taking another example 'On the Way to Work', it might be useful to ask how different *the* Walk would be if it were entitled 'Going Home from Work', and so on.

A larger person's way of moving is different from a smaller person's. Seeing this type of diversity is beneficial, as it offers the actor experience of different centres of gravity, different qualities of weight, types of gait, and so on.

In this work, each actor seeks Neutral for his own person and his own body: a body with particular shape, size and energy. He is therefore released from comparison and the temptation of thinking 'He's got it. I'll do the same.' There's no point imitating another actor's Neutral.

Receiving Feedback

Within the language of movement there is no right or wrong, only appropriate and inappropriate. If an actor infers that his work is 'wrong', he risks throwing something precious away.

Once the actor has received feedback, trying to 'fix' something quickly is ill advised. The issue may be a consequence of something not yet understood and it will not help the actor to work on it at this stage.

IN CONTEXT

A successful actor must get used to the idea of others valuing what he naturally has; when, for example, his quickness, his fluidity, or an expressive turn of the head are recognized and repeatedly complimented. To him, these are mere idiosyncrasies. Comparing the equivalent success in another artist – say, a singer whose voice is naturally wonderfully deep, or a dancer whose leap is naturally extraordinarily high – can be helpful. Movement gifts, particularly our own, are too often dismissed.

Notes to a Tutor

Within the feedback, comments and film titles, reference may be made to cultural difference, skin colour or sexuality. This needs careful unpacking and it is the tutor's job to hold the space and create a safe environment. The tutor's choice of language can also keep the actor 'on track' as he finds a more sophisticated way of seeing (for example, the tutor might drop in 'masculine' and 'feminine' as clearer descriptors than 'male' and 'female').

It is important to take great care of the quality, structure and tenor of feedback within the process of exploring Neutral. The actor is likely to feel more exposed in these exercises than he might feel, for example, in text work. In this mostly silent environment, the giving and receiving of accurate feedback is essential to diminish any sense of vulnerability and build confidence. (See additional online resources: *Feedback*.)

Moving On

A growing recognition of the Epic within the pedestrian means it is time to move on to Stage Two.

Figure 3.1   One of sculptor Antony Gormley's wonderful life size cast iron statues on the beach at Crosby in North-West England. Photograph © Ian Bramham Photography/Getty Images.

Stage Two: From the Pedestrian to the Epic

From this stage onwards, the work is about realization. It is not a time for the actor to work on any feedback notes, but impartially to observe himself and others.

A principle of Neutral, for this process, is that it is set apart from the messy everyday world or the world of the play. It is seen as a place of possibility; somewhere with no constraints of time or space. Of course this is neither realistic nor practical, but conceptually it offers clarity to the actor.

Understanding Physical Action

See Practical: *The Difference between a Mime and a Physical Action* (p. 81)
See Practical: *The Physical Action* (p. 82)

Sawing the Log is an exercise devised by Lecoq to explore the Neutral. The actor performs an unfamiliar Physical Action in order to find its essence.

The Physical Action should not be confused with 'mime'[4] just because it involves a saw and occurs within a movement context. A tell-tale sign that it is mime is if the audience is compelled to look at an empty space in which the object is imagined. With a Physical Action, the focus and the actor's intention are only on connecting with that action. The audience looks at the actor's body to read the story, not at the empty space.

An action that is offered within an acting exercise may require adding as much detailed personal context as possible. Here, the Neutral creates a framework in which the actor focuses solely on the action. His performance should be deliberately pared back.

Sewing is a physical action, but it can also express inertia (think of the imposed domesticity of Jane Austen's world). Within a play, the action of sewing may be used to reveal a character's inner state. Perhaps the small amount of energy used – the lack of physical action – evokes a repetitive, monotonous existence.

When the Physical Action is embodied, however, it can be 'the action of all actions', an action of the whole body, including the breath. To embody the Physical, the actor needs to commit all his energy; he needs to 'drive' the Action.

Sex and fighting dominate the action in film and television. Perhaps this is because they are the most easily understood ways of communicating physical

---

[4]Mime here is understood as fulfilling the task of creating the unseen objects for an audience.

action. There is a likely connection with both the actor and the audience. But what if an actor could commit the same, persuasive energy to other, less hackneyed actions?

It is important for the actor to understand that en-route to finding this fuller physical commitment, his action may not be read by the audience in the way he intended. Performing a fully involved Physical Action like *Sawing the Log*, he may be surprised, or even shocked, to learn that the audience saw him, instead, killing a baby on a Friday morning; or that he looked like he was punching a small child.

These impressions of his action are not so alarming and are in fact an affirmation, when he realizes, that he is committing the necessary energy to the Physical Action and it is only because this energy is tight and 'bound' and spatially restricted that the story of killing the baby came to mind, not that he is a horrible person.

The actor may receive any number of film titles for his *Sawing the Log* ('Quiet Misty Morning'; 'Gentle Giant'; 'Kneading the Dough'; 'Violent Colouring In'; 'My Lawnmower's Not Working'). They all offer something to the actor and, unravelled, they provide him with specific physical goals.

Moving into the complete exercise

Once the essence of the Physical Action has been understood, he can begin to appreciate what happens to his body when shifting to and from a fully involved Physical Action to the more physically passive actions. This vision is unequivocally offered within the full journey of *Sawing the Log*: hearing and watching are sandwiched between two bouts of Physical Action. Other areas of the actor's learning (e.g. living in the now, animal efficiency, elements, flow) may also surface in these explorations.

Stage Three: The Neutral Mask

A First Encounter with the Mask

See Practical: *First Encounter with the Mask* (p. 83)

It is important for the actor to capture and reflect upon his first impressions of the Mask. The story the actors-as-audience see and then verbally offer may not be what the actor is feeling; he may be described as funny when in fact he was angry and sad. Being the Mask and responding to the Mask as a light-hearted and playful interaction leaves room for creativity. There is never a time when the Mask is not offering, never a time when the audience is not receiving.

A Neutral Journey

See Practical: *A Neutral Mask Journey* (p. 85)
See Practical*: Stories of the Space – Pathways* (p. 87)

Lecoq devised several Journeys for the Neutral Mask. These allow the actor to fully engage with every moment, never contemplating the past or anticipating the future. Doing something repeatable and simple takes the actor into the essence of the Journey. He experiences the self as part of the world in every moment and as the Neutral he experiences and tells the story of the particular Journey.

The following journey is one particularly suited to the actor:
The Journey starts in a white mist and its stages are: sleeping; walking; standing; walking; standing; the mist clearing; seeing the sea for the first time; throwing a stone into the sea.

As well as offering him the Journey, it includes actions that he might not have paid much attention to and yet has to bring to life over and over in every play or film that he does.

As with the rest of the work, this is a taught exercise and dependent on an audience.

IN CONTEXT: EPIC

The actor may offer an Epic message through an everyday action. This is not because he has been directed to do so, or because he has taken on responsibility for the symbolic, but because he has, instinctively, found a way of touching an essence.

A Note for Tutors and Actors

When using the Mask as a teaching and learning tool, it is essential to understand the power it hands to the tutor/observer (whilst simultaneously making the actor vulnerable). The Mask gives the tutor/observer permission to look at it, but if the tutor is the only one feeding back, it can, over time, appear that he has 'special powers' of acute observation. In fact the Mask is doing most of the work, making the body stories very apparent. The tutor must always take time to stop, question and appraise his transaction with the actor. The power must at all times be acknowledged as a result of working with the formidable potential of the Mask, which is where it should remain.

Practical Section: Stage One

Colour as a Shared Abstract Physical Language

This exercise works only in a group situation. The group is divided into two (Group A and Group B). This is a very simple, quick exercise to increase trust and awareness of a shared physical language. It celebrates the shared human experience, without getting to a stage of focusing on the cultural associations and symbolism of certain colours.[5]

Group A

- Choose a colour from the primary palette and together locate a particular example of that colour in the room (without Group B seeing or hearing you).

- Without any discussion or preparation, take to the space.

- Check you have space around you; put on a blindfold to liberate you from seeing each other.

- Become the colour at the same time as everyone else.

Group B

- Observe.

- Suggest which colour it is that you are watching.

Groups A and B

- Stop and take stock.

- Don't let either your initial response or any of the excitement 'get away'.

- Don't feel silly about being excited about something that might seem so obvious. Don't stop being excited about colour. Avoid becoming too rational.

- Swap group roles for a different colour.

---

[5] Lecoq devised an exercise that moves on to explore the diversity of colour.

Groups A and B

You can go on to explore other colours, but it is not essential. Once you see each group's blindfolded movement-responses, the task is done. You can then go on to play with the colour palette with confidence.

- Try (without a blindfold) moving from, for example, red through to orange through to yellow.

- Allow the breath to reveal the embodied response to the texture and volume implicit in the visualization.

- Allow the shape-changes to take on the blended part of the colours.

- Let some physical aspect deteriorate as another develops; something reduces as something else blossoms; something fades as something else becomes more vibrant; let strength and weakness coexist.

IN CONTEXT: COLOUR

Keeping in mind the exercise above, in which colour is translated to a shared physical language:

What colours are described or used in the script/play?

What colour is your costume?

Does this offer any clues about your character? Does it match your idea of your character, and if it doesn't, can the difference or even the surprise of the choice add a different dimension to your character which you had not seen before or realized?

What is the colour, or colours, that come to mind when you think of your character?

What colours do you imagine your character likes?

Becoming Someone as You Talk about Her or Him – A Preparation Exercise

This is an exercise for the individual within a group – an exercise for you to realize just how many embodiments you carry from the pool of people around you. It's amazing what you absorb of a person's persona when you love or care for them.

- Choose a relative, or a very close friend, someone you know intimately enough that you will be able to embody her or him without having to sit down and think of how s/he moves.

- Have a partner ask you questions about this relative or friend – not too personal, as this is a real person (so something like this everyday question: 'What does your brother do for a living?').

- Allow yourself to demonstrate her/his mannerisms when that is appropriate in your answers, just as we do in real situations as part of description.

- After a number of questions, the questioner can continue with the questions but start to address you as the person described (e.g. 'How long have YOU worked there?').

- After the exercise, notice how much you have in your body-knowledge of this person: her/his rhythm; posture; certain nuances; idiosyncratic movements, and so on.

- Notice how these emerged easily out of your empathy, understanding and possibly even love of that person.

- Notice how you were not mimicking. You hold a physical knowledge of that person's way of being in the world, an essence, maybe the thing that you love about them.

- Take this understanding into your observation of other people.

'The Walk' – Beginning to Understand Neutral

This is an exercise for the individual within a group. This exercise uses a walk as a familiar action; a part of your life. This necessitates some research:

- Ask yourself: 'What is a walk?'

- Understand the essentials of what a walk is. Start with the broad strokes; the obvious. For example, it takes you from A to B. Is it, in fact, possible to walk without moving yourself across space? Not really, so it is clearly a pretty major element of a walk. This is an obvious statement, but you need to locate and take on the obvious above all else.

- Put your findings in an order.
- Highlight the essentials.
- This is starting to sound like a paper exercise but put the pencil down! Keep it as a dialogue with your body and the minute it becomes dull to explore, stop. It will not help you to plough through this as a task. Keep the question open; the answer will arrive.
- Look at analysts' and practitioners' studies of walking (for example, Mabel Todd, Alexander, Feldenkrais). (See Chapter 2, Practical: *T'ai Chi Slow Walk.*)
- Ask yourself now: 'What is the Walk?'
- Consider the responses of artists, writers, poets, and lyricists. You are not answering the question, but rather spending time understanding the question.

The brief for the next part of this exercise is divided into two: one for the actor-as-observer and one for the actor-as-performer. To begin with, the group (who become observers) form two lines. Facing each other, approximately two metres apart, they create a pathway between the two lines through which one actor-performer can walk.

Actor-performer

You undertake this only once.

- Walk up and down the pathway created by the group.
- Aim for a walk that is without adjective or adverb (that is, it could not be said to be walking 'slowly', 'quickly', 'nervously', and so on; it is simply 'walking').
- The length of the working space through which you are moving can never be infinite, so turn at either end to walk back in the opposite direction. The turns at each end of the room are not included in the expression – you and those observing you are focusing only on the Walk.

Actor-observer

- Observe the Walk of the actor on the pathway. What is your first impression of this Walk? Make up a film title for the Walk. Call it out. One observer writes down the titles as they are called out.

- The film title is the imaginative articulation of your first impression; it sums up the story of the walk that you see. Make the title fresh – absolutely off-the-top of your head.

- Avoid existing film titles as these are evoked not by what you are actually seeing but by old associations.

- Don't inhibit this impression by, for example, trying to work out which part of the body is leading. Anatomical details are examined in the next stage of the exercise.

- Make sure that you refresh your mind each time a new actor sets off: different film, different cinema, different protagonist – unknown to you, and so on.

- Respond out loud. You do not have to force this; it may take time to join in with verbalizing titles and that's fine. The practice in a group should, however, allow you space to verbalize what is in your imagination, as well as saying what you see.

- Try out the walk you are observing in your own body. You can leave the line to do this and then rejoin. Do this as part of the observation, with the actor continuing to do the Walk.

- Use your observation and the information of the film-titles that have been called out and resist directly copying the actor walking.

Actor-performer

- Remember at all times that what you are doing is 'the Walk', not just 'a walk'. You are not 'strolling' or 'ambling' or 'power walking'. The task is about upping your game – turning 'a walk' into 'the Walk'. Occupy yourself in offering what it is 'to walk' (as an action without adjective or adverb).

- As the observers offer their thoughts about your Walk out loud in the form of film titles, keep walking.

- Become more fully occupied in the Walk, neither listening in nor shutting the observers out, as they call out film titles and discuss them. Try not to change or lose the qualities the observers discuss as you walk.

- Remain open and practise 'belonging to' the audience. To help you with this, loosely imagine your Walk is also in a film called 'The Walk'. There are no other expectations of you, other than offering 'the Walk'.

- After you have stopped working, you will be able to reflect on – and slowly analyse – the observations and projections you received from the audience: all the wonderful descriptions, adverbs and adjectives from which 'the Walk' is aiming to free itself.

- When the group has finished analysing your Walk and you are gently stopped by the tutor, some notes may be given. They may not chime with what you felt as you walked, but they are unarguably what the audience saw from the outside.

- Remember that you are being observed as an actor working in the studio, doing the Walk – you are not being looked at as you in the real, daily world.

- Laugh if you want to after you have stopped, and write down your own thoughts.

Actor-observer

After a few film titles have been suggested, one of the titles can be selected for the group to examine.

- What is it about this person's walk that brought this film-title to mind?
- Examine and play with each word within the title, in the context of the walk you are watching.

Actor-performer

- Write all titles and notes down.
- Pick out the immediately accessible body notes mined from the titles.
- Take these away with you to work on in your own way over time.
- Keep the rest of your notes in original form for future reference.

Outer Stillness on Text

Work with a partner (if alone, you could use video playback).

- Find text that is not only meaningful to you, but that needs to be spoken out to the world – to someone. It needs to be text that you know and understand, but that you are also willing to use for exploration and play.

The body habits that are tied to communication are traced through this exercise: facial tics, gesturing hands, and the indications made by various body parts on certain words. This exercise gives you the chance to identify what is essential and what is incidental in the movement of your body 'on text'.

- Perform the text as you would 'normally': at your tempo and with a full, open heart so that your partner can register the level of passion and intensity invested.

- Now perform again, but this time, remove all gestures and all other body or facial movements without tensing up.

- Convey the passion and the story just as you did before. Note: this is not a vocal exercise. It is a physically-engaged, body exercise.

- Aim at connecting to the heart, guts and brain of the text.

- Your partner points out to you the movements that occur as they happen (or you could use video playback), and you can try to still them.

- Try to identify the responses and reasons for the movements: perhaps some are compensatory, belying a lack of trust in the text; some may be tics that occur with particular speech patterns; some that over-embellish the text may be due to a lack of trust in you being interesting enough, and so on.

- Try to maintain the stillness. Your partner should notice if the passion that was there in the first version is diminished now as you try to maintain stillness and investigate the movement.

- To offer the same level of passion will mean genuinely connecting to breath, thinking through the text, being in the present and experiencing the dilemmas.

Although you may have immediate discoveries that change you, there will also be other discoveries. These can be acknowledged and worked on over time, in other areas of practice, as well as when working on Neutral.

Key points

When undertaking this exercise, don't become cross with yourself for the movements you make without realizing or wishing to – try instead to be happy that you know something about yourself that you didn't know before. You are now armed to work in new ways with a knowledge of your instinctive movements. Acknowledge any emerging depth of connection that occurred because you 'got yourself out of the way' and remember it – this is 'less is more'.

IN CONTEXT: OUTER STILLNESS

Allow yourself the opportunity to experience the text with 'you' out of the way and let the text offer you physical information.

Practical Section: Stage Two

The Difference between a Mime and a Physical Action

An actor being asked to mime something is the equivalent of a runner being asked to do a back somersault: it is an entirely different discipline. Still, it's worth you having a go just for you to appreciate the difference.

Knowing the difference between mime and a Physical Action might help you clarify further what is meant here by 'Physical Action'. The action itself (the human intention and response to the environment) is the drama, whereas in mime the performer is responsible also for creating what is not there, that is, creating illusion.

Do the Physical Action of opening a door that isn't there:

- See the door as a barrier between two spaces. Stopping to indicate the barrier is enough.
- Open the door in the simplest way. The interest must be kept with the actor coming from one space to the other. It's the story that counts, not the accuracy of the illusion.

Now attempt the mime of opening a door:

- Approach the door.
- Reach for the handle, isolating the movement of the arm and, then having decided what sort of handle it is,
- place your hand on it and turn or press down, keeping the arm fixed to show the hand.
- Extend the arm; swing the door open on a perfect arc.
- Keep the hand on the handle as you walk around the imaginary door.
- Release the hand from the door and place the other hand on the inside handle.
- Now extend the arm, keeping the body in position, and give the illusion that the door swings again in a perfect arc arriving at exactly the same starting position but with you on the other side.
- Let go of the handle.
- Turn to face the room.

The audience is now much more interested in the illusion of the door than anything the actor has to say.

IN CONTEXT

When a director tells the actor to just mime it, this usually doesn't mean 'mime' but rather to do a Physical Action.

The Physical Action

Sawing the Log[6] is offered here as an example of an exercise that allows you to fully explore Physical Action. This is for the individual within a group. The group, as audience, sits along the front of the room in straight lines on chairs.

- Place one chair in the space, where you want to be in relation to your audience.

This exercise is offered in two stages. Note that the brief for the next part of this exercise is also divided into two: one for the actor-observer and one for the actor-performer.

Part A: 'Sawing the Log'

Actor-performer

- Enter the space alone; the space is empty apart from the one chair.
- Offer the Neutral 'Sawing the Log'. You can use the chair as support.
- Establish the Physical Action.
- Decide for yourself when to end the action.
- Remain in the space to receive any feedback.

Actor-observer

- Offer feedback about what you saw and loved, still using film titles. The titles offer useful information about the quality of the action you are observing. They help highlight the degree to which this 'Sawing the Log' has achieved the Epic and realized the possibilities of the Action.

Part B: Adding the Rest of the Story

When you have an understanding of Sawing the Log, add the rest of the story. Use the space and the chair for the following:

Actor-performer as the Neutral:

- is sawing the log;
- hears an aeroplane;

---

[6]This is a Jacques Lecoq exercise. The versions of Lecoq's exercises in this chapter are Ewan's interpretation responding to specific stages in the actor's process.

- watches the plane as it crosses from stage right to stage left;
- returns to sawing the log;
- remains in the space for feedback.

Practical Section: Stage Three

First Encounter with the Mask

This exercise is for the individual within a group of four or five actors.

One actor at a time explores the set tasks wearing the Mask, with the others as audience experiencing the Mask from the observer's point of view. Keep the initial encounter with the Mask short, and frequently switch roles so that learning can be maximized. This is essentially a playful encounter.

Play in the Mask

- If there is a choice of masks available spend time choosing the Mask for you.
- Enter the space.
- Turn away from your group, look at the Mask and with the Mask held in both hands at chest height, lower your face into the Mask. With the Mask in place, make any adjustments to the elastic, and so on. Lift your head and, after a beat, turn to face the front.
- Do whatever you and the Mask want to do for and with the group as audience.
- This must be an episode of freedom, so allow yourself a childlike, playful discovery of gestural, stylized or abstract movement. In this way you can begin to make a relationship with the Mask (however raw), establishing what works and what doesn't for your audience.
- Establish an idea of the basic rules of the Mask – starting with finding the distance you need from the audience in the space. In order for them to read the Mask they need to take in the whole body.

Once you have played in the Mask for a short time:

- Feedback your experience to a partner or the observers.
- Receive their feedback/impressions.
- Capture in writing this first experience.

- Include both your initial personal response to wearing a mask and being the Mask.

Questions to consider asking might include:

- Is the Mask liberating?
- Is it claustrophobic?
- Do you have a preference for abstract movement choices or emotional choices?
- What did you respond to?
- What did you find out?

Look through the following after your first encounter with the Mask:
Basic rules of the Mask to be discovered through play:

- Really look at the Mask before wearing it, so you know the face you are going to become.
- Do not use a mirror with the Mask.
- Don't touch the Mask.
- Keep the Mask facing the audience.
- Know the necessary distance between the Mask and the audience for the body and Mask to be read.
- Do not speak in the Mask.
- Turn away to take the Mask off.

Encounters with the Neutral Mask

This time, you and your audience take on equal status and equal agendas.

The Mask can offer actions, stories, emotions, abstract shapes – anything it likes. In turn, the audience, too, can make demands for anything it wants from the Mask. This works well as a dialogue. So, for example, the audience might ask for the Mask to be in fear. The Mask offers fear, but this may be read as being inquisitive and comical. If the audience feeds this back, you as the Mask can choose to continue to try to offer fear or you might take the response as inspiration to find comedy.

Actor-observer

- Use your acquired experience from the previous exercises in offering feedback.

- Take responsibility. Offer immediate and almost continuous response to what you see. Neither the actor working nor you should be waiting for the other. A continual flow of feedback is a crucial part of the game. Bouts of silence are clear signals of faltering stamina.

- Say out loud, immediately, your top-of-the-head first impression of what you see. You are no longer restricted to presenting film titles, and what you say now, should, through a build-up of practice, be more sophisticated.

A Neutral Mask Journey

This is an exercise for the individual within a group, and is done in the Mask by one actor at a time. The other actors work as observers in the audience set-up as for the Physical Action Practical.

- As the Neutral, lie down in the space, in a posture on the floor that tells the audience you are sleeping.

- Seek the optimum sleeping position: the clearest, simplest story of the Physical Action of 'Asleep' in your body.

- Remember, it is the Neutral sleeping, not the way you sleep, but *the* Sleep.

It may be that each actor takes turns to offer the shape of sleep, or it may be that the tutor offers Lecoq's own solution[7] as a place to work from.

- Open yourself up to the physical discoveries, for instance, of the essential difference between the breath of being awake and of being asleep.

- Through research and opening yourself up to exploring your physical expression, you may happen upon a large number of stories of sleep, of death and of rest, on the way to finding the Neutral Asleep.

If you have taken time to explore sleeping, you can go on to explore a full Neutral Mask journey.

- The Neutral sleeps surrounded by a white mist.
  The Neutral wakes surrounded by a white mist.
  The Neutral gets up surrounded by a white mist.

---

[7]But giving this here would undermine the process.

The Neutral stands surrounded by a white mist.
The Neutral walks forward surrounded by a white mist.
The Neutral stands surrounded by a white mist.
The Mist clears; the Neutral sees the sea for the first time.
The Neutral picks up a stone and throws it into the sea.
The end.

The Mist

Like everything else, the mist is accepted totally by the Neutral. The mist removes all barriers, obstacles or boundaries, including any spatial differentiation between the Neutral's space and that of the general stage and audience. It offers, instead, infinity.

- Allow the mist to help liberate you from outline and offer you acceptance of the lack of boundaries; to take away the walls and beyond; to truly do its job. When you do this, your presence is strengthened: it is a mistake to think that by imagining a big outline around the space around yourself, you create a big presence. If you no longer have a boundary, rather than being made invisible by the mist you become endlessly visible. This is the Epic. Allow no boundaries. Having no outline means you must be touching the audience; they must be in your space.

Key points

As with the exercise on *the* Walk, take inspiration from any number of sources in seeking the essence of the actions: paintings, poetry, myths, the science, the Archetype, or the Neutral itself.

These simple actions are your main vehicle of expression so spend time getting excited about the diversity of each of them expressively while looking for the essential universal stories of each.

From time to time you can go on and experience the Journey afresh and discover and take with you whatever the Neutral makes visible.

IN CONTEXT: CHARACTER'S JOURNEY THROUGH THE PLAY

What is the essential physical journey of your character through the play? Allow yourself to experience the essence of each part of this journey without affectation to then give to your character.

Stories of the Space – Pathways

This is for one actor in a performing space with an audience. Since this exercise can be done with or without a mask, it doesn't obey the Mask rule of facing front. The Mask enables the audience to see more clearly.

- As the Neutral you travel along a set of pathways (refer to diagram).

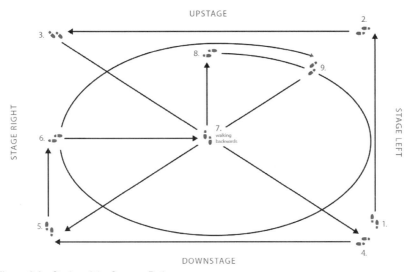

Figure 3.2 Stories of the Space – Pathways.

- Receive your feedback.
- Note for yourself the differences between the pathways; for instance, walking along the back of the space and walking along the front of the space?
- What is the rhythm of the walk down the diagonal? And across the centre from stage left to stage right, and so on?
- Where do you want to stand?

IN CONTEXT: STORIES OF THE SPACE

Each time you work a character within the same performing space, you learn something new about the space. If you are in a new venue and you get the chance to be in the performing space on your own, walk the space. Let yourself be as neutral as possible to physically experience where the space opens up, where it is warm, or where it is cold, and so on. Do this while imagining the audience is there.

4

IN THE MOVEMENT STUDIO

OVERVIEW

Conflict exists all the time in the body, between the mind, the emotions and external forces. The work in the studio must reflect this and actively prepare the actor for that complexity. Conflict can be an actor's best friend. It should be as present in acting and movement classes as it is in everyday life.

Actor Engagement in the Movement Studio[1]

Simple Action

See Practical: *Simple Action* (p. 93)

Working in the movement studio, especially if he is with others who have a dance background, the actor may feel he has to pretend to be a dancer. This is not the case. An actor in leotard and tights is still an actor. He has to be able to do what an actor has to do.

The actor is asked to stand in parallel and roll down the spine. He does what he is asked but, possibly, feels constrained by having to follow a particular form. Or he may not question the structure, thinking it's 'a movement class thing' as he steps outside of himself as an actor to meet the movement work. At worst, he may slip into a mindless 'zombie' state, believing this is what is required. It may be a shock to him to realize how wide of the mark this is. Movement work

---

[1] Ewan's process of work in the studio with the actors.

does not ask the actor to lose his energy, his sparkle, his breath rhythm or his place in the world.

Breaking a Habit of Movement 'Overwash'

See Practical: *Using Images to Break Narrative* (p. 93)

When engaged in movement, the actor should not be preoccupied with 'doing a swing', 'creating momentum' or 'flowing through an exercise beautifully'. He is required to be wholly present in each moment. An exercise of extreme dynamic contrast designed to leave no room for him to 'tell his story' can offer him such practice. Each action within the exercise must be fully inhabited and distinct. At first this is hard for the actor, however, once he has connected images to the movements he can confidently enter into and experience the journey of the exercise. The image is never known by anyone but himself – it dosen't matter how it sounds or appears, it only matters that it works.

Relationship with Music

See Practical: *Relationship with Music* (p. 94)

Different types of music elicit different responses. Everyone develops a personal repertoire of movement responses to fit the types of music they hear. These are the 'moves' they always do. Over time an expressive map of these music-response connections is built. The actor must explore beyond this map to avoid being restricted by his habitual movement responses. He is given time to stop and listen to music in order to interrupt his habitual route between listening to the music and moving. He listens and experiences his response in stillness without any plan to 'move it'. He is then free to explore a freshly discovered response to what he hears. Encouraged to assume that he can embody whatever it is he has just experienced, he gets on with moving according to a non-predetermined impulse.

Locating the Essential Expression in Movement

The actor needs to be able to locate and immediately offer the expressive potential of any moment. With nothing of his own imposed on the movement, the actor becomes the vehicle of its expression. A swing, for example, has an inherent freedom that evokes childhood, but the actor does not need to execute it like a child; the movement speaks for itself. The actor must not work to 'clean up' the exercise, but live within any conflicting experiences a moment offers. (See Appendices: *Building a Swing*.)

In the studio the actor needs to practise delivering what he believes is being asked of him, instantly and without self-consciousness or apology. He can do this in the knowledge that his skills will improve as he keeps offering. This is not throwing himself in unsafely, but trusting his actor's mindset.

He may, for example, be asked to jump in the course of an exercise. The physical action of the jump fits within the virtuoso range of dance or gymnastics and requires skill to execute it efficiently. In the search to supply this necessary skill, the jump is likely to lose its natural impulse – the feeling is abandoned.

A jump holds something of happiness within it, yet it rarely looks 'happy' as the actor tries to attain it. Rather, it can seem aggressive or desperate, with a fixed smile the only clue to its inherent intention. However hard someone is jumping, however 'good' he is at jumping, it's not a 'real jump' until the essence has been found and is 'lived'.

Recall a jump now, maybe from your childhood, along with the need you had to jump and the exhilaration of leaving the earth for a moment. The movement was, in part, about freedom. It was charged and vital and the impulse that took you away from the earth's crust came from a sense of being safe: you knew you would come back down to earth.

It is the physical articulation of this understood experience that makes the jump whole; it captures the essence of the action, which is then able to be 'owned' and acted. The actor can then develop his technique through exercises whilst always offering – expressing – the essence of the movement.

Reclaim What was Always His to Have

See Practical: *Locate the Conflict* (p. 96)

When the actor encounters an exercise that he perceives as a dance move, such as repeated turns across the diagonal of the room, he has to see this as an actor and not as a dancer: that is, he is turning around fast on himself as he travels from corner to corner across the room, not executing chaînés/pirouettes (as described in Chapter 1). The actor has to identify the raw experience, which in this exercise is of the conflict of spinning whilst crossing the room. It might help to imagine himself as a cricket ball, travelling and spinning through the air.

Maintaining the Conflict

Conflict is an actor's best friend. His work cannot centre on making actions and events look easy. Theatre is the space for engagement with conflict, which sits at the heart of being human. The actor is living and expressing the response to a series of given factors that are influencing him at any one time and which are manifested in that conflicted movement. When technique improves, conflict in the body can unfortunately become resolved as the actor is more physically able to achieve two or more simultaneous actions. To lose the experience of conflict in the body is to lose something fundamental. In sharing his experience of conflict in an exercise such as *Turns Across the Room*, he may, in spite of the undeniable exhilaration they offer, feel foolish or intimidated by the 'realness' of the work. This may make it hard for him to prevent the inclination to conceal his response, either through an assumed obligation to do so, or by clenching the muscles in the body to block the experience. He has to be enabled to commit to each and every stage of an experience. He needs to exist in a place where there is no self-censoring, nor hiding behind technique, steps or moves.

The Hybrid Exercise as a Vehicle for Expression

See Practical: *Using a Hybrid Exercise for Expression* (p. 97)

A Hybrid Exercise is a name given here to describe a preset and learned sequence of movements with expressive potential offering some aspect of fitness such as stretching, muscle strength or endurance. It is derived essentially from a variety of sources of movement styles and practices like contemporary dance, yoga, Pilates, and so on. A complete yoga exercise, such as the 'Sun Salutation', is tied into yogic doctrine, but there are elements of it that could fruitfully exist in a Hybrid Exercise.

In a Hybrid Exercise, movements no longer belong to any practice; there is no 'story' attached, nothing is sacrosanct. The actor can therefore discover and develop the raw, physical experience. Like other forms, a Hybrid Exercise is designed to be repeated time and time again. In this way the actor realizes and uses the essentials of what the exercise offers. (See Appendices: *Side Stretch*.)

Only once the actor has ownership of the structure and the essence of the exercise, can he highlight or prioritize a particular aspect. He could for example heighten an experience of weight or explore his relationship with the exercise through different qualities of breathing (athletic/animal/expressive); different music; different spaces; emotional journeys, and so on. The exercise becomes a spacious arena for expression, a journey of body and imagination.

Part One: Actor Engagement in the Movement Studio Practicals

Simple Action

Doing an exercise as a Simple Action using as an example *Rolling down the Spine*. (See Appendices: *Rolling down the Spine*.)

- First of all, alter your point of view of the movement form: start seeing the movements as actions (motivated movement): leaving, going somewhere, returning, and arriving back.
- To make this more accessible, do the exercise standing opposite someone else.
- Start with a moment in which you meet his gaze.
- Find the feeling of leaving that shared gaze. Start rolling down the spine. Keep your 'eyes in your head' (eye-line in line with the head movements).
- Do not allow your mind to plan ahead.
- Experience the aloneness of the journey as you roll down and then back up again.
- Arrive back upright; 'eyes in your head'.
- Have a moment to have really arrived.
- Feel the weight that the exercise has given you.
- How has the journey changed you?
- Then repeat several times.
- Start to experience other aspects that the movements offer you, such as the retreating into self as you roll down, the opening as you roll up, and so on.

Key points

You start in door plane, move into wheel plane, and end back in door plane. Breathe out on each action (rolling down and rolling up).

Using Images to Break Narrative

This is best done at an early stage of learning an exercise. Here the 'Swing, Stab, Release' is used as it is an example of an exercise that offers extreme and contrasting movement dynamics. (See Appendices: *Swing, Stab, Release*.)

- From the sensations you experience in the exercise, find a different image for every moment. Each image should highlight the quality and offer a completely different world.

- Create a map of images.

- Make sure that the image matches each particular movement and accurately creates its essence, quality and mechanics. Your images need to offer your body time, place and structure, so that you can meet not only the quality of the movement but also the whole exercise, including its rhythm and timing.

- An image can be of anything: it can be abstract or fully materialized. Sometimes it may not be possible to put it into words. If an image (however seemingly amazing) doesn't work for the movement, it is worthless. Likewise, an image that may appear to you as clichéd, odd or even disturbing is worthy to be used – if it works. No one else knows what your image is anyway.

- Test the effectiveness of each chosen image in action. Have someone watch you to see the effect of the image on the movement. It may have one element that needs adjusting to meet the exercise. For example, 'skiing down a mountain' used as an image for the swing may result in too much vigour. It might need a small adjustment – in this case, to 'a post-drink last ski of the day'.

- Interrupt each moment by one that is new and completely different. Shift from one reality to another, without constructing a linear storyline or narrative in which moments are related or form progression. For example, check that each image is unconnected, for example: the Swing: skiing down a mountain; the Release: a suicide lying in a warm blood-filled bath (the sides of the bath create the straight parallel lines within which the movement works).

Relationship with Music

Question your relationship and then explore and reinvigorate it.

- Plant the following questions in your mind:

  What is your relationship with the music?

  How do you listen?

  Do you see pictures?

  Do you see patterns?

Can you feel your response?

Do you travel through the music as a story?

What does your mind do?

- Now lie on the floor in a movement studio and listen to a piece of classical music that is unknown or barely known to you.

- Commit fully to both listening and to the mind's responses. Trust your responses.

- Allow yourself to puzzle over the earlier questions, knowing that the answers will not necessarily translate easily into words. Nonetheless try to find a way to articulate them.

- Stop and take note of your response (but in the knowledge that it might be only one of your responses or a transitory response that you manage to write down).

- Lie back down on the floor and listen to the music and again allow yourself to be with it.

- Articulate the responses with your body, just as you see or feel or sense them.

- Do not plan or prepare yourself or limit your expectation of what can be physically transferred from this inner experience. Your mind, for example, may be flying. Try to embody that sensation.

- Embody everything that you imagine, however intangible it seems.

- Do not perform them for anyone; you are simply physicalizing whatever the internal responses happen to be.

- Fiercely resist doing the 'moves' you know, the ones you are proud of and always do.

- If you do find that you are still responding in a habitual way, take one idea from your habitual response and expand on it.

Key points

If you are someone who doesn't get on with classical music, this may be because you have not encountered it often. Take some time to become accustomed to the form.

If you know that you struggle with being in the present tense and it is hard to remain present using the same music repeatedly, then you may need to use a fresh piece of music.

- Having done this with classical music, leave a gap of a week or so and then do this exercise with other music.

- Break any habitual responses by allowing yourself to listen and experience.

IN CONTEXT

Two very different questions to be considered:
What music do you associate with your character?
What music does your character listen to?

Create a playlist for your character. How does your character listen to music?

Locate the Conflict

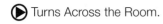 Turns Across the Room.

A familiar dance turning step is used here as an example of an actor prioritizing the story of conflict.

- Start in the back corner of the room (upstage left) with your shoulders along the diagonal line (facing the front). Your pathway across the space is a straight line to the opposite corner.

- Slightly bend your legs to give yourself a low centre of gravity.

- Get into a ready position but keep it soft around the edges.

- Your arms start in front of you as if holding a large bowl at chest level.

- Open your right arm out.

- When you are halfway around, let the left arm follow in the same direction, giving you the momentum to complete the turn, closing back into the starting shape. This movement of the arm helps to turn you.

- If you have not done this exercise before, give yourself permission to discover it.

- When faced with technical information before you have moved, redress the balance in your mind before you set off, putting the essence of the movement in front of all the other information.

- Ask yourself: 'What is the essence of this exercise?'

- Let your preparation include the undeniable exhilaration the turns offer; don't conceal your response or clench your muscles.

- If somebody demonstrates the movement, use images to help you retain information as you watch. Watch with your heart.

- Repeat the turn continuously. You may imagine yourself to be like a cricket ball just released by the bowler's hand.

- Step your feet round each other as you turn. Stay low with bent knees.

- As you turn, you move along the diagonal to the opposite corner.

- Keep spinning. You are doing circles (*indirect*) in your personal space and a straight line (*direct*) in general space. This gives you two spaces to play simultaneously.

- Keep upright/perpendicular throughout – don't lean forward. However, don't become preoccupied with getting it right at the expense of allowing the movement sensation to be visible.

Key points

Commit to each and every stage of the experience, without self-censoring, displaying or hiding behind the technique, steps or moves.

IN CONTEXT

Translate this to a character: *indirect* in personal space and *direct* in general space.

Using a Hybrid Exercise for Expression

See Appendices: *Side Stretch Breakdown*

This takes the Side Stretch as an example, but is applicable to a Hybrid Exercise of your own invention.

First you need to know the sequence without thinking about what comes next. You also need to have discrete images throughout that release you from 'doing' the exercise, and instead allow you to experience the movement fully. Then you can begin to use the form to explore different expression. Heighten the experience, letting any feelings arise. This does not have to be 'dramatic'; allow the experience to infiltrate each of the movements and as they change, let the feeling shift also.

Breath as journey

Experience a journey of 'expressive breath'. Note that this is not to be confused with 'breathing through the exercise' where breath pattern is matched to the rhythms of the individual movements.

Do the exercise with the idea and sensation of the breath invoked by a fairground roller coaster ride:

- It may sound silly, but allow your imagination to come into play: pretend to hand over money for the ride and actively climb onto a roller coaster. Take up the starting position of the side stretch.

- You are on board. Once the roller coaster starts, let go to the inevitable breath journey of the exercise. Be present with the movement taking you for a ride; allow the breath to connect with thought and feeling.

Now go through the Side Stretch with other focuses and provocations, which relate to other learning experiences. For example, consider:

Spatial planes

- Experience the changes from door plane to table plane to wheel plane, and so on.

- Acknowledge the different levels through which you are moving.

- Acknowledge the feeling at the beginning of the Side Stretch of the two-dimensional reaches to the sides and of existing in the door plane. (See Appendices: *Additional to Dimensional Scale.*)

Weight

- You might experience the weight as power and strength or notice the difference when it is with or against gravity.
- If it helps, you might imaginatively change the density of the air to be thicker and so on.

Music

- Allow yourself and the journey to be internally or emotionally in relationship with music. (It is not set or choreographed to the music.)

Landscape

- Do the exercise in different spaces: on a beach; on a mountain. Then recreate these experiences in the studio.

Emotion

- Impose an emotion at the outset and see what happens as you move through the exercise.

IN CONTEXT: PRE-REHEARSAL WARM-UP

If you use this exercise as part of your physical warm-up, it can also exist as a canvas for whatever you are exploring in rehearsal. You don't need to force these explorations.

If you are developing a character, you could also let the character do the exercise and without changing the actual form of it, note how this is a different movement experience.

5
OBSERVATION AND TRANSLATION

OVERVIEW

As a translator of ways-of-being in the world, the actor requires detailed and efficient processes of collecting and bringing as much as possible of the world into the studio.[1]

Observation

Observing is more than seeing.[2] For the actor, it must engage all his senses. Observations are not to be filed away 'in the brain', but stored in the body, live and ready for use.

The process has three stages. The actor starts by looking outwards: he looks at the world, then at the influence of the world on the person and then finally at the person himself.

Observing the 'World of the Play'

See Practical: *Exercises in Observation: Observing the World of the Play* (p. 110)
See Practical: *Creating the World of the Play: Sound, Touch and Scent* (p. 111)

As an observer in the real world, the actor's eye is naturally drawn to character and plot. In any given situation he will home in on individuals and their stories. This is fine but it blinkers him to the world the character is shaped by. In order

---

[1] Ewan's process of work in the studio with the actors.
[2] See J. Berger, *Ways of Seeing*, London: Penguin, 1970 – this is not a recent publication but it is still vitally relevant for the purposes here.

to develop a selective eye and a distinctive vision, he must expand his focus to take in the 'stories' of the space.

Any space, in any given world, influences the people in it. The physical environment – and the interaction with it – determines what people do, how they feel and how they behave. Call to mind a place you have visited – a coffee shop, perhaps – and take a moment to imagine it as it exists now. As you sit reading this you can picture it; you know the life of that world. You can recall a sense of its space and its rhythms. It has an atmosphere independent of specific plots or individual characters. You can sense the different body it gave you for the time you were there. The space was reflected in the way you moved. This world is, therefore, already a part of your 'embodied' range of movement expression.

The subtle story of space is only revealed through careful observation. Some spaces offer a more immediate sense of 'connection' than others: standing in an ancient church, for example, it may be possible to sense the imprint of all the people who have carried out centuries of ritual in the space. It is the actor's job to embody this 'sense'.

The actor should visit a broad diversity of places. Each will reflect its culture, society and systems. These places are likely to become the worlds of plays the actor might encounter in his professional life. By taking the eye to 'the world of the play', and away from individual characters, the actor accesses an understanding of how space shapes and motivates human behaviour. He can then paint a picture of the world in his body.

The actor should not be reliant on set, soundscape or lighting to create a given world. Using the observations he has stored in his body, he can call up the essential experience of any time or place. He can transport an audience through the way in which he embodies an environment.

Observing a Specialist at Work

See Practical: *Performing a Specialist Physical Action* (p. 113)

To discover the influence of the world on a character, the actor now shifts the focus of his observation to the characters and the way they relate to 'their' worlds. The actor observes the skill of a specialist at work. He sees how the specialist's body and movement are shaped by interaction with the 'world' of the skill: the mechanic, for example, is influenced by his functional environment – the grease, the noise, the hard surfaces. The more the actor observes the influences, the more he has to offer the character. He discovers what to bring into the studio and what to create without needing to learn the whole specialism himself. He does not become a skilled mechanic in order to embody and communicate the mechanic's world. Work done with this Specialist Physical Action can then transfer to any physical action undertaken by the character. Even an action as simple as taking a sip from a cup tells something of a person's world – the way in which the cup is held, the movement of the head, and so on. For example, a surgeon preparing and drinking coffee is likely to have a precision and efficiency not possessed by the regular coffee drinker.

Artistic representation – paintings, sculpture, poems, prose – all offer perspectives on an action. These are undoubtedly a valuable resource. However, for the actor, there is nothing to beat actually seeing or, even better, interacting with a specialist at work.

Looking Directly at the Character Himself

See Practical: *Looking Directly at the Character Himself* (p. 117)

When an actor then goes on to observe a person, he can easily identify some of the influences of the world on that person. He actively looks and questions why the person does something in a particular way. The number of influences is so great that to take only the information from one person in creating a character is invalid unless the character he is portraying is that person.

Seeing a character as a collection of combinations of influences (including genetic traits), many coming from the world of the play, offers the actor an accessible and fruitful way to construct the physical life of a character. This involves asking himself questions based on observation and collecting and identifying separate pockets of information, for instance, how someone dresses, her/his build, physicality, gestures and so on. This skill becomes extremely useful later when constructing character from an imagined reality. (See Chapter 8.)

Collecting People for the Future

In his observations an actor may 'find' a character for a play he dreams of doing. A man who seems to him the very embodiment of Macbeth might get on the same train. With this 'way of seeing', the actor is equipped to capture information very quickly. If he notes it down he can easily recall that person in the future if and when he gets that part.

Observation Prompts

By committing to memory BWTS (Breath, Weight, Time and Space), the actor has a short, accessible physical checklist.

Breath is integral to life, so integral that the actor can easily forget to look for it or utilize it. However, it is one of the actor's most important vehicles of expression. It is included here – and at the top of the list – to develop a habit of noting it during all observation.

Weight, Time and Space are three of the four Motion Factors[3] as defined by Laban and are present in all movement.

The actor can carry BWTS with him both in daily life and in the studio, drawing on them as observational cues as he begins to understand more of their meaning. Each chapter of *Actor Movement* details the way these observation prompts are perceived and used at different stages of the work. The actor gains multiple perspectives on BWTS through working with them in different ways. It is likely that his relationship with these four words will develop to the point where he will see BWTS in everything.

How to See More

Body language

See Practical: *The Park Bench* (p. 118)

So many exercises that the actor encounters develop his eye and ability to read the body. The ones that exercise this directly, as well as develop this skill, remind him that at all times he has available to him the great game of reading body language, and therefore every day he can take pleasure in being an actor. (See Chapters 3 and 8.)

POV

See Practical: *Capture an Essence of your Current POV* (p. 119)

Often the decision to be an actor means that a person has stopped to take stock and, to some extent, drawn a line under his previous life experiences. In doing so, he inadvertently cuts out transferable elements of his past point of view (POV). A previous life, as say a builder or an accountant, offers the actor knowledge and understanding that can enrich his current expressive potential. The life experience of a younger actor (for instance, being a teenager at school)

---

[3]Flow is the fourth Motion Factor. However, it is not used as one of the key prompts (see Chapter 8).

is equally valuable. Subjects studied recently or long ago, from fine arts to physics, can all prove rich resources.

Early Exercises in Translation

The actor has the potential to translate all things into performance. In this context, 'translation' is the means by which an actor uses his body to manifest the observations and impressions he has accumulated throughout his life. It helps for him to trust in the understanding that there is not one movement, or one thing in the world, that is created from nothing: everything comes from something.

'If You Can Achieve One Perfect Moment …'

See Practical: *'If You Can Achieve One Perfect Moment … '* (p. 119)

As a 'translator', an actor has to have an embodied understanding of the reach of the human condition. Through his work he must therefore achieve a broad and mature scope of comprehension, quite possibly before reaching that maturity himself (in terms of age or life experience). Actor Movement can facilitate this by providing shortcuts, through work such as the Paintings Exercise.

In the Paintings Exercise an actor works to physically recreate a 'classical' painting in three dimensions. The exercise entails observation and the reading of a painting to be translated to one moment of embodied stillness: a perfect physical understanding and evocation of that painting. The actor can extend and extrapolate from this exercise. However, if he can achieve 'one perfect moment' of embodied truth, it is a starting point from which he can then aspire to fully inhabit a role throughout the length of a four-hour play.

In his capacity as translator, the actor relinquishes any expectation of himself as artist. He needs only to illustrate the action. However, as he studies the finer details, he begins to read the movement captured within the subject/s (breath-shifts, posture, touch) and starts to see the world from the artist's point of view. As his appreciation of 'the small things' grows, he keeps looking and starts really seeing. He is only required (at this stage) to be open to the artwork. He encounters beauty and is able to translate it to the studio. He realizes colour can be translated, texture can be translated. After all, all he is creating is that 'one embodied moment'.

Incorporating the three stages of observation ('world'–'character in the world'–'character'), the actor discovers the advantage of translation over copying. The actor creates a new artwork – a three-dimensional painting in the working space. This new artwork expresses not just the action of the original, but what the actor loved about it – something a copy could never do.

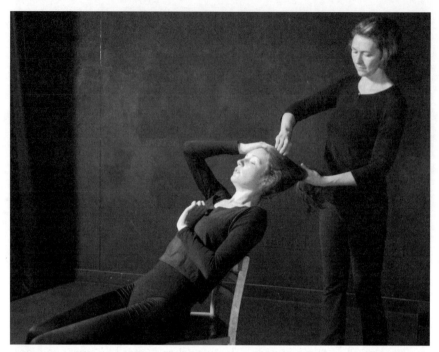

Figure 4.1   3D recreation of Degas' *La Coiffure* with actors Vivienne Bell and Sinéad O'Keeffe. Photograph by Todd Padwick.

Shortcuts to Physical Information

Translating from other art forms gives the actor confidence to embody an array of experiences he may not have encountered in real life.

It is commonplace to talk about the actor's need to be 'grounded', but what does this really mean? Consider the experience Paul Delaroche's painting *The Execution of Lady Jane Grey* (National Gallery, London; see www.national gallery.org.uk/paintings) offers to the actor. The axe-man is portrayed as though captured in the 'pre-moment' of physical responsibility: the moment before wielding an axe cleanly and effectively to execute a young woman. This weight of that moment is clear in his body. 'Grounding' is illustrated in one, wholly embodied moment of stillness. If the actor were to recreate this moment, the questions he might ask would be to do with the location of the weight; where it sits in the body; how the weight affects the movement; if it pulls downwards, sinks, drops or drags; or if it implodes, rises, drifts away or even dissipates. The actor can focus on the weight as intention; or perhaps as responsibility, determination, timidity, disinterest or as emotional weight such as anger, and so on.

Do This with Each of the Prompts

The actor-in-training might discover, for example, that the ownership and articulation of weight in his body is a harnessing of the weight that comes from being 'lumbered' with responsibility. This fuels an excitement the actor can take into his everyday body work: he now appreciates the potential of Movement Fundamentals (for instance, work on weight) to express narrative and human truth.

Figure 4.2 3D recreation of Delaroche's *The Execution of Lady Jane Grey* with actors Lynsey Murrell, Sinéad O'Keeffe, Vivienne Bell, Nina Fog, Luke Norris and Matt Tait. Photograph by Todd Padwick.

A painting carries both epic statements and the fleeting emotions of its subjects. It offers basic body and gestural language. Intriguingly, the breath in a 'captured' moment still possesses the rhythm of life.

A painting by a master allows the actor to investigate all the Factors of movement. He can see that time exists in something that is essentially timeless. To discover how he can read the painting with the search for time in his mind, he looks first to the narrative; to the movement of off-balance and mid-action. In understanding the drama of the pre- and post-movement, he can ask himself what he 'knows' of the speed of each of these movements. It is then that he can begin to see time as a quality within the painting. Space is expressed through the gaze of the characters, the placing of bodies in the composition, their proximity to objects or to each other, and the artist's depiction of the space beyond the bodies. Colour and texture enhance the 'felt' quality of the space.

The artist's understanding of three dimensions becomes evident when the actor who has translated the painting in the studio is able to walk into the space, as if walking into the painting itself. Now he can move around and between the bodies. He sees how his picture – and the artist's – works from every angle.

The actor should spend time contemplating the painting, excavating its substance. The painting doesn't change or disappear; it gives him all the time he needs to learn.

The painting also offers something else, an 'extra' that is worth highlighting. It might be easier to understand using a textual equivalent. When an actor 'owns' a phrase of Shakespeare (through speaking or performing it), he also owns in this moment, something of Shakespeare's astounding, verbal intelligence. If the same actor places himself 'inside' a painting by Velasquez, he will own something of the painter's body intelligence. The intelligence of great art is there for all to receive. This is quite the opposite of the exclusivity sometimes apportioned to it. It does not require prior knowledge, academic proficiency or intellectual ability to access it. It requires only the confidence of the actor to understand that this is something to which he can relate; something he can 'own' for a time, and translate. (See Chapter 4, Practicals: *Using a Hybrid Exercise for Expression*; Chapters 7 and 8).

IN CONTEXT: PAINTINGS AS CHARACTER RESEARCH

The actor can look to paintings as research. When he finds something in a painting that offers an aspect of the character he is researching, something in a figure's posture, perhaps evocative of era or class, the actor can go a step further. He can physically experience the posture, holding it long enough for it to feed him its meaning.

An actor researching a period role might benefit from 'living' several postures from a variety of paintings from a particular era: an eighteenth-century body, for example, that is holding a quill pen, and another that is sitting with legs up on the table whilst gesturing in conversation, and so on.

Identifying Metaphor as a Direct Resource

See Practical: *Taking the Physical Metaphor Literally* (p. 125)

Metaphor is a very particular medium of translation. The actor develops trust in his instinct to allow a profusion of metaphors to manifest themselves in his performance. However, he can also consciously choose to craft and embody them. A young actor who connects to the imagery or sensation of a metaphor can understand and evoke something of another person's life experience even if he has not himself been broken-hearted/at death's door/strangled with fear, and so on. Embodying a metaphor allows the actor to identify with the experience, even when the story is different from his own. Methods for this are detailed throughout this book, particularly in Chapters 7 and 8. The actor must be hungry to take this on: he really is serving the play when he can bring to life metaphors from the text or of his own creation. Now he is a master of translation. (See Chapter 4, Practicals: *Using a Hybrid Exercise for Expression*; Chapter 7 and Chapter 8.)

IN CONTEXT: PLAYING WITH BOTH IMAGE AND METAPHOR

The actor can be awake to metaphor – to how he might use it to relate to and serve both his character and the bigger picture in the world of the play. It is accepted practice for fellow artists – writers, set designers, directors, dancers – to consciously use metaphor as part of their craft. So why shouldn't the actor? His job is to say as much as he can with what he has – and this includes his body. So why should he not consciously use physical metaphor as language? For example, the character may be pensive with turbulent thoughts. The actor may wish to manifest this by stirring his coffee in a way that acts as a physical outlet for the internal rhythm of the character (the stirred coffee becomes the metaphor for these turbulent, circular thoughts). In this way the metaphor provides the audience with stimulating information without the actor needing to 'signpost'.

Part Two: Observation and Translation Practicals

Exercises in Observation: Observing the World of the Play

Observe the 'worlds' of selected institutions and venues which have both formal and informal environments. Capture the essence of the space, not the story or the event that you find within the space on that day at that time.

- Choose and visit a place to observe: a court of law, a meat-market, an A&E waiting room, and so on.

- Look past any activity in the space and instead look closely at the space itself. Note down as much as you can as if you were a designer: its real size and the size it feels to you; its temperature; its colour scheme; its atmosphere, and so on. Use all your senses to note the sounds; the textures; the smells; the quality of the air, and so on. Experiment with depriving yourself of your strongest sense in order to heighten your other senses.

- Note how the architecture of the space manipulates the movement of the people within it. Observe how the space channels people, telling them how and where to move. If it helps you, imagine yourself as an architect or a town planner.

- Look at the ritual(s) of the space: walking in a library (never running) or facing the door when standing in a lift.

- Pick out the particular features that affect the use and feel of the space: the height of the ceiling in a cathedral; or narrowness of a corridor; the echo of an empty house, and so on.

- Feel the tempo, pulse and rhythm of the space. Notice, for example, how often something happens, and when there is a change in the activity and rhythm of the space. Can you see the rhythm as a musical score?

- Ask yourself: 'What time of day is it?' 'What time does it feel like?'

- Acknowledge any simultaneous time frames that might exist: 'the working day' for some may in fact be the middle of the night.

- You may want to compare the atmosphere of a space at specific times of the day. An A&E department in a hospital, for example, is very different at two o'clock in the morning from how it is at two in the afternoon.

- Make time to absorb the atmosphere of the space by bringing your whole attention to it without any questioning or prioritizing of information.

- Compare this with another place that shares one of its aspects (such as history or ritual), but that is different in other ways (such as a church and a court). Try to capture this difference.

Note that in some situations it might be possible and easier to be part of an activity in order to 'blend in', but always keep the emphasis on observing. Join in with bingo or a tea dance, for example.

In the studio

If in a group situation, physicalize and share your observations through creating an example of what one of your observed spaces was like.

- Choose one of the places you observed that inspired you the most.

- Bring that place to life with a group of 'recreators'. They must also have been to the place, but are guided by you.

- Make sure to try out the essential and specific differences you found between this and another similar place.

As a separate exercise:

- Try just one Observation Prompt at a time, for example, Space – being outside. What is your gaze when you are thinking?

- Bring only this specific observation back into the studio.

- Try a different Observation Prompt another time, for example, Breath. What is your breath like after you have been running?

Key point

Once you have experienced an aspect of BWTS in the studio, you can trust it to be in your personal 'bank' for later recall.

Creating The World of a Play: Sound, Touch and Scent

This is for a group of actors working on the same play. Sight, for most people, is the dominant sense. Take away sight and all other senses are heightened. A small group create an experience for the rest of the cast. One blindfolded actor at a time is guided through a world of the play created for the other senses.

- First, you need to work out what the essence is of this world.

- For example, if you are working on *The Arabian Nights*, what are the essential ingredients of this 'world'? They could be the smell of incense, or the sound of ankle bells; the swish of drapes and the fragrance of sweet flowers and fruit may also spring to mind.

- If you are working on *Macbeth*, on the other hand, how do you evoke the sense of castle? You may need the crackling of a huge log fire; the echoing sound of feet on stone; the sense of cold and damp air; the cold nose or wiry hair of hunting dogs; draughts; the sound of distant wooden doors being locked; a howling wind, and so on.

- Prepare the sounds and the objects that are going to offer the experience of this world. It really doesn't need a lot to create a magical atmosphere.

- A soundscape of the sea might be conjured with just a plastic bowl, water and rice; the waft of a sea breeze with a large piece of card; maybe the smell of seaweed or vinegary chips can contribute to a general sensory impression. Lay the actor down on a soft surface on a towel, shine a bright light on him and place his hand in a tray of warm sand.

- Keep it simple. Try things out for yourself first. Be imaginative; it is amazing what works when blindfolded. Do not let the actor see how you created this sound, touch and scent scape until afterwards. He can then see how little you used to create it.

Each actor begins outside the working space in which the world is going to be created.

- If there are instructions to give him, do so in advance. He needs to be secure and relaxed throughout this experience.

- Meet him and blindfold him.

- Hold his hand or his shoulders and lead him into the world.

- Guide him through it. Try not to let this interfere with the experience for him. Make sure neither to abandon him nor overwhelm the experience with your presence. His body can then experience the world and his body memory can take from it what he needs.

Note that it might be the case that taste is an important part of this atmosphere. Bear in mind, however, what it might be like to have food put into your mouth, particularly if you did not like that particular food, or had an allergy to it. Taste is an important sense, but in this context it might be better accessed through smell.

IN CONTEXT: ATMOSPHERE OF THE PLAY

This is only realistic in a long rehearsal process. In a room near your rehearsal space, you could design and create a set-up to offer the atmosphere of the world of the play for each of the cast to experience blindfolded, one at a time. Depending on the size of the cast, other members could also create a world, so that everyone gets an experience of a created landscape and the atmosphere of the play.

Performing a Specialist Physical Action (SPA)

- Choose a Specialist Physical Action that you would really like to investigate and would personally enjoy experiencing. It may be something from a play you are working on or have worked on in the past, or something that might come up in your acting. Make it something that stretches you, that is unfamiliar or out of your usual remit, but still within the bounds of possibility for you.

- Remember that any specialist activity is 'perfected' and has something of the performance in it because of this.

- Seek out, if possible, a definitive specialist of your chosen SPA. There is nothing to replace this live research – being in the environment and seeing it at close quarters, asking questions of the specialist, and so on.

Equipment

- Consider what you need and ensure you are not working with something that is entirely unsuitable. The actual equipment or tools required for the SPA will not always be appropriate. Again, only what is essential is required: for example, if the character was a butcher demonstrating splitting a carcass, he could not be wielding a chopper on a real carcass. In the same way, when demonstrating chopping skills as a commis chef, he might 'cut' already pre-cut vegetables with a blunt knife. A specialist might be employed for the specialized part of an action. In film, a shot of beautiful writing with a quill pen, for example, would be an inserted shot of a calligrapher writing on the paper. Yet, you would more than likely still offer the whole essential action for the wide shot. Learning calligraphy isn't the task; it is learning the SPA which is essential.

Break up – reveal the actions and intentions

- Remember, you are not miming here. If there is any part of the action that requires imagination to create something, remember that the difference between a mime and an action is in your intention. A mime may ask your audience to look at what is not there; you need an audience to look at you engaged in the action as you inhabit the world of the play.

- Select the components of the SPA that you are going to offer. Discover what is essential by asking how little you could do to convey it. Identify and break down the skills you are going to work on.

- Avoid looking at how other actors have done this action. This is confusing and dilutes your response.

Don't just look to the physical action to learn the physical action

- Find other ways to access, learn and practise the physical skills required in the action. Imagine that you want to do a SPA of playing the guitar. It may be that you do not play that instrument, but you can touch-type on your computer. Can you transfer the essence of touch-typing – precise use of the fingertips in a sequence – to an understanding of playing notes on an instrument? Or, if your SPA is fly-fishing, you may not be able to do that in real life but you might be able to play tennis. Can you transfer the essence of a tennis serve – to throw the ball up and flex your arm behind you, hit the ball and send it to a particular destination – to casting your line?

- Try looking to other art forms for interpretations of your SPA (painting, sculpture, poems, prose, and so on). These are all forms that may capture the essence of your action. However, be careful to avoid straight 'copying'.

- Do not add personality to the character. Here, you become the definitive character of your SPA.

- The specialist skill and the era within which it exists should offer you the change of body necessary for the character. It should change your person/personality.

- Let the SPA shape your body's movements. If you bring a character body to the task, it may distort or block the efficiency of your chosen action. In drama this kind of conflict may be helpful, but in this exercise it is not. What is the SPA telling the audience about the world of the play?

- Use the 'Efforts' (see Chapter 8, Part One) to help identify the different qualities of the SPA.

Develop and fine-tune your chosen Specialist Physical Action by asking the following questions:

- What parts of the body are involved in the SPA?

- Which body parts are not involved? Are these free or held? (See Appendices: *Creating a Fixed Point in the Space.*)

- Break it up into individual actions. Don't be surprised at how many this turns out to be. Work on each one separately.

- Then divide each action into three sections: beginning, middle and end of the movement. Each of these also possesses its own quality. Now you are able to concentrate and perfect one movement at a time just as a musician might do with a piece of music.

As you work you can identify exactly where the problems are and address any missing information. Once you have mastered your action, ask: what is the character's relationship to the action?

- Without throwing away the mastery of it, find your character's idiosyncratic way of doing the action.

- First find which parts of your body are not involved in the SPA and are therefore free to 'act'. Try out some random movements with these parts, simply practising moving them in isolation without interfering with the SPA. Include isolated body parts such as a twitching eyebrow.

- The actions before and after the actual core SPA are valuable: they help to illustrate which parts of the body and how much of the person is engaged in the SPA. The information within these 'tops and tails' is useful in crafting other pauses or interruptions as necessary. (See Chapter 8, Part Two.)

IN CONTEXT: THREE STAGES

You can divide any physical action into three stages. Each part of the action can then be understood and established as a distinct part of the story. This yields three times the information, communicating more about the character and the situation than first meets the eye. This can also sometimes clarify your character's movement, for example, the action of turning your head to the front from facing the back can be broken down as:

- Facing away.
- Turning head.
- Arriving facing the front.

You need to have full physical capacity in play to fill each of these individual moments. (See Chapter 3: Neutral and the Epic.)

Put yourself to the test as a specialist of your Action

- Try the SPA blindfolded, if safe.
- Try the SPA with different mindsets and with different feelings. Try it with different Efforts for the character, different personalities. (See Chapter 8, Part One.)
- Try doing other things at the same time (if possible) like talking, laughing, crying, singing, looking somewhere else, and so on.
- Work at maintaining the specialist's respect for controlled action, whatever his emotional state. A dentist doesn't drill right through the patient's jaw just because he's angry.

Choose an everyday action. Transpose some of the qualities of the SPA you have worked onto this other action, for example:

- Imagine you are a builder building a wall; transfer this skill set to making a sandwich for a packed lunch. Maybe there are physical actions in the play that the character undertakes to which you can transfer the SPA movements.

IN CONTEXT: SPECIALIST PHYSICAL ACTION

If you are taking on an SPA it shouldn't be all-consuming and you should not feel obliged to learn the whole skill. Once the decision has been taken about what element of the SPA can be seen and from what angle, you can begin the specific learning. You can gain a tremendous amount by having in place your SPA before rehearsals commence. See any physical action as a bonus rather than as an imposition.

Looking Directly at the Character Himself

Start to look at people in general – in order to discover more about each of their worlds. This may be as a planned observation exercise or as you go about your daily business. When you notice something interesting about someone, get your enquiring mind going; observe the environment as well, locating its part in the movement you see in the person.

- Gently enliven your curiosity by allowing something to invade your eye.
- Don't work at seeing something. Use the things that make you physically curious; things that make you – for example – put your head on one side, raise one eyebrow higher than the other or half open your mouth.
- Here is an example of questions and observations that arose from watching a woman on a bus:
  - At first glance she seemed very relaxed or perhaps even defeated but something in her body language signalled that she needed to be somewhere quickly.
  - How is it possible to see that she is in a hurry?
  - How do you know that?
  - How can you see that?
  - Where is this visible in her body?
  - Why does she look relaxed?

    Curiosity paid off. She had handed over responsibility to the bus: she retained only an aspect of hurried intent but without the power to do anything about it.

From this observation you would have information to recreate a similar moment of someone in a bus, in a hurry. Even better, you would have 'banked' a physical expression of 'handing over responsibility' that is transferable to lots of other situations (for example, for a character that assumes a passive role in an emotional situation where someone has taken over).

- At first glance, situations may appear very different from one another, but see if you can transfer something you have discovered to another situation.

The Park Bench

This is a partner exercise within a group, and just one example of many 'reading body language' exercises that you can do in the studio to sharpen your eye. It is a brief light preparation exercise, not a long improvisation. It requires a group as an audience. Two chairs are placed slightly apart in the working space to create a park bench.

- Improvise: two people on a park bench, who don't know one another.
- One of you sits on a chair as an imaginary bench in an imaginary park. You settle into your own imagined reality of this situation.
- The other actor enters the park and sits on the bench (another chair). Shortly, after the second actor's entrance, when you are settled into your realities, you are both asked to freeze.
- Two people from the audience pick up the chair with you on it and move it to the other side.
- Then you unfreeze and restart the improvisation still sitting on your park bench, accepting that the story is affected and may be completely different.
- Allow the relationship to emerge between the two of you; whether you are people who know one another or are strangers.

The game continues, but the chairs can now be put anywhere in the space, which also changes the situation.

Key point

This exercise is helpful for developing reading and recognition of the stories through body language and proximity, as you observe people in the real world.

In the initial improvisation you may not have realized the detail of the story that was there, but that story is made very clear when the bodies are subsequently rearranged.

Capture an Essence of Your Current POV

- Sit alone as yourself (not in character) holding a particular feeling, or thinking about a person. This works best with the memory of a heightened moment in your life.

- Be aware of the life of things around you.

- For example, let's say a leaf falls past your window; the clouds drift across the sky; an ant is crawling on the window ledge. Something will catch your eye and you will, at the edges of your consciousness, connect with a particular aspect of its movement. If it is the ant to which you are drawn, it may be the pace at which it moves, or the fast rhythm of its little legs, or, that it is moving on relentlessly; or it might be its linear pathway which inspires your empathy. The quality of movement that particularly stands out will match a physical quality of the feeling you are experiencing.

- Your attention doesn't shift to anything that you are seeing; all this time you are still thinking of your heightened moment.

- Take on the movement. Let it inform your next action. This is not asking you to be an ant. In identifying with one aspect of the ant's movement you have revealed an aspect of your personal POV.

- You have identified an essential movement quality which is now available.

When you have explored this exercise as yourself, you can then do it as your character.

If You Can Achieve One Perfect Moment ...

▶ If You Can Achieve One Perfect Moment ...

Translating 2D Painting to 3D

This exercise is for the individual in a group. You translate a painting of your choice to three dimensions in the studio with a cast of actors.

The solo actor can adapt this process using a painting with one character in it. He positions himself in relation to the physical world and focal points of the painting. Note that portraits where objects are placed to serve the character are not ideal for this exercise.

- Visit a gallery and find a painting to which you personally respond. If choosing is challenging, persevere: there really is a painting hanging on one of those walls that is for you.

- Look for paintings which have more than one person in them. For example, see 'La Coiffure' by Degas in the online gallery of the National Gallery, London, at www.nationalgallery.org.uk/paintings

- Your choice of painting will be somewhat restricted by the availability of a good quality colour reproduction of it: postcard, print, and so on.

- Describe your visit and the choice of painting, either out loud for someone else to write down, or to yourself in your journal. Describe the whole experience: for example, what you were wearing, where you were, what drew you to the painting. Was it the colour? Was it the light? Was it the painting's depiction of textures of, say, fabric or skin?

- Be concerned with whatever it was that attracted you to the painting.

- Keep particular note of what you liked and what affected you so that you do not lose these as you discover more about the painting.

Choice of painting

Some paintings are obvious 'actor paintings' because of their drama or narrative, but be aware that something non-narrative can be just as rich.

Plan your recreation of the painting

- Choose your cast out of your group.

- The actors should wear neutral clothing and use only essential props, such as weight-bearing objects.

- The translation of the painting is your vision of it only; it is not your cast's idea of it.

- Do not use this painting as a creative launch – don't alter anything or make anything up. If you cannot see something – say the subject's feet are hidden by a table – read the rest of the painting as it will help you fill in the blanks.

- Aim to recreate it as accurately as you can, so that what you read in the original painting now reads in the three-dimensional 'painting'. Remember the artist spent hundreds of hours on this painting and has done the creative job for you already.

- Work with your actors to recreate the painting in a studio space.

- When the three-dimensional 'painting' is ready, present it to your

audience. They should look at it from the front as they would if
encountering it in the gallery.

- So, gather the audience where you wish them to be. Ask the audience
to turn their backs (or shut their eyes) and then invite them to turn
around (open their eyes) when you are ready.

- Receive the audience feedback: let the audience say what they got from
the painting, what they loved, and so on. Do not show them the original
painting; their role is not to compare. (See additional online resources:
Feedback.)

- Look at the painting yourself with fresh eyes after this feedback.
What have you achieved? Look at the notes you wrote about your
first impression of the painting. Have you excluded or veered away
from something you had envisaged because you decided this was
not possible to achieve? If this is the case, work out how to make it
possible. Be true to your initial impression of the painting along with the
feedback and rework your painting.

- Show it again.

Relationship between 2D and 3D

Looking at how the artist has directed the viewer's eye through his use of space
in the painting will give you a key into the 3D translation. In *'La Coiffure'* (*Combing
the Hair*), Degas's two-dimensional vision translates to three dimensions easily
and perfectly, displaying his deep understanding of crafting three-dimensional
space in two-dimensions.

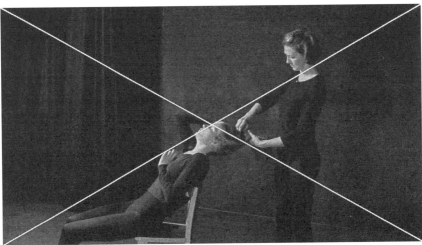

Figure 4.3 Video grab with overlaid on-screen composition lines. Vivienne Bell and Sinéad
O'Keeffe.

- Walk into your painting – into the places the artist could not paint because it is behind his subjects.

- Look at the painting from any angle; each angle from which you look offers you a view of what seems to be a different painting. The views are not sculptural because each angle tells the story of the two-dimensional painting: the side of it, the back of it, and so on.

- Look at your spatial use within the frame that you have given yourself. What are the spatial relationships between the characters, for example, levels, diagonals, spirals, linear shape, spacing, and so on? If the painting works, it can be viewed from any angle and it will translate from two dimensions to three.

- Keep going back to the painting itself to supply the information as to how these relationships should be formed.

- Show it again.

- Receive feedback. Go back to work on your painting. Be aware of the richness of the material with which you are working – the actors. They are live; human and existing within three-dimensional space. Think of what else you might have neglected to translate through focusing exclusively on the bodies in the painting: perhaps the textures or colours can also be translated to your recreation whilst still staying absolutely true to the painting.

- Show it again.

IN CONTEXT: CREATING DEPTH OF FIELD

Paintings are useful because they are equivalent to the two-dimensional frame of the screen or proscenium arch. When working on a play, this heightened awareness of the two-dimensional plane of the audience's framed perspective can help you to use spatial choices in relation to the depth of field as an expressive tool (particularly on a raked stage).

Bringing the painting to life

- Look again at the notes from your first visit and at the thing that you loved about the painting. Keep this as the driving force and do not allow yourself to be diverted from that. Ultimately, what you love about the painting is all that you can offer.

- Maintaining the moment of the painting as the focal point, create the three seconds of action/movement before the moment of the painting and three seconds after.

Some paintings seem to lend themselves to this. They are a captured moment in time and so it is easier to create the flow of movement into and out of that moment. However, all paintings have a life to them and it is the life in that moment that you are concerned with and not the naturalistic narrative of it.

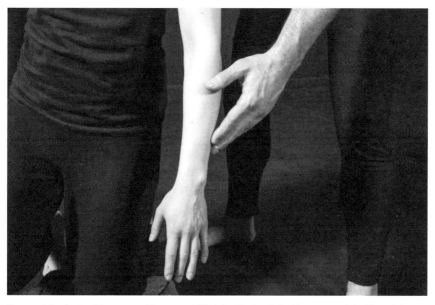

Figure 4.4 Gestural language. Close-up of (Sir John Brydges) the Lieutenant of the Tower's hand on Lady Jane's arm with actors Nina Fog and Matt Tait. Photograph by Todd Padwick.

- Identify the moments within the journey of the breath in each body/ character in the painting, that is, what is happening at the beginning of the in-breath, the middle of it, the end of the out-breath, and so on. These will help you fathom the journey to and from the painting.

- Decide the expressive nature of the breath of each actor in the stillness of the painting. Is it the breath of thought, of emotion, of human response? Is it, for example, light, or thin; held or released; mid in-breath or out-breath? Does it evoke a colour, and so on?

- Examine how the actors can manage to maintain the sensation and placement of breath without holding their breath. Question how they can start and stop without adding in an inflation or deflation linked to the action of stopping and starting.

Once you have the three seconds before the moment and three seconds after:

- Work out a simple mechanism for your actors to arrive in the painting together after the 3 seconds before.
- Work out how they commence the three seconds after holding the painting, using a signal (such as a clap) from you.
- Work out the coming to a stillness as a soft 'sketch' to end.
- Invite the audience to view the painting from the front again but now with the added 3 seconds before.
- In the stillness of the painting invite the audience to 'walk through it.'
- The audience can lie on the floor, peer over a character's shoulder, or look at the painting from a character's POV.
- Your cast is to stay in the moment of the painting. The painting must not dissolve or change until the audience has left the space and seen it once more as the front-on (two-dimensional) version.
- Then give the pre-decided signal to the actors to do the 3 seconds after.
- Receive feedback once more.
- Look again at your original notes of why you chose the painting. Revisit your painting if necessary.
- You can now add sound, smell, drapes, lighting, and so on.
- Prune back anything that gets in the way and ruins the essential feel of the painting.

IN CONTEXT: PORTRAIT OF YOUR CHARACTER

When you have a character and are in the rehearsal process, you can imagine you are to have your portrait painted. Go through the process of preparation for it: where you want it to be painted; what posture you are going to adopt; whether you would be involved in an activity, and if so what that would be; what you would wear. Decide what would represent your character best, and how best you could be captured in a moment of time. If it makes it easier, imagine the portrait is going to be used for the front of the programme and needs to speak clearly of who you are in relation to the play or film.

Taking the Physical Metaphor Literally

Taking 'Falling For You' as an example.

'Falling for you' is a familiar colloquial phrase that speaks of beginning to allow love to take some control. In this context, see the whole phrase as a physical action. To fall is an obvious physical action. 'Falling for you' is also a physical action. See how much you get of the meaning from the action of 'falling for you'.

For this example you need a partner, although the partner does not have to do anything. You are going to do/give this action for/to this partner.

- Stand in front of partner.

- Make eye contact and keep it throughout.

- 'Fall' for your partner: fall from the ankles, keeping in one piece, not collapsing. At the last possible moment, simply step out of the fall towards your partner. You will end up standing a little closer to your partner, still holding eye contact.

- You have just 'fallen for him/her'.

- The fall part is the bit you allow to happen – you cannot 'do' the fall, so focus on allowing the sensation of this short moment.

- The metaphor isn't 'landing for you' or 'lunging for you' or 'falling by yourself'. So don't draw attention to the landing. Maintaining eye contact will help. (See Chapter 2: Falling.)

- Now you can choose another metaphor.

- Take it seriously and literally.

- Put it into action.

6
TRANSFORMATION: ANIMAL AND ANTHROPOMORPHIC

OVERVIEW

Acting is a process of transformation. At first it can be difficult for the actor to transform into another human: people are so complex and individually characterized that it is hard for him to know what to change and what to retain. Transforming to another animal can therefore be a useful 'staging post' in the process of characterization.

This chapter is in two parts.

Part One: Animal Study. This section describes a process of transformation into a non-human animal, using close-up and consistent observation of real animals.

Part Two: Anthropomorphic Study. This section describes a process to develop a human character from an animal study as well as offering a process to work with an animal study as inspiration for a scripted character.

Part One: Animal Study

Other animals have very different movement qualities from humans and from each other. They are also more consistent across their species. Each species has its own limited, yet clearly defined qualities. There is no possibility of confusion in deciphering what makes a cat a cat and what makes a horse a horse, and so on. An animal's uncomplicated identity contrasts with the actor's complicated persona. When working on an animal, an actor can't really say 'I'm a bit like that character.' He is forced therefore to make choices unrelated to his own behavioural patterns. The animal's morphology is an unalterable fact and therefore demands consistency on the part of the actor. Its physicality makes demands on the human body that could never be invented by an actor.

The process described here represents a merging of two, complementary disciplines:[1] Peter Elliott's focus is on working with actors to achieve realistic animals and creatures and it usually involves animatronics or motion capture. Ewan's focus is on the developmental process, working with actors on their capacity for transformation through ownership of process and, movement vocabulary, taking animal study on into anthropomorphic study.

The first section of the chapter offers an animal study that can exist in realtime (at the pace and rhythm of everyday existence). This is followed by more complex ideas, leading to a study that can exist in both realtime and condensed time (actions that take place over a long period edited into a short amount of time – a template for the time-shape of a play).

The second section explores the means by which the actor can take animal work into anthropomorphic character development. (See additional online resources: *Actor-In-Training Animal Study Brief*.)

The Zoo

See Practical: *Choosing an Animal for Your First Study* (p. 139)
See Practical: *Preparation for First Session After Observing Your Animal* (p. 139)

Zoo visits are essential for this study. Observing a live animal has clear advantages over the use of film or photographs. Close proximity to the animal means research comes straight from the source. The zoo provides the actor with a close-up of the animal's living, breathing body. Perception is immediate, without edit or prejudice. The animal's behaviour may be altered by captivity, but it is still authentic.

Some animals are not suited to a first study; these include chimps, snakes, fish and insects. Chimps are unsuitable because they are too similar to humans; snakes and fish because they are limbless (the actor must invent too much); insects because they operate as part of a larger system (for example, an ant colony). These are better taken on as later studies. There are, however, more than enough animals from which to choose.

Living in the Now

Unlike humans, animals live in the present tense. They live in direct response to nature, taking every moment as it happens. Living in the now is an essential skill for the actor. He is continually being asked to recreate moments in a way

---

[1] Elliott and Ewan's process of work in the studio with the actors. Elliott is a renowned specialist in the film industry.

that makes them seem as though they are happening for the first time. For humans in contemporary society, this is difficult as so many of our actions are preconceived. Animal study enables the actor to respond to the moment in a process of continual improvisation. Every movement is motivated, with an inner driving force and an outer manifestation. For the actor to experience total transformation, the work must be both internal and external.

Imagination/Observation Percentage

See Practical: *First Session in the Studio* (p. 140)

Transformation as a process can be seen as an 'equation' balancing observation and imagination. In the early stages, the work is approximately 80 per cent imagination and 20 per cent observation. The animal, at this point, offers the actor freedom rather than restriction. As the process develops, the ratio of observation to imagination changes: the actor's imagination is increasingly informed by what he has learnt by watching the animal. When the actor now tries aspects of his animal's behaviour that he has not observed in real life, these derive from effective observation of what he *has* seen. His developed physical understanding of the animal supplies the necessary missing information. For example, he may never have seen an elephant run at full speed (there may not be space in the enclosure), but he intuitively understands how this might be from having watched the elephant walk: 'inhabiting' the animal tells the actor what to do.

Hierarchy of Information

There is a necessary hierarchy of information to be made in any study. A hummingbird, for example, flaps its wings incredibly fast. However, it does this in order to keep its place in the air, so for the actor-as-hummingbird, the stillness the bird achieves is actually more important than the flapping. A giraffe is a quadruped – it walks on four limbs. However, in order to access the height experience of the world's tallest mammal, the actor may choose to be bipedal.

Actions that are Physically Unachievable

Being confronted by animal actions that are unachievable – such as flying, swimming, running at speed – can lead to the actor dismissing them outright. However, instead of being blinded by the overall action of, for example, flying, he can observe the detail contained within it and work out what he can do. If working on a bird, he might perfect the take-off and the landing and offer an accurate study of flying with the actor trusting his imagination. For a swimming animal such as an otter or an alligator, he can enter and exit the imagined water and likewise offer an accurate study of swimming in the studio space. A bat hangs upside down. The actor could spend years training to do that or he could shift to the bat's perspective, making the world around him 'upside down'. If the actor believes what he is doing, an audience will too.

Observation Breakdown

See Practical: *Observing Your Animal* (p. 141)

This is the actor's opportunity to practise a full character observation process. By concentrating on one animal, he can develop an approach that is at once methodical and empathetic. He becomes aware of technical aspects including 'the living backbone', breath rhythm and transitions (how the animal gets from sitting to standing/walk to run/high space to low space). Through precise observation, the actor builds a vocabulary of his animal's behaviour and brings it into the studio.

The actor is only watching a small portion of the animal's life and the animal does nothing for the actor's benefit. It is a cliché to say that an actor must love the character he is playing. However, clichés are built on truth and the actor needs to love this animal and foster a passion for knowledge about it as he builds the journey to transformation.

As well as the zoo observation, the study is backed up with as much other information as possible: books, magazines, wildlife photography, film footage (DVD and internet), discussion with a zookeeper, and so on. In this way, the actor comes to see and to know the animal in all states (sleeping, hungry, angry, cautious, playful). He imagines the animal's life as a whole, seeking to understand what time means for the animal, connecting with its rhythms and the way it sees the world.

A good animal study arising just from observation and mimicry is almost certainly a happy accident. It would also be difficult to repeat. Effective transformation depends on a fully developed, interrogative process.

By using a mnemonic,[2] the actor has the acronym BBWSWRB (Bumble Bees Would Say Wasps Read Badly) as a memorable working order of seven key aspects for animal study. These may be recalled repeatedly when observing and subsequently when working on transformation to animal or character.

---

[2] Thank you to Lyndsey Campbell (Central acting alumni) for coming up with this mnemonic.

1 **Bumble – B**ackbone

2 **Bees – B**reath rhythm (Heartbeat)

3 **Would – W**eight (Centre of gravity)

4 **Say – S**pace (The way it uses the space)

5 **Wasps – W**ay it sees the world (Eyes)

6 **Read – R**hythm of life

7 **Badly – B**alance of senses

Each aspect takes its turn as the centre of attention, but the others always remain part of the picture. Some aspects are strongly related to others (for instance, Breath and Weight).

First and foremost among these aspects, the actor needs to observe and understand the animal's backbone and breath.

Backbone

The actor needs to see past the outer shape of his animal and work from an understanding of the backbone. This is the core structure from which all major movement stems and the key to other physical attributes. For example, the lion owes the power of its back legs to the stability of its backbone. The spine twists, arches and undulates. The animal's centre of gravity continually shifts along it.

The backbone offers the actor essential character information. When transforming into a lion, he must explore and maintain this moving backbone, recognizing its influence on, and relationship with, other body parts. With other animals, it may be necessary to consider the power of the arms or wings. The massive wingspan of the vulture, for example, is supported by its backbone. In every case the backbone *is* the animal.

Breath rhythm and heartbeat

Breath and action have an interesting and complex relationship. The animal does not take a new breath at every step. The actor has to look hard to discover the breath rhythm and match the speed of breathing to the activity. There are clues to breath rhythm in the way an animal moves. The ability of an animal to respond quickly, for example, may indicate that it has a fast breath rhythm.

Transformation to the animal does not require the actor to change the way his body functions. For example, a very small mammal such as a mouse has a minute diaphragm and an incredibly fast breath rhythm. This is impossible for the actor to sustain; he might hyperventilate. The actor can, however, retain his animal's breath rhythm and heartbeat in his imagination. A lizard can slow its breathing to the extent that it appears to have stopped altogether. The

Figure 5.1   Lizard – Inland Bearded Dragon. Actor: Reece Richardson. Photograph by Patrick Baldwin.

actor, while not actually holding his breath, has to find this same quality in his stillness. He experiences what it's like to still his breath for a short time and retains the sensation and effect while he carries on breathing. He only allows real breath to influence the movement when it is both fitting and possible to do so.

Weight/Centre of gravity

Weight goes hand in hand with the centre of gravity, so they are always worked on together. The centre of gravity in all animals is greatly affected by the smallest of movements; it's a continual game of tiny shifts. The placement of the centre of gravity, and the range of shifts around it, is specific to each animal. Everything that walks, biped or quadruped, has to change its centre of gravity – releasing weight from one limb and transferring it to another (just to take a step).

An actor tackling an elephant study should neither block out the issue of the animal's weight – which is impossible physically to attain – nor force the issue by moving in a heavy, lumbering way. Through breath rhythm and shifts in the centre of gravity, the actor can achieve an accurate sensation of the elephant's weight, and the movement of that weight.

It is essential to find the 'sense' of weight as well as how exactly the animal uses its weight. The delicacy of movement, for example, of the feet of a rhinoceros may surprise the actor who is studying it. Animals that move between air, ground and water offer the actor a playful exploration of weight. Rather than focusing on the arms as a starting point for a gibbon's brachiating (swinging from branch to branch), the actor needs to investigate and trust in the mechanics of shifting his centre of gravity. He has to imagine and create the shifts in weight without really hanging or brachiating.

By embodying the mechanics of a movement, the actor can live its essence without having the environment – or the body – in which the movement is normally carried out. Imagination can fill any gaps. The result of this expansive and imaginative exercise is an actor who physically understands the effective use of the centre of gravity when undertaking human character transformation.

Space/The way it uses space

An animal creates a defined use of space in relation to its behaviour, its territory, its predators, food sources, and so on. A rat, for example, moves expertly around the edge of a space following each contour, avoiding crossing an open space as much as possible. A lion, on the other hand, can easily walk right through the centre of the space.

The actor gains much by working outside in a real landscape. He can create spaces for himself that replicate the animal's nest or den, and then can later recreate them imaginatively in the studio. (See Chapter 5.)

Rhythm of life

The rhythm of an animal's life is connected to its metabolism: grazing animals, for example, eat most of the day and move fast only when necessary. The rhythm of life also relates to the animal's life span, social grouping and survival mechanisms.

The way it sees the world

The position, physiology and function of an animal's eyes are essential pieces of information for the actor that each help to feed the imagination: a chameleon, for example, moves its eyes independently so it takes in two views of the world that each eye can react to. Rabbits have almost 360-degree vision but a blind spot to the front. (So when a rabbit looks at something sideways it is because it is the best view it can get.) Working both technically and imaginatively, the actor works out what attracts his animal's attention and how it perceives its environment. Effectively, the actor learns to see the world through the animal's eyes. Each animal has its own perception of the world. It belongs in its own microcosm of what's important and what it can ignore.

Figure 5.2   Sloth Bear. Actor: Nina Fog. Photograph by Patrick Baldwin.

Balance of senses

Humans are predominantly sight-driven. A dog will hear someone approaching and has probably already smelled him. The human looks to the dog's reaction to realize someone is coming. When undertaking an animal, the actor cannot alter his sensory perception, but he can rebalance his awareness and change his reaction to stimuli.

Senses the human doesn't possess, such as a bat's sonic sense or a lizard's hypersensitive sense of smell can be imaginatively accessed and translated to movement (through working with the bat's seemingly erratic, radar-guided flight path or the lizard's way of 'tasting' smells with its tongue).

Sounds

See Practical: *Sounds* (p. 144)

Most animals use sounds as part of their behavioural vocabulary. These sounds are an important part of the physical study. In order to make any animal sound, the actor must access its location, its timing and the volume of breath required. Sounds made by some animals are a major feature of their behaviour. These offer obvious vocal physicality. For example, the loud, guttural roar of the lion shows the use of his diaphragm; his whole body is involved in the action of panting. The sound a rat makes, although far more discreet, still offers access to the animal's inner landscape and rhythm of communication.

An accurate sound can lend atmosphere (even to the actor making the sound). It may evoke the part of the world the animal comes from or the amount of space in its habitat. Equally, the actor has to find the reason for the sound in order to hit its particular quality (loudness, clarity, and so on). He must then allow that motivation to inform pitch, reverberation and tone.

Improvisations: Working in Realtime

See Practical: *Improvisations in Realtime* (p. 145)

The first stage of the improvisation process involves being his animal in real time. So the actor lives in the now in realtime. He attempts to do the same amount of activities that he observes his animal doing in a given time frame. In fact, when working on some animals the actor probably always does a slightly compressed version of realtime: a leopard in realtime may sleep for an hour, walk twice round his cage then go back to sleep again.

Non-interaction

Individual actor-animals don't relate to each other. It may be that a lion is working next to a golden lion tamarin or a vulture next to a rabbit. Neither disturbs or connects with the other.

Motivation

See Practical: *Motivated Thoughts Out Loud* (p. 146)
See Practical: *Stream of Consciousness* (p. 146)
See Practical: *Short Concentration/High Curiosity* (p. 148)

This is a journey of discovery and the actor always looks to the animal for information: the imperatives of its daily life translate into motivated thoughts. This basic cost analysis translates pretty closely to human needs, wants and values. How do animals think? Do they think in images? Do they dream? He can only surmise, but through exercises and extended improvisation in animal study the actor can explore what it is like to exist without the intellect interrupting or overriding motivated action.

The Working Process

See Practical: *Working Technically* (p. 149)
See Practical: *Ongoing Process in Realtime* (p. 150)

The process combines resolving technical challenges and being completely involved in being the animal and takes place in a combination of outdoor and indoor sessions. A studio space facilitates technical focus and the boundaries of the room offer structure to preparation exercises. (See Practical: *Mirrored Speech*; See Appendices: *Body-Parts Leading*; *Linear/Circular Pathways*.)

Shifting between observation, improvisation and technical work is the core of the process. Each time the actor returns to watch his animal, his experience in the studio and his research refresh the need to observe and redirect his eye.

The Leap – How an Actor Steps into and out of his Character

See Practical: *The Leap* (p. 150)

The actor should be either fully himself or fully animal. Insufficient clarity on this point leads to some confusing half-in/half-out state of being which does not exist. By using a mechanism, with practice, he can shift instantly from human to animal and vice versa. This is 'The Leap'.

The trigger

The Leap relies on a trigger: a completely transformed moment chosen from the study that is as wholly different in as many ways as possible from the actor's own human movement and motivation.

IN CONTEXT: THE LEAP

The actor needs to be helped to trust that he can change states immediately, making 'The Leap' into and out of a transformation. It can be taken into work situations where involved preparations are inappropriate. The word 'Action!' on a film set, for example, means just that: immediate action for a take.

Group Animals

See Practical: *Group Animals* (p. 151)
See Practical: *Colony, Pack and Herd Games* (p. 151)

Sometimes the goal is not the detailed study of an individual animal but the study of a group. It is about being one part of a whole. This process includes responding to the rhythm and survival needs of the group, leading the actor to think in terms of a 'chorus'. The understanding of this can be supported through developing appropriate games. There are games that provoke distinct animal characteristics such as the herd instinct, predatory behaviour, or family dynamic.

Developing a Specific Warm-up for the Animal

See Practical: *Creating a Personal Animal Warm-up* (p. 154)

In order to develop an appropriate warm-up (and subsequent cool-down) for his particular animal he can create specific, bespoke exercises and games to support the sustained physicality. For a tiger study, his preparation might involve isolating and experiencing an action of the limbs and reaccessing, for example, the heavy weight in the paws by imagining the wall as the floor and 'walking' or pawing against the wall.

Zoo Set-up

See Practical: *Zoo Set-up* (p. 154)

At the end of stage one, the actor can take on the experience of being his animal in a zoo set-up within the studio space. His study is by no means the finished article, but he has acquired enough information that he can let the situation of being viewed in realtime push him to deepen his learning and his transformation to his animal.

Condensed Time

See Practical: *Adding Condensed Time to Your Improvisations* (p. 155)

The work at this stage becomes more performance oriented. The actor offers a study of his animal using condensed time. Condensed time for an audience includes everything they want to see. Condensed time for the animal contains everything the animal ever does. It is only the time span of the progression of

activities that is condensed; the inner rhythm of the animal does not change. As in a play, the actor does not move faster to show what happened in, say, the three days or three years in which the play is set. It's an edited version of activities within a compressed time frame.

Alternating between Condensed Time and Realtime

The performance might even include repetition of activities that an audience enjoys. To progress from real to condensed time takes practice. The actor has to learn how to select work for condensed time just as playwrights must edit down action for plays. The actor can practise offering, for example, the experience of being bloated/sated one second and being hungry the next without a journey in between. This heightens the actor's need to 'live in the now' and in this he finds further release from his own intellectual interference.

Although he will know all the things that he wants to fit into his improvisation, these activities must not be choreographed as this would mean that the actor was not living in the now.

The Performance

See Practical: *Performance Format* (additional online resources) (p. 155)

If the study culminates in a performance shared with other actors and an audience, the condensed time improvisation is now his solo performance, while other actors perform their animal study in realtime as background characters. This process works in rotation, each actor experiencing both solo and background. The background actors should carry on living as their animal without detracting from the actor in the 'spotlight' who is working in condensed time. The background actors provide the 'world of the play'. Each actor pulls focus on cue. He has to follow all the usual performance criteria.

There is no doubt that this performance is for an audience. It will be entertaining – animals, after all, are a delight to watch. For the actor, this works well as his first character: his Animal Study becoming a benchmark of possible transformation when undertaking future human characters.

Part One: Animal Study Practical

Choosing an Animal for Your First Study

- First visit the zoo as a 'tourist'. Put aside any difficulties you may have with zoos. This is for work – it is not about asking you to change your principles.

After the visit you will have mentally mapped the zoo, taken on board the spectrum of animals on display and experienced a connection with one or more of the animals.

- After a reasonable gap, reflect on your tourist visit and choose one of the animals that stayed in your mind – one with which you connected. This is your study animal.

- Don't choose an animal because you think it will be a 'good' one for you to take on. Choose the one you want to work on. Any animal, no matter which you choose, is going to be vastly different from you. All animals offer the possibility of complete transformation from the human animal. Some animals appear harder to achieve than others for differing reasons: a mouse because it is so fast and light, a gorilla because of its detailed physical vocabulary, an elephant because it has four limbs and a trunk, and so on.

- Do not shy away from your number one choice because it may be too difficult: some of the biggest challenges bring about the most creative answers.

- If an animal has been chosen for you by a tutor, don't waste your time trying to work out why you have been allocated this particular study subject: go with it.

Preparation for First Session After Observing Your Animal

It is now time to return to the zoo for your first study visit.

- Capture your initial impression. Don't stay at the zoo too long; this observation is simply a first meeting with your animal.

- If you are trying out movement in public, be clear that you understand the difference between displaying and just being visible while working. Don't draw attention to yourself.

- After leaving the zoo, consolidate and begin your extended research: fire up your imagination; use all resources.

- Find appropriate replacement foods so that you can replicate the way your animal eats. For example, cooked spaghetti or gummy worms could substitute real worms for a bird. Use your common sense: steer clear of any food that you could choke on (such as nuts) or anything you could slip on. Avoid miming eating.

First Session in the Studio

- Be clothed appropriately to move as your animal: wear knee-pads if you are studying a quadruped animal.

- Lie on the floor, close your eyes and take yourself through a relaxation exercise.

- Now, visualize your first visit to the zoo to find your animal; to reaffirm and heighten the experience.

- Track through the visit you made to the zoo in detail (buying the ticket, talking with a friend, what you said, what mood you were in, what you were wearing, what the weather was like) until the moment you arrived at your animal's enclosure and watched it for the first time.

- Recall and visualize what your animal was doing; take everything from memory and do not make it up.

- Take in the animal's breath rhythm, physically empathize with this (feel it as you watch it in your mind's eye) and then

- Fully adopt the breath rhythm yourself.

- Visualize its backbone and, as you do, empathize with this shape and form and then adopt its backbone as much as is possible, still lying down without employing your limbs.

- Next, as you lie there, visualize and take on something of the animal's weight: feel it give into, or lift out of, the ground.

- Now, without planning or hesitating, 'become' your animal. Be fully involved: throw yourself into being the animal without being inhibited by what may or may not be right.

- Use the sounds of the animal, even though at this stage they may not be accurate. This doesn't mean that you should make them up, however – aim for accuracy even if it is not yet possible.

- This is your first improvisation in realtime; keep to the behaviour you observed on this first study day. You won't have enough information at this point for a long improvisation. Do about ten minutes.

Observing Your Animal

Take a notebook and maybe a sketchbook. Look for specific things as you observe the animal, once more using **B**umble **B**ees **W**ould **S**ay **W**asps **R**ead **B**adly (Backbone; Breath/heartbeat; Weight/centre of gravity; Space; Way it sees the world; Rhythm of life; Balance of senses):

Backbone

- Look at the shape of the backbone, including the animal's neck and tail.
- Look at its length.
- Look at its size and at how the limbs extend from it.
- Find where the movement begins – see the backbone in sections if it helps.
- Look at how it moves: watch the backbone as the animal goes from sitting to standing; as it prepares for flight; as it lies down; as it runs, jumps, and so on.

Breath/heartbeat

- Observe the influences of the breath on the movement and behaviour of your animal.
- While watching your animal, physically empathize with the breath. Attempt the actual breath, even for a short time, and then transfer the quality it gives you into your whole body. From this, imagine the heartbeat – its internal rhythm.
- Re-experience the actual breath-rhythm you found.
- Commit it to body memory.
- Back in the studio, demonstrate the rhythm of your animal's breath for yourself by transferring the pulse of the breath to a normal human walk. Make each step on an out-breath. Do not do this as your animal: this exercise is not simulating stepping as your animal; its purpose is to clarify the observation of your animal's breath rhythm.
  (See Appendices: *Jumps, Sounding the Breath on Landing*.)

Weight/centre of gravity

- Look at the weight of the animal: at how heavy or light it is.
- Look at the distribution of the weight.

If you can locate its centre of gravity, ask yourself:

- What is the range of shifts around the animal's centre of gravity?

- When and how does it use its weight? When does it resist gravity, or give in to gravity?

- How does the animal maintain its centre of gravity through the larger actions?

Space

Observe your animal's behaviour in relation to its environment. Look for facts. Find out about the following:

- Watch the way the animal uses the space, maybe noting it down as a floorplan.

- Look at how much space it takes up (include the space above it) and how big its world is.

- Where in the space is it comfortable? This could be related to activities, but also its place on the food chain. The meerkat is quite low on the food chain so nests underground in a burrow – a different world from the open spaces above.

- What level does it live on? Under the ground; on the ground; at height; in the sky?

- So, does it want or need to be above or below other animals?

- Which spatial planes do you need to 'know' movement-wise? For instance, as an owl you may inhabit, and therefore 'know', the door plane when standing and sitting, and know the table plane when flying. (See Appendices: *Additional to the Dimensional Scale*.)

Figure 5.3 Owl standing and owl in flight. Copyright (left) © Eric Isselee/Shutterstock and (right) Jim Cumming/Getty Images.

The way your animal sees the world

Thinking both technically and imaginatively, work out what attracts your animal's attention and how it perceives its environment. Look for facts. Find out about the following:

- How are the eyes positioned? Are they front-facing? Stereoscopic? Or are they at the sides of the head? Does that offer all-round vision?
- What is outside the animal's field of vision? What is the focal distance?
- Do the eyes move? How much do they move? Does the animal blink?

When you have the facts about the eyes themselves, you need to know how the animal sees and what it tends to look at. For instance:

- Is it attracted to movement?
- What does it see that motivates it?
- Watch your animal to see if you can begin to see the world through its eyes; try to imagine how and what it thinks.

Rhythm of life

Observe your animal and you will see important information about its rhythm of life in any of the activities your animal is engaged in – it is always there. Do not look for particular information; rather, focus on the whole picture which starts to add up. This is the everyday rhythm of life, the rhythm manifested in the metabolism of your animal.

- How often does the animal need to eat?
- How much does the animal sleep?
- Does it survive on speed, stillness, camouflage, body armour, safety in numbers?
- What is its breeding pattern?
- Does it belong to a herd, a family, a pair-bond or a flock?

No individual question can give you the definitive answer, but collectively the answers should tell you the animal's rhythm of life.

Balance of senses

Know the facts; look for facts. Find out about the following:

- Notice actions that reveal the balance of senses: the way, for example, a nose leads, searching the air for scent; the pricking up of the ears; the open mouth or the flicking tongue 'tasting' the smell, and so on.
- Put the senses in a hierarchy.
- As you watch your animal, take on the purpose of the senses for yourself – what it reacts to and how.
- Think about what you want to recreate of the environment when you are in the studio to offer yourself an equivalent experience of the balance of the senses. For example: spray some perfume or scented deodorant onto a piece of card and get someone to hide it for you to find by looking with your nose.

Sounds

- Have some knowledge of your animal's sounds from the beginning.
- If you do not know the sounds it makes, start with an imaginative approximation of the sound based on your research. Don't strain: the quality and accuracy of the sounds will increase as the study progresses.
- Learn as much as possible about the context and meaning of the sounds. The sounds are not just an empty replication: they should still possess the communication and meaning of the animal's original sound. For example, calling across a long distance is different from doing a sound as loudly as you can.
- If your animal is one of the very few silent animals (such as the giraffe), do not invent sounds.

Improvisations in Realtime

▶ Animal Study Improvisation.

If you are working in a group, when you are improvising as your individual animal do not interact with any of the other actor-animals. Use the idea of the zoo and make invisible boundaries, avoiding crossing into others' spaces. If you have to cross another actor's space, do it without acknowledging him, or his animal's food.

If you can, identify someone to watch you and feed back to you. If alone, set a video camera on a tripod to cover your working area for playback observation. Remember that at this stage the animal study improvisations are not performances.

- Choose an area in the room and create a space to facilitate a 20–30 minute improvisation.

- Decide a length of time for the improvisation and set a timer.

- You need some sort of delineation of the space – perhaps a few chairs or an upturned table. Place any food you wish to use within your spatial boundaries.

- Take the space as yourself, remembering that you should never be in a half-in–half-out state. Leap to your animal. Any thought of how you are doing, or how to apply your observations, should have been left with the person who existed before The Leap.

- Live in the now as your animal with no plot, no plans; you are not working technically. Use the sounds of your animal.

- Do not cut out the outside world. Acknowledge it by allowing it to feed your motivation. A passing police siren, for example, may make your ears prick up, or a speck of floating dust may grab your attention.

- Within another improvisation you can create an outdoor 'home', in the corner of a garden by a tree, for instance. Maybe add a very small, enclosed space as a transporting cage. Imagine being released into your enclosure after it has been cleaned.

- Hide food that you can forage for later. French bread, for example, can be used as a substitute for meat. Enjoy the texture, the pulling and the chewing, as though this were the real food.

- At the end of the predetermined time, leap back to yourself.

- In order to retain the physical memory of the improvisation in your body, avoid huffing and puffing and demonstrating how hard you have worked and what pain you are in.

- Stretch out any particularly stiff muscles.

- Receive any feedback from a partner.

Motivated Thoughts Out Loud

This practical relates to the thoughts of the animal as it sees and takes in the world.

- Identify your animal's motivations through research, observation and improvisation.

- When you are being your animal during an improvisation, speak its thoughts out loud for just a short time.

- What words are you using? At first you may find that gaps are filled by your own thoughts, or that the thoughts are articulated as ideas. For example, a thought like 'I think I am hungry' can become motivated, something like 'Must eat', 'Where's food?'. Motivation may become looking for food with the thought out-loud 'It's not here' interspersed with sniffing 'Not here', and so on.

- Once you let go of the need for your thoughts to be various and interesting, the animal begins to exist.

- Gauge the difference in motivation immediately after you have done this.

- This practice should be added to your improvisations and need only be done in small doses.

Preparation Exercise: Stream of Consciousness

This is an attempt at the experience of thinking in the present tense. It can feel as if it 'scrambles' your brain, but it is an important step into freeing you from the constraints of structured language and, perhaps, opens a small window into a stream of consciousness.

For this exercise you need a partner of similar height and someone to call out the instructions. It is in four stages.

Stage one: Mirror exercise

- Decide who is A and B.

- The leader (A) starts to move in a way that B can easily mirror, not moving too fast. Remember not to turn away (sight is the communicator). Accuracy is the important factor; being creative and clever is nothing without accuracy. The game is not to catch the other person out. It is important to save laughter for the end of the exercise, so that the exercise isn't disturbed.

- The leader is changed at regular intervals by the caller: A leading, then B leading, and so on. The changing from one to the other should be indiscernible. After a while the changes should become more frequent, taking the exercise to a stage where the caller states 'No one leading.' Remember not to stop or hesitate in the changes of leader.

Stage two: Mirrored speech

- Remain with the same partner and same set-up, but maybe stand a little closer together.

- Focus on each other's mouths, and again one of you leads and one follows, changing at the caller's command.

- This time, mirror each other's speech, speaking exactly at the same time. The leader should speak slowly and articulate his words for the partner to mirror. At this stage, you can say anything as long as you do not stop.

Stage three: Mirrored speech with rules

Same partner, same set-up. Undertake mirrored speech, only this time with a new set of rules:

- No gaps in the speaking.
- No repetition.
- No making a list, for example red, yellow, green.
- No telling a story.
- No referring to yourself, for example 'I went to the store.'

So what you are left with is a stream of unconnected words. This is a form of stream of consciousness.

- Don't censor either yourself or your partner.
- Try not to break concentration.
- If the exercise progresses satisfactorily, nobody will lead.

Stage four: Stream of consciousness

- When the caller shouts out 'Nobody leading', turn away from each other and walk around the room, continuing your own stream of thoughts out loud with the same rules (but now unrelated to your partner).

- Keep yourself released, free, easy, open and available: let go of any preconceived ideas, any censoring of yourself and be in the now with the words just falling out of your mouth.

- Stop after a few minutes.

Key point

Observe how this leads you to submit to a continuous thought process.

Short Concentration Span to High Curiosity Ratio[3]

▶ Short Concentration/High Curiosity.

Wear the clothing for your animal study. The exercise takes about 15 minutes.

In this exercise you use a short concentration span to high curiosity ratio. To the modern ear, the voiced thoughts may sound unintelligent. However, for a creature living in the wild, a short concentration span is essential. Possessing a concentration span long enough to read several chapters of *War and Peace* at one sitting would endanger its life, some other creature could jump on its back and eat it. High curiosity is also essential. In the rest of the animal kingdom there are no supermarkets and no internet shopping: the animals have to search for their food, and curiosity facilitates this hunt.

- Select a number of objects and place them in front of you. These objects should be (as far as possible) indestructible, of no value and not dangerous. Choose the sort of things you could give a giant baby to play with: shoes, newspapers, old clothes, cardboard boxes, balls, and so on. Avoid food, metal, sticks, glass or pens.

- If you are in a group, place yourself in an invisible 'bubble' and don't make eye contact with anybody else.

- Sit with the objects in front of you.

- View them as if they were brand new to you, but don't show any sense of awe or wonder: see them merely as objects to be explored using all the senses. Do this not as your animal but as yourself.

- Use your hands, feet, nose and mouth. Sounds should be allowed to come out naturally (grunts, murmurs, groans, sighs, and so on).

- Be naturally curious: sit or lie and wait for something to want to be investigated; it should only take a few moments before you find

---

[3]This acting exercise was designed by Peter Elliott for studying primates, but it can offer you a way into living in the now, uninhibited by convention or language.

yourself playing with something: banging or stroking it, or whatever else occurs. You will either get bored with it or something else will grab your attention.

It must remain a non-intellectual process. Do not make it happen: let it happen; no working at it. If you find yourself looking at the objects at arm's-length, you are probably being too intellectual.

- After about five to ten minutes, allow your 'thoughts out loud'. These are not mumbled, but really spoken out loud. Let the thoughts tumble out of your mouth: what is motivating you, what you like, don't like – not just as a list. 'What's that?', 'That feels nice', and more. The thoughts need to be emotionally connected. Again, do not over think this; just let it happen. (See Practical: Thoughts out loud).
- After a few minutes of thinking out loud, put the thoughts back inside. Do not rush this process.
- Continue the exercise for a few more minutes.
- Then rest. You can now laugh if you want to. This exercise is experiential, so no judgement should be made about whether it was a 'good' or 'bad' result.

Additional stage

- Before ending the exercise leap to your animal and continue as your animal for about five minutes (See Practical: *The Leap*).

Working Technically

This is the chance for you to isolate the problems or the challenges discovered while trying to be your animal and work through them practically. Working technically suits some people; improvisation suits others. Both are necessary and you must not blur the two; at any one time either work technically or immerse yourself in being the animal.

- Make a plan of what to work on. Make a list of all the challenges that seem impossible. Look at what you have been avoiding (the giraffe running or the otter swimming, and so on).
- Give yourself a finite amount of time and stick to it. (See additional online resources: *Personal and Professional Self*.)
- Consider constructing costume bits that offer a sense, for example, of a tail or a nose. Use these to offer yourself a one-off playful experience of

a specialist skill of your animal. For example, if you are a crocodile, you might want to have a go at lying on a skateboard and using your limbs to travel at speed.

- Spend considered technical time exploring BBWSWRB, one by one. Highlight the experience of each aspect as you improvise your animal.

Key points

Ten minutes of fully-committed work on a technical aspect, or ten minutes in a fully-involved improvisation is highly productive. You can schedule in or add together as many ten-minute slots as you want, but by working in assigned time slots you remain in control of the process.

Ongoing Process in Realtime

This is a continual building process of observation, research, improvisation and working technically. Altogether you should aim to make about eight to ten zoo visits, any number of technical 'ten minuters' and about 15–20 improvisations of varying lengths in the studio and outside.

The Leap

 The Leap.

You must be able to leap from yourself to your animal and from your animal back to yourself. Your leap must be an instant and total transformation: there is no transition state.

- Choose a 'trigger' to leap from human to animal. It could be a sound and/or a movement. Locate a moment that is in every way different from what you are likely to be doing (passively standing in the studio before the leap is not an option). This will prevent any blurring of identity.
- Make sure that it doesn't rely on outside factors, such as a table to jump onto.
- Acknowledge that your body memory is capable of holding a fully-crafted motivated moment as the trigger to make that leap.
- Avoid caution; just transform.
- Practise the leap between yourself and the animal. Rather than thinking about what changes you have made, identify anything that

hasn't changed or transformed. Track through your whole body: fingers, eyebrows, feet, face, hips, and so on.

Group Animals

This is an exercise for a group. All decisions are made by the group. Each person in the group has to be able to achieve all of the choices. The level of detail that an individual study demands would encumber the discovery of a group identity. The aim is to achieve broad-stroke information, although accuracy is still important.

- Choose a group animal to observe together.
- The group identifies BBWSWRB and works on the group animal in the same way as on the individual animal by observing, having technical time and through improvisations.

For group studies, you do not do condensed time or thoughts out loud.

- Each member of the group takes a turn to step out of the improvisation and observe: look for uniformity, spotting any little differences – like the way in which the feet contact the ground, the way the face is used, and so on. Discussion should lead to a collective decision about the technicalities of these movements.
- Within the group 'live in the now', sharing the same codes, the same motivations. There are no signals and no plans; just a group identity. To an outside eye you should look like a family, a herd, a flock, a pride, and so on. One flamingo, for instance, may start a call that is quickly picked up by the others and builds to a cacophony of honks which dies as quickly as it started.

Colony, Pack and Herd Games

All these group games work best in a large outdoor green space.

The Penguin Game – Colony

This game involves a rebalance of senses and the resulting shift in body language. The actor begins to look like a penguin simply because he is shaped by the action and by the motivation.

- Group members are double numbered (two 1s, two 2s, and so on) so that they are in pairs but are not next to their partner in the space and do not know who their partner is with the corresponding number.

- The group is spread across the space.
- Walk around with your eyes tight shut.
- Keeping your eyes shut throughout, start calling your number.
- At the same time listen out for your number being called somewhere in the space and start to make your way towards the sound.
- When you find the other number, have a small celebration, after which you fall back to the sides of the space and watch the rest of the game.

A penguin that only listens or only calls out cannot find its mate and pair bond.

Wolves – The Pack

This is an exercise for a group of six. This game begins with army platoon work. Explore the group need, function and strategies:

- Choose a leader. Develop a team strategy for travelling efficiently, whilst staying in a tight formation and communicating without words.
- Choose the actor who can run the fastest to be the prey. He is set free.
- The task of the pack is to hunt the prey, using long-distance loping (travelling with long easy strides at an easy pace) as the most efficient rhythm of a pack of wolves (or army platoon) – they cannot sprint. This is in opposition to the prey's speciality of sprinting at high speed over a short distance. Use unspoken strategies to surround and take down the prey as a whole group. It is no good arriving early or late to the kill: if early, you may get injured; if late, there may be nothing left for you to eat. If you manage to achieve a 'kill', you should surround the prey and pounce towards him, but do not ground him. You want to avoid injuries, and over-enthusiasm can be dangerous. You should, however, enjoy the sounds of a feeding frenzy.
- Once your group finds its timing and rhythm and all are in sync, it becomes a functional, menacing 'machine'.

Herd – Grazing Game

This game demonstrates cost analysis. (If you cannot be outdoors for this, scatter lentils on the studio floor before the game.)

- Select about three 'hunters' (lion/lioness) and pull them out of the group. The rest of the group becomes 'a herd' (there is safety in numbers).

- The herd spreads out, with enough space between each of you to allow for grazing: too close and you will be standing on each other's food; too far apart and the safety element will not be felt.

- Pluck one blade of grass (one lentil) at a time without pulling up any soil or root.

- You cannot watch and eat at the same time, as the animal's eyes and mouth are both in its head, and its mouth is close to the ground as it eats.

- You must feel and rely on the herd; one of you will always be looking out.

- The herd should fall into the rhythm of life of a herd, most of the day every day given over to eating.

- The herd cannot sprint, but can run longish distances. The hunters can sprint fast over short distances. So a slow languid cat-and-mouse game has evolved: if the herd can stay just out of the sprint distance of the hunter they should be fine.

- Hunters should be patient and look for opportunities tactically to separate a victim. When a victim is selected, surround and go in for the kill. Do not ground the victim, but hold them and vocalize the success.

- Both sides must play by the rules of the savannah. The animals live there all the time and have found ways to survive without continuous paranoia. Energy is food. Wasted energy means needing more food.

- The games end after a kill, or when the herd has felt the herd mentality and worked in a rhythm that could go on ad infinitum. The handfuls of grass should be inspected and anyone of the herd who is found with insufficient food should be declared a non-survivor.

Other games can be explored for other groups of animals (e.g. flocks, prides, families, pair-bonds, troops, etc.).

Key points

As well as informing you about the make-up of a group and its function, these games highlight BBWSWRB and are therefore also useful to do as part of your preparation towards an individual animal study. These games should always be done without aping the animal group by which it is inspired. A game should work even without you knowing the animal it is based on. The game informs you.

Creating a Personal Animal Warm-up

Working as your animal, especially in a long improvisation, leads to physical challenges. You must prepare for these by creating your own specific animal warm-up. Each actor and each animal study will have different requirements.

- The first step is in identifying what you, as an actor, need to help your body prepare to go into your animal study. It needs to prepare you for all the unfamiliar muscular and vocal challenges of your animal. Create games and exercises, using BBWSWRB as prompts.

The following examples are not a prescription, as all needs are so variable.

- The golden lion tamarin has rapid, sudden head moves; it seems to continually check its environment, focusing on one place after another. A partner stands in front of you about one metre away. He moves his hand rapidly from one spot to another. He clicks his fingers at each point. You move your head and eye focus to his hand on each click.

- The otter has a fluid backbone. Placing about eight to ten traffic cones or markers on the ground about one and a half metres apart, you can quickly weave your way through them, working on the fluidity of the backbone.

Zoo Set-up

This is the halfway point in the animal study process.

- If you are in a group, half the group can become the general public visiting the zoo. Their belief that they are looking at real animals is essential.

- Choose a space and create a slightly more defined 'zoo environment' within the space than the one you have been creating for improvisations.

- Define a pathway for the public.

- Be clear about your spatial boundaries and what the space needs to contain (for example, a table for lying on; a stand for your food; a water bowl, and so on).

- Leap into your animal in realtime. As in a public zoo, assume that you could be visited and stared at and commented on by the zoo visitors. What is your perception of any visitors? Do you take any notice at all? It is important that you do not speak thoughts out loud during this improvisation.

The experience of the zoo set-up consolidates your study of living in realtime. This marks the point at which to move to the next stage.

Adding Condensed Time to Your Improvisations

- Start the improvisation in the same way as the realtime improvisations: prepare the space, prepare any food and props, take the space as yourself then leap to your animal in realtime.

- Undertake about ten minutes of being your animal in realtime. During this time you could try 'thoughts outloud' to deepen your motivation.

- At some point, switch into condensed time for no more than two minutes. This is the time to include all the things you love about your animal – as many states as possible and as many dynamics; in other words, being your animal at its most interesting. Keep your animal's rhythm of life and breath-rhythm consistent. Make it a seamless edit of events.

- After the two minutes is over, switch back to realtime for about another five minutes. Then leap back to yourself.

Check afterwards:

- Did your animal's inner rhythm speed up?
- Did you include everything you wanted to?
- Did you show all the things you love about your animal?

If you take your animal to performance, this is your two minutes to pull focus and spotlight your animal.

Remember, it is only the time that is condensed: the inner rhythm of the animal does not change. What makes both realtime and condensed time 'real' is being in the present tense.

Performance Format

This is an exercise for a group.

- Take the space and be your animal. Live in the now without relating to the other animals. Each actor has already done his leap and is his animal in realtime. Once the audience settles, a bell is sounded signalling the beginning of the performance.

- Live in the now, in realtime, to establish the atmosphere. Let the audience soak this in and really get a sense of what is in store for them.

- After one minute, another bell is sounded. This is the signal for the first animal to start. The animal must start by pulling the focus; it is a clear moment that enables the audience to know who they should be watching. If this is you, your sound or motivated action tells an audience you are in the spotlight.

- Be in condensed time for two minutes until the bell rings again and another actor takes the spotlight, at which stage you return to realtime.

- Use only tried and tested props and food. You have enough of a challenge living in the now, improvising and being open in front of your audience without added obstacles. (See additional online resources: *Performance Brief for Tutor*.)

IN CONTEXT: CONDENSED AND REALTIME

As a character in a play your role is not necessarily the main focus. Having lived in the background as your animal and developed a trust in existing in realtime, it is evident that it is not necessary to stick with passive/sleepy type activities or turn yourself into a statue. You can have energy and yet not distract from the focus of the foreground. Once you have worked in both the real and condensed time in the animal study performance, you can confidently take the skill back into the play.

Part Two: Anthropomorphic Study

This offers two processes[4] for working on a character's physical journey: one for devising a character and one for a scripted character.

"Can I call you back? I'm with a piece of string."

Figure 5.4   Cat executive on phone, playing with string on his desk. 'Can I call you back? I'm with a piece of string.' – Issue Publication Date 01/17/2005 Leo Cullum/The New Yorker Collection/ www.cartoonbank.com.

Devising a Human Character from an Animal

See Practical: *Animal to Human Animal* (p. 160)

Anthropomorphism is normally thought of as giving an animal human character-istics. In this case, however, it is about creating a human character that develops from the study of an animal. For the actor, this is not some form of 'cartooning' but a full anthropomorphic transformation. It is derived from detailed study of a particular animal and taken into a fully-rounded human character with a

---

[4]Ewan's process of work with the actors.

complete inner landscape. The information is acquired completely from the animal as source; it is translated, but not made up. Humans, like other animals, live and breathe and are motivated. It is more likely that the actor will find the information for a complete transformation into a character by working from another animal than from a fellow human being.

Finding a Voice

See Practical: *Finding a Voice* (p. 162)

Having met the beginning of his anthropomorphic character, it is time for the actor to take him outdoors to the park. At this stage the character is going to be larger than life and the voice is going to match this.

A Human Playground

See Practical: *A Human Playground* (p. 163)

The first time the character meets other anthropomorphic characters is in a highly structured social occasion with an activity in which they all take part. This is an organized match of rounders (baseball). Each character saw this game advertised locally. The 'animals' have never met before and all arrive, in character, at about the same time. The game is important in different ways to each character. This game is a miniature world, a playground in which the actor can discover and build on his anthropomorphic character. The intellect is now working alongside the animal instinct; as a human, socializing the character will, at times, have to battle with itself to stay in the realms of civilized behaviour. There is no need for psychological drama; simply lining up to bat offers him ample opportunity to develop how to communicate.

Social Improvisation

See Practical: *Social Improvisation* (p. 164)

Back in the safety of the studio, the actor starts to explore playing with the scale of his anthropomorphic character. The idea is to take the character further towards being socially acceptable. The character should not look like an actor at play, but like a real person: the actor retains everything that his character came from, but in such a way that the character now belongs in the real world.

Revealing and Making Choices

See Practical: *Revealing and Making Choices* (p. 165)

Through this process so far, the work has evolved with physicality informing character development. It is now time to look at making the character sociably acceptable. This is the time to make choices. The studio, as playground, offers the actor a more controlled environment than outside to start looking at detail and working for precision. It is a chance to work all the aspects – BBWSWRB – separately, to feel and understand the individual effect of each.

Anthropomorphic Group Animals

See Practical: *Group Animals* (p. 168)

The actor's established group animal study holds a wealth of information. This group work can very quickly and with little preparation be translated into a human ensemble piece.

Anthropomorphic: From Animal to a Scripted Character

See Practical: *Animal as Inspiration for a Scripted Character* (p. 168)

For a character that already exists in a script, the process of anthropomorphism is different. It does not involve an animal developing or changing into a human. But neither does it change the animal study process. The animal that the actor finally selects for study for the character offers a constant mirror to the character. The animal itself presents the actor with inspiring choices about the way a character operates in the world: the motivation for movement, the rhythm of life and the way it sees the world can all be taken into account. It may be that the actor can envisage an animal when he thinks of the movement of the character he is working on. Equally, he may know something of the character's innate behaviour or personality and that, too, can inform his decision of which animal to choose to work with. A character develops through rehearsal.

Choosing an Animal

See Practical: *Choosing an Animal for a Scripted Character* (p. 168).

Using a mixture of animals as inspiration leaves no room for the character to form and grow. An animal offers choices of great clarity and if the actor used, say, two animals, it would be difficult for him to take himself seriously; there is no such thing as a monkey-giraffe, and mythological creatures would require a different process. In this scenario, the actor would lack the inspiration from something real with which to work.

A person cannot choose who he is, and a character is shaped as much by what he hides as what he shows. For instance, it is immediately obvious to see how a gibbon would offer fruitful information when working on the fop in a Restoration play. However, choosing an animal for the character that needs to hide behind his foppishness – perhaps a wolf – may give the actor even more with which to play.

If he has done a full study in the past, the information can be absorbed quickly. He will know and quickly navigate the stages of the process, as well as recognizing when he is successfully inhabiting the animal.

Part Two: Anthropomorphic Study Practicals

Creating a Devised Character from Your Animal

This work is developed as a process, rather than relying on instinct or intuition. This gives you a range of tools and provocations to use later when devising characters.

Animal to Human Animal

For this exercise you are in the studio. Your starting point for this is your animal study and as in your animal improvisations you:

- Prepare the studio space with food and 'stuff', as you did for your animal. But this time with additional nesting and home-building objects: clothes, coats, scarf, bag, shoes, chair, table, and so on.
- Now take the space and leap to your animal.
- After about five minutes, settle down and go to sleep.
- During your sleep something happens: a strange mutation, an operation, and you now have human arms and legs grafted on replacing your animals limbs. Everything else is still the same; in all other ways you are still your animal, including your backbone.

- You wake up.
- Let your animal discover any advantages it now has as it gets on with its life.

Figure 5.5 Mr Vulture just after his operation. Illustration by Toby Elwes.

- Accept the situation. Work with complete physical conviction. There is no need for your character to look at these new limbs in surprise, or try them out like a newborn. He just gets on with life the way a three-legged dog seems not to dwell on the missing leg but gets on with using the three it still has.

- If your animal study is of a quadruped, and you choose to be on all fours (on your knees), you will have to make the journey from quadruped to biped during the improvisation. Don't make a meal of this. Let the animal's motivation solve this, for example, its need to look over something could lead to the discovery that your legs straighten to take you up to that height and then once there your animal has discovered its human legs.

Figure 5.6 Mr Vulture adjusting to his human arms and legs. Illustration by Toby Elwes.

- Or, if your animal has wings, it may find that it can use its hands instead of its beak, but it may also find that its beak is still useful too.

- Or, it may find its arms whilst involuntarily stretching, and so on.

- Once a discovery is made it becomes part of your animal's vocabulary

- Don't throw anything of your animal away; the human arms and legs are the only change.

- Your animal can now start using its new limbs to continue nest-building. Carry on for at least ten minutes.

- Then add human intellect and be aware that adding intellect to an animal doesn't imply a low IQ.

- Carry on with nest-building and home-making. Talk to yourself. Verbalize the continuous story going on in your now human mind. You can try thoughts out loud. Note that this is not yet the voice of your anthropomorphic character.

- It is important to avoid the extreme ends of age – your character is not defined by his age.

Key point

- Try not to plan in advance what you think you might do as your animal in this improvisation. It is all about discovery.

You have just created the first stage of your anthropomorphic character.

Finding a Voice

This is an exercise for the individual, working outdoors.

- Start as your animal for five minutes. Heighten your awareness of the breath of your animal.

- Leap to your anthropomorphic character (remember BBWSWRB).

- After you leap to your anthropomorphic character, go for a walk around the park and talk to yourself out loud.

- It is time to find a voice.

- Use the breath rhythm of your animal; sounds may translate as exclamations.

- The voice must be informed by the physicality. Don't fall into the trap of coming up with a cartoon or caricature voice that takes over the physicality.

- You may find a place for a translated version of your animal's sound like the whoop of a gibbon, the snarl of a lion, and so on.

Key points

Keep it grounded and real to itself. Trust the depth of the animal study that is embedded within you; the work is all there for you to build on.

A Human Playground

▶ Anthropomorphic improvisation: Rounders game (baseball).

This is an exercise for the individual in a group, working outdoors.

- Arrive at a game of rounders as your anthropomorphic character. Imagine having seen an advertisement for it in the local paper. You may have chosen to go because you are a solitary animal and (your intellect) thinks that it would be good for you to meet people. Or you may be energetic and think it will be fun, and so on.

- Follow the normal rules of improvisation: you want to be there and want to take part and there is no need to invent a lengthy back story. Let your character evolve.

- Two appropriate team captains are chosen from amongst you (it is not going to be the mouse).

- The captains choose their teams; this can offer you lots to deal with – you cannot break social rules but your feelings are going to be affected.

- A coin is tossed to decide who bats and who fields. The captain of whichever team fields, organizes his team members into their fielding positions.

- The batting team line up.

- If you, as yourself, have a competitive nature, you may have the dilemma of wanting to score a rounder (home run) but at the same time needing to remain in role as, say, a tortoise. Restriction or challenges can become springboards for you. You can find out more about your character by not making it to the base than by letting your own competitive side win.

- As much time should be given over to socializing as is appropriate during a game: small talk about the game as you line up to bat (this is not psychodrama), an introduction as a runner meets a fielder at second base, or having a break at half-time with some cut-up oranges could be good ideas.

- Participating in the game informs your physical choices. Experiences parallel those to be found in a play: interaction; involvement; listening; exclusion; inclusion; simply living; feeling, thinking and so on.

- Occasionally leap back to your animal. Through this stage of the process, you have to keep as much as possible of your animal.

Social Improvisation

This is an exercise carried out in twos or threes. You are back in the studio and then go on into the real world.

- Partner up with one or two other anthropomorphic characters.

- Decide on a type of established relationship that you find interesting: for example, the rhinoceros and the bush baby as a married couple; the hawk and the kangaroo as brother and sister.

- Find a space and spend time together, getting used to each other's rhythms, sharing the space with no interaction. This might be a couple existing in a living room. Keep it simple. Do not create a plan or backstory.

- Keep things slightly larger than life.

- Let the improvisation develop slowly and accept it; use the rule of improvisation. It will offer more discoveries if the relationships are positive and functional

- After about 15 minutes, when the relationships have found validity, are not overworked and, though still slightly larger than real life, seem realistic – and without throwing anything away – work at fitting into society by making some parts of your character private.

- Take your anthropomorphic character into the real world. So go out to the shops or down to the café for a cup of tea.

- You should look like a real person; you may of course, be one of those slightly more extreme people – there are many of them out there and, like them, your character has learned how to be perceived as 'socially acceptable' – but not someone who would disturb the general public.

If you are working alone then you can still do this process. Set up a space, maybe choose a radio programme to listen and respond to and just spend time with yourself existing in your anthropomorphic character in the same way. Wait until it feels real and then take that person into the real world: order the coffee, read the paper in the café, and so on.

Revealing and Making Choices

This is an exercise for the individual in a group, back in the studio.

Your anthropomorphic character now belongs to you. It is time to deconstruct it. For this you need some indoor games. It is not necessary to keep the relationships on which you have worked.

- Play an indoor game like cards or dominoes with other characters. If working on your own, you could play Patience or Solitaire. Listen to the radio so that you have something else to react to.

- Start as your full anthropomorphic character. After about ten minutes, focus on one of the key aspects you should now know so well: BBWSWRB.

- Start with the backbone: keep the other key aspects present deep inside, but the focus is on the backbone. Don't add anything else. This is your chance to identify how highlighting just one aspect can physically and mentally influence your character.

- Move the focus to another aspect and repeat.

- Give each aspect time enough for you to feel its influence – about five minutes on each one.

- Imagine a camera zooming in on different body parts, maybe focusing on your feet or your hands or moving into a close-up on your face. Better still, have someone do this with a real camera to capture the effect of each aspect at work.

- Leap back to your full animal several times during this process to reinforce its influence.

- To maintain your character's motivation, keep the game going as your character interacts with the other players.

IN CONTEXT: ATTENTION TO PHYSICAL DETAIL

During a rehearsal process as a human character, you might wish to look at how expessive you are actually being with different parts of the character's body. For instance you might imagine for one part of a rehearsal, that the curtain is raised only enough to see your character's feet. In a film this may happen in a very real way with a close-up of, for example, feet or hands.

IN CONTEXT: BBWSWRB

You can use BBWSWRB to clarify choices for a human character even without using an animal as inspiration.

When looking at the character using BBWSWRB, it helps if you use both the character's instinct and the person he chooses to reveal to the world.

Backbone

Every character has a different backbone. There are descriptions that allude to the backbone as essential character notes; phrases like 'spineless' or 'he has no backbone' allude to a lack of courage. These can be worked with literally. The focus here is on finding the inner character's backbone. The backbone is the hanger for the way his whole body moves. It affects which body parts lead, dominate or are neglected. The backbone can tell an audience about social class and status.

Breath

The character literally breathes the world in and breathes himself out into it. Breath, therefore, tells us about his relationship with the world: breathing fulsomely and fearlessly, for example, may give the experience of accepting the air, the world and everything in it. There will be clues about the character's emotional breath rhythm in the text.

Weight/Centre of Gravity

It is not so much about how heavy or light the character actually is and more to do with his effect on the world: the 'impression' he makes on the world; his intentions; his responsibility – how much or how little he carries and where he carries it define his centre of gravity.

Space

How much or how little space the character takes up relates to status. His inner character will also need to inhabit certain spaces at certain times. These may directly oppose the space the world has placed him in or the way he wants to use the space.

Way it Sees the World

His essential POV. This is taken care of to a certain extent within your acting process. You can bring it back to the body, however, allowing it to inform the other aspects of BBWSWRB, which will in turn affect a character's actions and his demeanour. Also, explore the way the character uses his eyes – whether he examines, peers, or stares; the speed he blinks; how much he moves them; whether he looks people in the eye, and so on.

Rhythm of Life

This manifests itself in the character's walk, his rhythm as he sits or other ways of being in the world. Is he relaxed or flighty; busy or restful; manic or calm? Does he burn energy or use it conservatively?

Balance of Senses

The human animal has a common hierarchy of senses, with eyesight being dominant. However, it is worth checking and adjusting – and not just when playing a character deprived of a sense. All characters have a different relationship with the senses. A musician, for example, will have a different relationship with sound than a blacksmith. Also, each character can alter their balance of senses when a situation requires it: straining to hear a faint sound; looking at a distant object; tasting an unfamiliar food, and so on. Rebalancing the senses is real and tangible and should never be faked.

These are a few examples, additions and reminders of the way BBWSWRB can apply to the work which is offered throughout the book. You can make your own connections and make a list of ways of working with BBWSWRB for yourself. Trust your instincts: the list you make will be the one that is most useful to you.

Anthropomorphic Group Animals

This is an exercise for a group. This only works if you have an established group animal. Together you are given a group identity, such as lawyers, burglars, surgeons, models, and so on. You are also given a situation.

- With almost no planning and not much talking (maybe 20 seconds), you do an anthropomorphic leap to the given task. As a group, of Meerkats, for instance, you might all become a group of art critics at an exhibition.

- Throw yourself into it and trust the group; trust that the information is already there.

- Keep these improvisations very short, about one minute long.

These are fun and light spirited and the results can be surprising.

Animal as Inspiration for a Scripted Character

If you have done the Animal Study as presented in this chapter then you will easily be able to work quickly through the process on another animal to the stage of 'living in the now'.

Choosing an Animal for a Scripted Character

- Research your character. Build an understanding of the character. Hold back from choosing an animal; choosing it at this stage means all you can arrive at is what you already have/know.

- Go to the zoo. You are going to find an animal. This is the easy bit, as long as you are relaxed and trust that it is going to result in a choice.

- Walk around the zoo and simply look out for your character as you visit each animal. Don't try too hard. The choice you make reveals the aspects of the character that stand out for you. When you have made a choice, leave the zoo and sleep on your choice.

Observing Your Choice of Animal for a Scripted Character

- With the decision on your animal in place, go back to the zoo. This time, put your character in the very back of your mind so that you can focus just on the animal. It can offer you something to give to your character.

Animal and Character Improvisations

- Track through BBWSWRB; realize the one/s that dominate/s, the ones you think are potentially integral to your character.

- Have an awareness of the one/s that dominate/s, but still maintain being fully the animal when you are improvising.

- Prepare the space in a simple human set-up with common activities relevant to the world of the play: a table, chair, pen or quill and paper, coat or cardigan – anything that your character might occupy himself with.

- Prepare yourself to improvise as both your animal and your character with clothing that serves both, as there is no time between leaps to get changed. This might mean, for example, wearing kneepads underneath your trousers if you are quadruped as your animal. Include suitable shoes.

- Do two types of improvisation, one immediately after the other: leap from your animal to character, then back to your animal and back to your character, and so on.

- You will immediately be conscious of some of the aspects influencing your character. You cannot build your character in a day.

- Trust that these improvisations will naturally feed into your character as you move through the different experiences your character explores in rehearsal.

- You may want to explore being your animal pre-rehearsal and at the early stage of rehearsal. However, the animal is your inspiration throughout rehearsals even if you don't improvise again once you are in rehearsal: you know how it would react, where it would go in the space and what it would do. If, for example, a vulture was in the room right now, it would know what to do. It wouldn't have to think about it – and neither should you.

Key points

If you are an actor-in-training, you will be trying out many acting techniques in which you make lots of decisions about your character's actions. In this process it is important to make room for your animal to make decisions for you: a large element of this is not about doing; it's about handing over to the work you have already done. This exercise needs space to develop. It's about trust.

7

A CHARACTER'S EMOTIONAL JOURNEY: SOLO DANCE[1]

OVERVIEW

Inner responses that do not feature in the play often get left to instinct instead of being physically explored. The path to a moment of outward expression may be ambiguous or inexplicit, but the action is fuelled by the inner landscape. Clarifying the emotions and feelings and experiencing their expression enables the actor to embody them. This project is a process for actors to explore emotions through their translation to dance. The solo dance is the actor's choreography of the emotional journey of a character from a novel. Investigating the emotional journey is probably the most valuable direct physical exploration an actor can do to serve his character.

Working with Emotions in Movement

There is often ambivalence in crafting and performing feelings and emotions; in one single moment they can excite a dynamic, yet overwhelming mass of responses. In many cases, they are either worked on with reverential intensity or left to the mystery of instinct. Both approaches are problematic. If the actor is expected to draw on memory, but hasn't had diverse and 'rich' emotional experiences, he may feel inadequate. If, on the other hand, the emotional memory is powerful, he may feel unsafe performing it. This process offers a

---

[1] Ewan's process of work in the studio with the actors.

progression of work focused on the precise movement of emotion. Through this the actor can craft and develop a vibrant palette of emotion in movement without confusion or fear.

The word 'emotion' is, at heart, an action word. It is, after all, derived from the Latin *emovere* (to disturb, agitate or perturb). Emotions engender strong and complicated responses in the body which are difficult to identify and recreate. A lack of clarity when aiming to express emotion precisely through movement is therefore to be expected in the initial stages. Experts have differing opinions on the definition, range and mechanism of emotions. For this exercise, four basic emotions – Happiness, Anger, Grief and Fear – are used as a workable option.

The Solo Dance process focuses on the physical expression of both emotions and feelings, and the crafting and performance of this 'physicalization'.

Project: Solo Dance – A Vehicle for Emotional Expression

The Solo Dance is self created material, expressing the inner life and emotional journey of a character from a novel set to a piece of edited classical music.

If an actor does not see himself as a dancer or a choreographer, the Solo Dance might be viewed as a daunting proposition: both in that it is 'solo' and that it is a 'dance'. These fears, however, can be immediately allayed. This is an actors' project, which gives a model for working with emotions. Dancers and non-dancers are equal on this journey. Actors who have never danced are not at a disadvantage, and those with a background in dance should not assume a head-start.

Though what is described here is a dance project, it is not dance theatre. Nor is it interpretive or creative dance. It is designed to develop a particular aspect of the actor's expression. Through the movement of the dance, the inner life of a human is revealed in a physically owned and 'real' manner.

Once he has completed this journey, the actor can draw on the Solo Dance process to explore the emotional journey of a character in a play. The actor can engage with the stuff of his character's dreams and nightmares – the dance allows him to 'embody' this felt experience.

The Four Stages of the Solo Dance Project

1 Research.

2 Instinctively creating material.

3 Identifying and crafting choices.

4 Fine-tuning the quality of the movement.

The first stage requires both time and a relaxed mind-set. If the first stage goes well, the second stage may be extremely short.

The third and fourth stages require some sort of objective eye, even if it is just the actor watching himself on video. With the lone actor in mind, this chapter offers substantial practical support (some of which may not be required if the actor is in a tutor-led process).

An extra final stage of the process – performance – may be added, depending on circumstance. This is a process-based exercise to gather a body of knowledge about a character; performance at the end of the process is not a prerequisite.

Stage One: Research

The research has two points of focus: the book and the music.

Choosing the Novel

See Practical: *Further Guidance on Choosing the Novel* (p. 186)

The actor chooses a novel from either classical or contemporary fiction that has touched him and left an impression. It should feature a character with whom the actor can empathize, to the extent of knowing something of what it is to be that person. Below are some suggestions:

Catherine Morland from *Northanger Abbey* by Jane Austen
Marlow from *Heart of Darkness* by Joseph Conrad
Sydney Carton from *A Tale of Two Cities* by Charles Dickens
The Girl from *Rebecca* by Daphne du Maurier
Mariam from *A Thousand Splendid Suns* by Khaled Hosseini
Francie Brady from *The Butcher Boy* by Patrick McCabe
Kafka Tamura from *Kafka on the Shore* by Haruki Murakami
Bertha Mason/Rochester from *Wide Sargasso Sea* by Jean Rhys
Grenouille from *Perfume* by Patrick Suskind
Kilgore Trout from *Breakfast of Champions* by Kurt Vonnegut

Why a novel rather than a play?

The actor always finds 'his' part in a play, while the reader loses himself in a novel. A good novel offers immediate and intimate access to character. It is therefore a useful starting point for the actor, as it allows him sufficient information to confidently access the inner life of a character. If the character of Dracula has just popped into your head, it's probably best to pop it out again. Dracula is an archetype. Archetypes represent some deep and particular aspect of humanity (the Warrior, the Wise-woman, the Fool, and so on). Other examples from popular fiction include Edward Cullen from *The Twilight Saga* or Gandalf from *The Lord of the Rings*. These characters exist in mythical situations, distant from ordinary experience. No one wonders what Gandalf has for breakfast. This exercise, however, requires a character about whom this question might usefully be asked.

An affecting novel seeps into the psyche. The character's relationship with the world is described in such detail, that the reader is a fellow traveller on the emotional journey.

This is a page from an actor's chosen novel.

'I'm not smirking. I'm smiling. You're the most amazing person.'

'I suppose I am,' she said, and her face, wan, rather bruised-looking in the morning light, brightened; she smoothed her tousled hair, and the colours of it glimmered like a shampoo advertisement. 'I must look fierce. But who wouldn't? We spent the rest of the night roaming around in a bus station. Right up till the last minute Doc thought I was going to go with him. Even though I kept telling him: But, Doc, I'm not fourteen any more, and I'm not Lulamae. But the terrible part is (and I realized it while we were standing there) I am. I'm still stealing turkey eggs and running through a brier patch. Only now I call it having the mean reds.'

Joe Bell disdainfully settled the fresh martinis in front of us.

'Never love a wild thing, Mr Bell,' Holly advised him. 'That was Doc's mistake. He was always lugging home wild things. A hawk with a hurt wing. One time it was a full-grown bobcat with a broken leg. But you can't give your heart to a wild thing: the more you do, the stronger they get. Until they're strong enough to run into the woods. Or fly into a tree. Then a taller tree. Then the sky. That's how you'll end up, Mr Bell. If you let yourself love a wild thing. You'll end up looking at the sky.'

'She's drunk,' Joe Bell informed me.

'Moderately,' Holly confessed. 'But Doc knew what I meant. I explained it to him very carefully, and it was something he could understand. We shook hands and held on to each other and he wished me luck.' She glanced at the clock. 'He must be in the Blue Mountains by now.'

'What's she talkin' about?' Joe Bell asked me.

Holly lifted her martini. 'Let's wish the Doc luck, too,' she said, touching her glass against mine. 'Good luck: and believe me, dearest Doc – it's better to look at the sky than live there. Such an empty place; so vague. Just a country where the thunder goes and things disappear'.

Figures 6.1 Extract from BREAKFAST AT TIFFANY'S: HOUSE OF FLOWERS; A DIAMOND GUITAR; A CHRISTMAS MEMORY by Truman Capote (Penguin Classics, 2000). Copyright © Truman Capote, 1958. Copyright renewed 1986 by Alan U. Schwartz. Used by permission of Random House, an imprint and division of Random House LLC. All rights reserved.[1]

[1] Any third party use of this material, outside of this publication, is prohibited. Interested parties must apply directly to Random House LLC for permission.

The reader's identification with a novel's hero or heroine can be so intense it is felt in the body: a literally visceral reaction. Why? Because the language is seeded with physically evocative imagery and metaphor.

The words the actor[2] has picked out are unique to that actor.

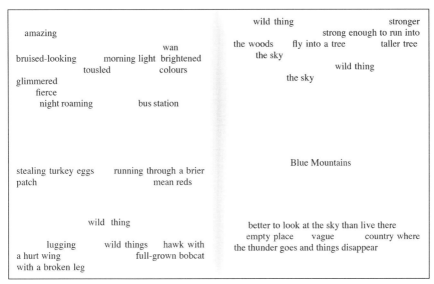

Figures 6.2　Extract from Breakfast at Tiffany's by Truman Capote (See 6.1 for extract detail).

A metaphor offering physical 'translation' of feeling may be implied in the text, rather than spelled out. Take, for example, the seminal passage in J. D. Salinger's *The Catcher in the Rye*, when the protagonist Holden Caulfield wonders where the ducks go to when the water from a lagoon freezes. There is no answer to his question, but the reader 'feels' the dilemma; being unable to land, not knowing where to go, being left out in the cold – these ideas are all open to physical exploration. No great deliberation or struggle to produce responses is required at this stage – the actor can be confident that he has received a physical and sensory experience just through reading the book. Keeping this 'body response' is of paramount importance as this is what liberates the actor when practical work on the Solo Dance begins.

[2] Rosie Yadid, (Central, 2014)

Choosing the Music

See Practical: *Further Guidance on Choosing and then Cutting the Music* (p. 187)

Music allows the actor to inhabit a world of heightened emotional response for which he must find a physical translation.[3] Classical music works best for this project – with some caveats.

Music that has prior associations, such as music that is composed for or used in film or advertising, can create strong imagery for the audience, which in some cases would compete with the dance. With choral or operatic music the lyrics are likely to become the focus rather than the dance. Dance music, including ballet scores, will work for this project, as long as the phrasing is not in 'balletic' patterns. Continuous, compelling rhythm, such as the strict meter of the waltz, is designed to impose itself on both listener and dancer. The rhythm of such music may hold the actor to ransom, robbing him of choices and limiting the possibilities of what he is able to express.

The music has its own journey, which will sometimes be 'moved with' and sometimes 'moved against'. There should be no expectation that the piece will reflect the character's journey in its entirety. As the actor listens to music options, he may hear moments in the chosen music which evoke the character's inner journey, or it might be that he initially only hears one very strong moment of connection. As the suggested length of the dance is only three minutes, considerable editing of the music may be necessary.

Stage Two: Instinctively Creating Material

Getting on His Feet

See Practical: *Raising the Stakes* (p. 187)
See Practical: *Identifying a Driving Emotion* (p. 188)

It may be that the only space available for the actor to move in is a small bedroom. Whatever the restrictions, the moment comes when he has to 'get onto his feet' and move.

There are many constructive, comfortable ways to initiate a piece of choreography. It might be tempting to use physical motifs or shape-creating tools (abstracting gesture, writing in the air, and so on). However, while these are effective starting points for creating movement, they have no place in this process. Developing material that starts in this way will, sooner or later, block the

---

[3] P. Bausch, *Le Sacre du Printemps* (DVD), Tanztheater Wuppertal, Paris: L'Arche, 2012. Seeing the film of this dance piece in 1980 on a tiny screen in a small studio was inspirational for Ewan as a student at the Laban Centre.

actor's own discovery of a physical language. His way in is to keep attempting to move and form into dance what he feels inside.

There is a temptation for the actor to clean up or 'accomplish' a movement; to become eloquent in a particular physical phrase and throw away material that is seen as 'no good'. This temptation should be resisted. Tiny, accurate clues as to what the instinct is trying to say may be obscured by more conscious choices. These clues are the substance of the dance and the actor must have courage to trust them.

> 'I tried solo dance again today and I was still stuck on the change. I tried for about an hour and I just couldn't get any further. I was getting more stressed at the fact that I couldn't *choreograph* a simple dance. But then I stopped. I lay down and just listened to the music over and over. I just lay there and I breathed naturally, and I relaxed. I actually completely gave myself to the floor and every muscle sank. I *felt* the floor on me for the first time.
>
> I then started to move. I wasn't dancing and I wasn't posturing, I just moved. *I wasn't thinking!* I now have the rest of my dance. *Yippee.*'
>
> Hannah Kaye in the First Year, 3-Year Acting Course

To allow instinct its full creative power, the actor must plunge to the centre of the physical response. 'Raising the stakes' – an acting term borrowed from gambling – is useful in this process. It means being bold and extreme with the vision and sensation of the emotion and the experiences of the character. The actor should have a sense of freedom from intellectual constraints. Emotions are not nice, tidy thoughts.

How is Improvisation Captured?

See Practical: *Tools for Improvisation* (p. 189)
See Practical: *If There are Gaps in Your Material* (p. 191)
See Practical: *Work on the Dance on Someone Else's Body* (p. 191)

A writer captures instinct in words. The words are there on the paper or on the screen. The writer will only lose his

Figure 6.3 Actor: Reice Weathers.
Photograph by Todd Padwick.

instinctive response, his equivalent moments of improvisation, by screwing up the paper or pressing 'delete'.

The actor works in a medium where instinct resides essentially in moments of improvisation. This means 'perfect moments' of response can easily be lost. Every actor has to find his own way of capturing a raw, instinctive response. He may video himself improvising and see the great moments on screen. He may, in sleep, see himself moving more acutely (and fantastically) and find himself writing down findings at three in the morning. It may be that inspiration is 'captured' little bits at a time by repeatedly rerunning the idea or leaving it and returning to it later.

Words 'translated' too fleetingly may result in missing the very thing that would turn the actor's expression into something extraordinary. Let's take the metaphor 'melted with grief'. The verb is in the past (perfect) tense. 'Melted' is a completed action rather than a transitional one. It is likely that the mental picture of 'melted' is a puddle on the floor. However, what if, having melted, the actor discovers that this is not the end? The melted state is fluid[4] and the fluidity allows the actor to move on. Change can occur; hope can occur. The puddle can become a bigger puddle; or run down a drain; be collected in a vessel; evaporate; or seep into the ground. The grief is mobile and exists in many forms.

A physical journey can occur by taking the metaphor seriously and responding in the present tense. (See Chapter 5: 'Taking the Physical Metaphor Literally'. Also see Transitions later in this Chapter.)

For a Stanislavski-influenced actor, it is established practice to ask five initial questions about his character: Who? What? Where? Why? and When? An actor in this process can use the same questions to build a full, three-dimensional picture of emotional imagery and metaphor. Again, taking 'melted with grief' as an example:

- The 'Who' could be the subject/character's self-identity prior to the situation: the character's essential persona, his stature or size, his emotional state (confident/bubbly/serious/quiet, and so on). It could be represented by a wax-like expression, or an ice-cold stare. Knowing this 'Who' will identify the way in which the character 'melted'.
- The 'What' is the melting caused by the grief.
- The 'When' is the timing. When did the melting occur? At night? In the day? Early or late in life? At the beginning of time or at a point when the future seems impossible? Each of these offers different possibilities for movement.
- The 'Where' is the emotional landscape, which may or may not correspond to the 'real' landscape of the situation. It may be a dream

---

[4] See David Weiss & Peter Fischli *Der Lauf der Dinge (The Way Things Go)* Short film/documentary, 1987).

world: the melting may have happened in a tight cramped space like a trunk, in a soft-earthed environment, or in an endless, silent desert, and so on.

- The 'Why' is the reason for the melting: why has the subject melted? From excessive heat? From lack of shelter? From lack of physical support or from lack of inner support (through being spineless, gutless, and so on)?

When physically manifesting a metaphor, it is the 'gut' that needs to be allowed to tell the actor what to do – because it does know. This process is not a paper exercise. If something doesn't work when he tries it out, the actor can just let it go. If it does work, it can be incorporated into his practice. It reflects the wider acting research process.

Emotional Breath

See Practical: *Emotional Breath* (p. 190)

'Athletic breath'[5] can interrupt the emotional journey. Preparation moments that honour the mechanics of individual actions – 'I'll quickly breathe in readiness for this unpleasant emotion' – may break the flow of ideas. The expression of anticipation is one of the few times when a form of breath preparation is justified. Otherwise, the actor should keep to the pattern of the emotional breath.

Stage Three: Identifying and Crafting Choices

This stage of the process is about identifying what has been created and crafting the choreographic choices. The material is revealed either to the actor himself on video, or to an observer. There should be an expectation that the material will be explored so that the essence of the movement can be drawn or teased out.

Transitions

See Practical: *Transitions* (p. 192)
See Practical: *Question Models of Symmetry* (p. 193)

Material which seems unformed and hazy may in fact be accurately connected.

---

[5] In an Actor Movement context this is an exaggerated demonstration of the out-breath and of the preparation for action on the in-breath.

Yet it can sometimes be sacrificed for the 'I've got a good idea' movements that feel accomplished but actually halt the inner journey. Life exists as a series of potentially surprising and often contradictory transitions. Work that deals neatly with a sad section followed by a happy section, and so on, does not reflect life.

When learning a dance, it is usual to try to make the steps as efficient as possible; in any case, steps naturally become more efficient with practice. In the context of the Solo Dance, joining steps up to make transitions between movements look smooth means that the 'story' of each transition is likely to be lost. The actor must resist the urge to let the foot simply 'step in' to transport the body to a new place because in doing so he is literally 'stepping all over' his emotional journey.

The physical transitions tell the story of the character's struggle or solution to emotional change. There are an infinite number of ways into and out of embodied emotional conditions. All the important questions and answers are found in the transitions:[6] the character may lift himself out of depression, fall in love, quell anger, or emerge from torment. The actor can stop and look at the actual physical translation of these shifts, that is, the movement the body has to make to allow for the change to occur.

Committing the Whole Body

See Practical: *The Face as Part of the Body* (p. 193)
See Practical: *Transposing Physical Expression* (p. 194)

The actor must allow his whole being, including his face, to transform. It is often forgotten that the face is part of the body. In the usual habit of daily life, the face holds a particular expressive role, expressing more detail than the body. In Solo Dance, body and face have equal responsibility; each should behave as expressively as the other.

Formed and Unformed Ideas

The dance is made up of formed ideas and unformed ideas. The formed ideas include dance steps, shaped moves and other existing movement vocabularies. The unformed ideas are the actor's practical, everyday movement: moves that are instinctive and idiosyncratic. Despite their differences, formed and unformed ideas can be treated exactly the same way in the studio.

---

[6] This is useful here – Calderone, M./Williams, M. L. *Actions; The Actor's Thesaurus*, Nick Hern Books, 2004.

Investigating the Formed Idea

Imagine an actor has designed and created a vertical movement, but when he performs this movement it is pointed out that it is at a slight angle. He was unaware of it, but this diagonal lean – although conceived and offered as a perpendicular movement – is in fact the unconscious expression of the emotion's very essence. Having noticed its existence, the next step is to analyse what it is and why it was done. In order to discover its logic, the actor can recall the feeling of the diagonal slant: is it weak or strong? It may be dreamy, quirky, supercilious, or through being scared or smitten by something or someone. Is it an uncomfortable deviation from stability? Does it come from sadness, desperation or dependency? Perhaps it is compensatory overbrightness? It won't take long for the actor to identify its quality. The actor can then allow the movement to develop. The diagonal, in this case, becomes part of the dance.

The quality of the movement may contain clues to the mechanics, just as the mechanics may contain clues to the quality. The actor might now ask himself about the direction of the diagonal: is it about pulling or pushing? From which point does the line emerge? And if it is extending out of his personal space, where is it going?

Revealing the Unconscious Elements of the Unformed Idea

See Practical: *Revealing the Unconscious Elements* (p. 198)
See Practical: *Personal Space in Relation to General Space* (p. 198)
See Practical: *Spatial Awareness – Thinking as Performer Now* (p. 199)

The actor may discover that, in his need to tell the story, he has choreographed the plot line. Recognizably human, everyday movement can, in the context of dance, be easily overlooked. It may also be executed on a purely gestural level. This means that it is at risk of being abandoned or lost in other moves.

Imagine an actor is stuck, standing and staring along a diagonal. When asked what he (as his character) is doing, he says, 'I am reaching out to someone but what I'm doing doesn't feel enough.' This is a good opening response and in a pause taken to understand it further, he realizes that he only thinks he isn't doing enough because he is not allowing the movement to be the expression of the feeling. The movement is in fact enough, but he must now allow the diagonal line to speak. The reach is now seen to express something of being alone; the stillness has a quality of isolation and emptiness. Questions may surface, such as 'Where in the body is the reach felt?', and 'What is the weight of the reaching?' Once the actor knows what the diagonal is giving him, he can question his feeling of being 'stuck'. Is it creative stasis or is its impotence in fact the essence of the action?

Imposing an Opposite Quality Using BWTS

See Practical: *Imposing an Opposite Quality Using BWTS (Breath, Weight, Time and Space)* (p. 196)

By imposing distinct qualities on the movement he has created, the actor sharpens up his existing physical responses. By forcing a decision and imposing on the action through what might be the 'wrong' choice, he ultimately finds the appropriate quality and the right 'fit' for each moment within the journey.

There is no need for the actor to have learned any established dance language. Nor should he attempt to take on the vocabulary of someone else (movement specialists and Laban practitioners included). However, BWTS (Breath, Weight, Time and Space) is inherent in every move he makes. BWTS could, for example, offer 'breathless', 'weak/powerful','fast/slow', 'straight/ curved' and so on, in different parts of the dance. Each element gives a different point of access. (See Chapter 5.)

Actor as Audience

If the actor is in a group situation, taking on the role of 'outside eye' as others perform the task will be a real advantage. When offering feedback, it is far better to speak about what is actually observed than to give praise about the 'amazingness' of the dance or the skill-set of the dancer. A tiny, isolated movement of, say, a foot, can make an impact on the eye, as though spotlit. The ability to recognize this expressive power can be taken back into the actor's own work and he can increasingly invest in the most subtle movement by the smallest body part. Similarly, receiving feedback from the group can be surprising. It is affirming to learn that the audience 'get it'; that they see and at times even feel the journey the actor is making. (See additional online resources: *Feedback*.)

Stage Four: Fine-tuning the Quality of the Movement

See Practical: *One Found Moment Can Be Replicated* (p. 201)

A self-generated dance offers a distinct advantage over work that is choreographed by someone else. The actor knows every movement; its inspiration and meaning is understood. The dance is a 'safe place' for the actor because he choreographed it with his body. When fine-tuning the material in relation to body and expression, the actor should take note of what can be seen as his specialisms.

For the student actor, this is the point at which a tutor can highlight and work on a particular movement, or work on the quality of the expression. It is likely that the same note will apply to a number of his movements, in which case locating and perfecting one moment may be more productive than working on a larger section.

Relationship with the World: The Music

See Practical: *Revisit Your Relationship with the Music* (p. 201)

The music chosen for the character relates directly to the emotional journey. It can mirror parts of it precisely and can sometimes run parallel. At other times it will oppose the journey or the emotion.

The actor develops the dance knowing the music; its differences and its similarities to the journey.

As an exercise, it is possible for the actor to do the same journey of the dance with another piece of music. The objective of this is to advance discovery of the character's emotions. It may be that within this new relationship the music is dominant; the actor must therefore dance to it. On the other hand, if the actor is falling, and the fall is inevitable within the emotional arc, he must 'go with it', experiencing and exploiting a conflict with the music. It is necessary to work out exactly where the opposition – and the synchronicity – lies. When he returns to the relationship with his music, he may find he needs to make more, or better, decisions.

Style

See Practical: *Permitting Style* (p. 202)

Reading out loud is different from reading to yourself. The necessary change in pace reveals the rhythm, dynamics and flavours of the writing. The novel has its own particular style of expression: it can be pictured as a hidden surface such as the back of a tapestry, with threads of emotion woven in and out. An actor taking on a character from a Jane Austen novel, for example, must be able physically to express a full emotional journey and not feel cramped by the period style of the novel. The style transfers to the dance from the book: it is revealed in the rhythm, dynamics and flavours of the dance.

Choreographer and Actor

See Practical: *Step into the Material as the Actor* (p. 203)

When the actor has his dance, it is time to divide his roles into choreographer and actor. As the choreographer he is outside the movement, whereas the actor is inside the choreography. The actor could not distinguish between these different roles before now, as the choreographer needed the actor to be in the dance while he created it. Now that each movement is fully owned, the dance is ready to hand over to the actor.

The choreographer may have choreographed something bold and challenging, letting a superb sequence do the work of telling the audience the scope of this feeling. On the other hand, the choreographer may have choreographed something bold and challenging which subsequently needs to be pruned back to allow the actor 'ownership'.

Before any pruning occurs, however, it is worth battling with the original creation. The big, courageous moments should not be cut away. They should be built up to, lived up to and securely inhabited. If the actor had known at the beginning of the process what he knows by the end, he might have chosen less challenging material. A certain amount of faith is required: what seems like a challenge may end up as a gift.

Relationship with the World: Shift Perspective

As a way of defining the character's conflict, it is valuable for the actor as choreographer to imagine using a camera (lenses, dollies, cranes, and so on). What view or angle would the camera offer to clarify and heighten the emotional journey? For example, for losing his grip on the world he might imagine a camera pulling back to make him appear to recede into the distance.

This idea of the right camera work to express the emotional conflict can then be translated to the body and the space as part of the dance. In the dance, the example above would be translated into the actor's body moving backwards in the space while his intention moves forwards. The resulting effect of the actor diminishing upstage offers him an experience of growing insignificance.

Preparation for Performance

See Practical: *Performance Space* (p. 204)

The dance may not be taken to performance but it is helpful to imagine a performing space in relationship to an audience.

The performance conditions demand a new level of work from the actor. However, as this is a dance of the inner journey, polishing it ready for performance may not be a good idea. He has nothing to hide behind: it is the body and his music speaking without text or props. All that exists is the actor, the space and the audience.

Solo Dance Process for a Character in a Play

An example of a an actor's[7] Solo Dance for a character in a play:

> Actor's Synopsis: 'In *All My Sons*, Miller examines the morality of Joe Keller, a 61-year-old manufacturer of fighter plane engines. Joe's dilemma: to allow flawed parts to be shipped out, putting the safety of pilots in jeopardy, or to allow them to be scrapped and his business to fail. His choice is a matter of self-survival – almost a message of capitalism and the survival of the fittest. The action of the play is set in August 1947 in the Midwest USA. The events depicted occur between a Sunday morning and a little after two o'clock the following morning.'

In rehearsals, the actor had been exploring a torso collapsed with age and emotional defeat for his character. The Solo Dance was his chance to explore the emotional journey of Joe Keller before and after the tragedy which defines his life. At one moment in the dance, for example, the actor is travelling down the diagonal of the working space with his arm held aloft. When asked what this is, he explains that Joe is holding the plane in the air. When this point is interrogated, it becomes clear it is an essential metaphor: by investing in that moment (that is, believing his arm to be that long, his shoulders that broad and himself to be that strong and open-chested), he displays responsibility, pride and purpose as he really holds the plane aloft, personally taking the weight of the airmen's lives. The actor had instinctively chosen the diagonal line to walk down as he holds the plane; a pathway which offers him the unstoppable power and status that the character holds in his community. This physical action is neither mime nor literal narrative. The dance, when revisited daily, lives inside his character's body memory and influences his character's movement.

IN CONTEXT: PROCESS FOR A CHARACTER IN A PLAY

With ownership of this process, the actor can create a Solo Dance for his character's emotional journey. He can continue to adjust his movement responses and choices as he develops his character in rehearsals. This works best as a private, start-of-day or end-of-day exercise.

---

[7] Alexander Neal (Central 2011) created a Solo Dance for his character Joe Keller in the play *All my Sons* by Arthur Miller.

Solo Dance Practicals

About the Practical Work

Some of the following practicals can be explored without working on a Solo Dance. They can be worked on solely for what they offer independently. They include a span of work that connects strongly with the ideas in Chapters 4, 5 and 8. Learning is of a progressive and lateral nature and the material can also be related to other chapters.

When working on a dance, the questions asked of you and of your dance can be taken on and explored with total confidence: they are there to increase expressive potential. You work with what is yours and it remains yours until completion, if and when you hand it to the audience. Working within this process can be seen as parallel to the way in which an actor has to work throughout his career. Even in a collaborative situation, you are essentially alone. You are always going to be in union with, or battling against, yourself in your search for character.

Practical Section: Stage One

▶ Extracts from Five Solo Dances.

Further Guidance on Choosing the Novel

Length of the novel

If the book is of a good quality, it's not really an issue how long it is. For example, Steinbeck's *The Pearl* or Hemingway's *The Old Man and the Sea* are both very short but ideal for this project. If you do select a long book, however, be sure to read the whole thing.

What sort of novel

- Genre-specific books – such as horror, sci-fi, crime, fantasy or romance – offer a distinct aspect of a character on a specific journey and are not suitable here. Agatha Christie's Miss Marple, for example, does not have an emotional journey. Children's books should also be avoided as they don't offer the complexity of the adult experience.

- Make sure you read the book before you see a film of it. Otherwise, you will be robbed of your own response to the book, as you would be if you took on board an illustrator's interpretation of a particular character. Any literature that you have studied academically also may obscure any personal inspiration.

- Autobiographical novels are not wholly honest; bear in mind that they are selective in what they wish to tell. So be selective.

- It's more likely you will have responded to a character of the same sex as yourself and empathized with her/him. If this is not the case, check that it is the emotional journey you connect with rather than the interest you may have in choosing a different gender. The emotional journey should be the focus and the reason for your choice.

Further Guidance on Choosing and then Cutting the Music

- Listen to several potential options with your chosen character in mind.

- When you can see how to cut the chosen piece of music to the desired length, do this as sensitively as possible.

Key points

Avoid being tempted to create a personal musicscape by cutting up and editing together different pieces of music to fit the different emotions of your Solo Dance, as this robs the music–movement relationship of reality.

Practical Section: Stage Two

Work instinctively but then question everything: start with instinct; follow with questioning; end with instinct.

Raising the Stakes

▶ Raising the Stakes: Inhabiting a Physical Dilemma.

As an example, imagine you have choreographed a balance in your dance as a seminal point in your journey.

- Offer the epic nature of this balance, where the character concerned cannot wobble – you absolutely cannot wobble because a wobble would take over and you would be left offering a pedestrian action: someone being a bit wobbly.

- Work out the extremities of the balance; the oppositional pulls.

- Work out any other imagined reality that creates the balance, including accurately creating any necessary fixed points, such as being tied to something, or stuck to a surface, and so on. (See Appendices: *Creating a Fixed Point in the Space*.)

- Imagine the balance; use your belief in your imaginative world – acting required.

- Differentiate between this and determination. Recognize the difference in your body between a gritting of your teeth, tensing and forcing your resolve, and the freedom of allowing yourself to live and breathe every moment to its fullest.

- Try it out; find this moment physically and inhabit it completely.

- You may not have a balance in your dance, so choose an equivalent moment from your movements.

- Raise the stakes of this moment. Heighten the identity of the drama. Be greater/bolder/more.

- Be in the present tense and commit totally to the essence of the movement – the physical expression of the emotion.

- Now try the opposite. Your world is spinning or tumultuous or you are lost and perpetually falling. You cannot be stable.

IN CONTEXT: RAISING THE STAKES

In rehearsal it can be quite difficult to read your own body as there is always so much going on. To develop an idea or clearly see what the experience is that you are working on, you might want (outside the reheasal) to take one moment and test out raising the stakes of that moment in just the way described here.

Identifying a Driving Emotion

'Stasis' might best describe the times when you are not moving at all but feeling a lot. It can feel powerful to have periods of immobility in your dance as an attempt at containing the emotions that are moving about inside, but be sure to question: are you the only one having a great time? It may be an honest reflection of your ability to realize and respond to the feelings which are occurring, but you also need to actually get on with the job of movement. Get past the movement of the character and start to discover the physical expression of the emotion on its own.

An example using 'pain' as a simile might help you with this instruction:

- Recall a time when you were consumed by pain.

- How would you describe that pain to a doctor? Not the you-left-lying-on-the-ground-gripping-your-knee-and-moaning in pain, but the pain itself, for instance: stabbing, dark, metallic, thin, or dull.

- Embody emotion in the same way, so that it is the emotion consuming you that is viewed – not the you that is denying/fighting/hiding/diffusing/deflecting/frustrating or masking it.

IN CONTEXT: YOUR CHARACTER'S DRIVING EMOTIONS

You can identify your character's underlying (perhaps never revealed) driving emotions and let them out to play as part of pre-rehearsal warm-up. (See Chapter 8, Practical: *Bottling Exercise*.)

Tools for Improvisation

You must ultimately create your own method of generating material and of accurately repeating and refining it without losing spontaneity. The following are extremely loose suggestions and should not override your instinctive response:

- As you set out to improvise, have in place a method to catch the raw early responses. You will begin to clarify what works best for you as you go along: for instance, recording, writing down, videoing or memorizing.

- Give yourself a time frame to work within.

- Embody the character at different points in his emotional journey.

- Find a moment when the character has a particular physical experience, such as rowing against the current, running barefoot through the woods, or rolling down a hill. Try embodying it.

- Walk or stand or sit or lie in the space as your character. Try being low to the ground, in the middle of the room, at the edge of the room, and so on; start to move …

Now forget the purely external aspects of the character's life and pay attention to his emotional journey.

- Explore the character's emotions any way you like – what if he dreamt of free falling or drowning? Can you freefall? Or drown?
- Embody how the character might behave physically if a particular emotion took possession of him.
- Allow yourself to experience being the landscape of the book.
- If you have a sudden breakthrough that tempts you to work on one bit in detail, note it down so you can get back to it later. That way you can continue to improvise and you don't lose the spirit of what you are discovering.
- Retain empathy with the character's emotional journey – your inspiration.
- Trust your instinct.

Key points

As you create material have the courage not to 'delete' it all.

Emotional Breath

Try this example:

- Find the emotional breath for 'a sleepless night'. Get beyond the actual breath of the action of tossing and turning and reach the mind in turmoil: the feeling of anxiety that prevents sleep. If, for example, the feeling is (metaphorically) 'seaweed slapped against rocks', find the breath that equates to this.
- Now ask these questions: where in the body is the movement? Where in the movement is the in-breath and where is the out-breath? At what point on the breath does the movement start?

Now select a section of your dance:

- Move from the emotional impulse and stay with the breath pattern that this offers.
- Accept that athletic breath may want to kick in as preparation for the mechanics of the movement in this section.
- Do not let this happen; instead, become aware of the breath of the emotion and yield to that journey. So, for instance, if you were going down to the floor, you would let the breath take you there.

IN CONTEXT: EMOTIONAL BREATH JOURNEY

As a one-off experience, inhabit a heightened emotional breath journey whilst working alone on a character. Do this as a character improvisation using his everyday movement or text. This may give you new information about your character's emotional map, which in turn informs the movement.

If There are Gaps in Your Material

- Don't keep starting at the beginning: you will wear it out.
- Try starting at different points.
- Be still in any uncreated moments: close your eyes, or even lie down, at these points in your dance and let yourself imagine these moments, physically shifting back and forth into the created parts with full commitment.

Work on the Dance on Someone Else's Body

This is an exercise for the individual in a group. If you are stuck on a section of your dance, it may help to have someone else move for you.

- You could ask several of the group to move for you. Offer the music, the metaphor or simile or, maybe, a collection of images and textures and a mixture of plot and feeling.
- Watch as they improvise. Offering an explanation of any of these means that you have to articulate your thoughts – no bad thing.
- Watch the individual physical responses to your instructions; see if you can see what you explained and described to your peers in what they offer. If you cannot see it, maybe you missed something essential in your instructions and this is all that is lacking.
- If not, keep watching them and look for something that you like and with which you can constructively connect.
- If you see one of the group doing something that you like, alert the rest of the group so that they can explore not the same but similar territory. Then you can watch several ways of physicalizing this material.
- You may begin to feel less stuck as they show you either a detail or a broad-stroke and whichever of these it is, one will illuminate the other.

Key points

Watching them can make you aware of how much more you have than you thought. They will not have demonstrated the deep understanding of the character that you have. However, they will have shown you a glimpse of what it is you know but hadn't necessarily managed to embody yet.

Practical Section: Stage Three

Understand the dance you have created by questioning each physical decision, honing and crafting your movement choices.[8]

Transitions

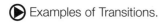 Examples of Transitions.

How can you better embody the emotional shifts rather than creating clean mechanical transitions?

- Look through your dance and pick out any times when you have glossed over a transition; when you have too efficiently moved yourself out of or into a different situation. For example, what if you were in a kneeling position and thought you needed to be upright for the next movement and from that kneeling position, you had simply brought one foot through and stood up.

- It might help to break down each action into smaller and smaller actions to locate the moment that needs the attention.

- Find where in the body the action was placed just before the moment 'the foot stepped in'.

- Now you have located it, you are on the road to solving how this transition might occur differently, maintaining the flow of emotional action through the body.

---

[8]See D. Humphrey, *The Art of Making Dances*, New York: Grove, 1959, for further inspiration.

Question Models of Symmetry

Check whether you have repeated to the left the same movement you have done to the right to even out the sides. This may be a habit from a dance or movement form you practise. It may be from your perception of dance. It might be in response to, and as a reflection of, the repetition in your music's patterning. It may be that a model of symmetry seems to affirm what you are 'saying'. Whichever it is, question it.

- Clarify the story of the space in the movement and decide:
- If not both, which side is the one to keep?
- If, after exploring this, you do use both sides, identify the differences between the first and the second sides in terms of movement, as each of these will possess a distinctive aspect.
- Use the ability to 'live in the now' to experience each side's full meaning.

The Face as Part of the Body

▶ Examples of the Face as Part of the Body.

- Allow the experience of the journey to playfully affect the face just as it does the rest of the body.

While it is assumed the face speaks volumes to the audience, often it actually tells it very little where feelings are concerned. (See Chapter 3, Practical: *Outer Stillness on Text*.)

- How is your face involved in your dance?
- Recognize that pulling faces is likely to be a demonstration of the effect of the emotion – 'a telling about' – and therefore tied to plot rather than the expression of the emotion itself.
- It is slightly different if you find yourself smiling. This can be telling the audience about the character being happy. It might be you trying to make the audience feel at ease with the dance. It might be your habit to smile. You might be doing it out of self-consciousness.
- If you find yourself with a blank face or mouth hanging open, this might be your attempt not to let the face interfere with the work the body is doing. It could also be that you are involved in feeling it all in your face as one wide-eyed, jaw-opened experience.

If the face is open and liberated from these holds, it can then match the emotion. Try this:

- Tuck your fingers in, then release the hand slowly and open all the fingers equally and simultaneously until your hand is flat and facing the sky.

- Now give it a simile: first, like the petals opening on a buttercup, then like a child about to be caned across the hand.

- Do the same action, but this time using the face.

IN CONTEXT: THE FACE

Work out when the face is visible to and able to be read by other characters, and when it is not. When the private face of the character is on view to the audience but the other characters cannot see it, an opportunity exists to share with the audience something of your character's emotional journey.

Transposing Physical Expression

The impulse of a movement can come from different places in the body; arms are the obvious place from which to express, while the legs are less obviously expressive.

Committing to Your Choice

You may find that your dance is predominantly expressed in your arms and that the quality of the movement has not been considered. This is not too surprising as this part of your body is habitually used for gesture and demonstration. If this is the case:

- Commit to whatever the movement is and place the whole experience of the expression in one part of your arm, as if no other body part could move – in your elbow, for example.

- Recognise a fuller expressive ability of that part, for instance, the elbow has the potential to express vulnerability when exposed, or when angular, to be used more aggressively, as if jabbing someone, and so on.

- With that particular embodied knowledge, you will know if the movement should continue to belong in the arms. Decisions can then be made about the rest of the body's involvement if necessary.

- If you discover that it is appropriate and meaningful to do so, you have the choice to shift the choreography to another part of the body rather than constantly resorting to using just the arms for the expression.

Transposing a Quality to Another Body Part

- Choose a movement and transpose it to another part of the body, keeping the quality and experience.

- Question why it was where it was. You may find a surprising level of ease when doing it in a new placement. It may have been where it was, as with the above example of the arms, simply because that was your immediate, most easy option.

▶ Transposing a Quality to Another Body Part.

Try this:

- Do the whole dance just with your legs and feet (often neglected).

- Discover how, through the heightened need to communicate, they can 'speak' for you. Do not change your choreography.

- Make sure the upper body is in connection with the lower body so that the legs and feet can offer impulses to the top of the body. They can then experience being the source of the momentum.

- Trust that the body will react to your legs and your feet.

- You may discover that by doing this, there are huge gaps in the body's ability.

- If so, apologize to your legs and feet and make sure you start consciously to bring them into the rehearsal room as sites of potential expression next time you do your dance.

IN CONTEXT: BODY PARTS

Looking at the character and body parts – head, stomach, chest, nose, genitals, and so on – consider:

- Which body parts are favoured by the character?
- Which body parts are neglected by the character?
- Where does the character lead from?
- Which body parts are left behind?

For instance, for a character that lives in his head: the head becomes his whole body/world and so the neck takes on the equivalence of legs just to transport him around.

Imposing an Opposite Quality Using BWTS (Breath, Weight, Time and Space)

This involves looking at the mechanics, the movement in the body.

You will connect with this idea if you have ever weighed the pros and cons, but followed your heart to the 'wrong' choice.

- Choose a phrase of your dance.
- Do this phrase as you have created it.
- Now do it again, but this time impose one distinct quality of either BWTS on the phrase (see guidance on the next page).
- After the experience of imposing each quality on your phrase, do the movements as they were choreographed once more.
- Find greater accuracy in the original movement of the qualities that you have just explored.
- Only change a moment of movement to the quality imposed if you are completely sure change is what you want.
- Be guided by the emotional journey as you go through this exercise.
- How does the quality of WTS change or affect the breath?
- Does moving in this way also change or affect the other two Motion Factors?

Use the following guidance when working on moments in your Solo Dance and imposing WTS. (See Chapter 8, Part 1.) (Breath was worked in an earlier practical.)

Weight

As you look at the aspect of Weight, keep in mind that the lighter or heavier expression of your choreography may have been influenced by your commitment, courage, or by fear of the project itself.

- *Light:* Envisage *light* as defiance of gravity, as though you leave no imprint; you move with a light touch.

- *Strong* and/or *Heavy*: Envisage *strong* and *heavy* as committed force and/or a giving into gravity. (See Chapter 5: Weight.)

Time

- *Sudden*: Envisage *sudden* without continuous movement. The *sudden* might quicken the move or break it in time, creating several stops and starts. Think of a musical instrument that specializes in *sudden*, such as a drum or piano, and feel what that is like.

- *Sustained*: Envisage *sustain* without any stops and starts. Think of a musical instrument that specializes in *sustain*, like the bowing of a violin.

Be true to the quality you are exploring: if it's *sudden*, it's *sudden*; if it's *sustained*, it's *sustained*.

Space

- *Indirect*: Envisage *indirect* as without direction; flexible; circular movement.

- *Direct*: Envisage *direct* as moving in straight lines with goals.

IN CONTEXT: IMPOSING CHOICES

Once you have found your personal way of working with this process of imposing choices, it may be useful to take it back into character work. It may be that you know a character you are working on well, but have not made physical choices because you did not wish to interfere with the inner detail you had started to accumulate. This physical silence can be broken with a bold (probably inaccurate) choice. You can then move onto more subtle and realistic options. The idea is just to try things out. The character knows which of the choices fit and you will always learn from the choices that don't.

Revealing the Unconscious Elements

When working on a moment in your dance, look at the mechanics of the movement to reveal its unconscious quality.

- Chose a moment in your dance, one you are not sure of yet.

- Describe this moment out loud to yourself – acknowledge both the shape and the mechanics of the movement.

- Keep the experience light of touch and stay in the present tense with the ideas when working on a moment from your dance. Whether it is a quality that needs unearthing, or the mechanics of a move that need clarifying, the moment of the movement can tell you what it needs you to do.

- Ask yourself the 'why' of each description. Allow these questions to come naturally from the movement.

- Clarify the movement; for example, the quality of the weight ('Why am I light in that bit of the movement?'); consider its energy ('Is it radiating? sparking? dispersing? held? gathering? bursting? ebbing away?'); its rhythm and its timing ('Why do I move abruptly on that bit?', 'Why am I holding my breath in that moment?).

- Look at the essence of the movement. You may need to ask, for example, 'Why do I move forward in that bit?' or, 'Why do I move down to the ground after that bit?' It may be that you are taking for granted the fact that you are moving in certain directions that have simply appeared in your dance.

Personal Space in Relation to General Space

This exploration is in two parts: the parts may merge or you may go back and forward between the two.

A process that demands being on your own, engaged in a personal journey, may, understandably, lead you to consider only personal space. This will result in a dance with an indistinct use of general space. At its extreme, this would lead you to an inward or body-centred focus where you might watch your own hands, or constantly look at the floor.

- Be focused, fully occupied and immersed in what you are doing, but be clear that immersion does not imply introversion.

It is important that you acknowledge introversion as additional and separate. For this you need to bring your attention to and clarify your expression within the general space.

- Recall the practice on the five Ws and the section on space, in which space as metaphor is introduced: the character's emotional landscape is not always the same as the 'real' landscape of the rest of the play.

- Allow yourself to discover the 'emotional' space.

- Now take this one stage further and let the general space become the rest of the world for you.

- Before considering general space further, choose a moment of your dance and look at this moment in relation to near space: how large is your kinesphere? What is the size of the space you take up in the world? How big, therefore, are you in the world?

The personal space must include your interior which also includes your breath; breath has its own relationship with the general space as air.

- When you breathe in, do you suck the world into you? Or, when you breathe out, do you deflate like a balloon? Or do you wilt?

IN CONTEXT: SPACE

Alongside asking yourself about the particularities of your character's personal space, consider your character in relation to the rest of the space, the general space, the world of the play. This may be experienced as a constant metaphor as you relate to and engage with it from your personal space. There is likely to be a difference in the texture, density or colour, for instance, between the two spaces.

Spatial Awareness – Thinking as Performer Now

Looking now at the general space:

- Bring an awareness of the 'performance space set-up' to your dance.

- Acknowledge that all of the performing space belongs to the dance. This is not asking you to 'move' through the entire space. However, by bringing awareness of the performance space to your choreography, choices regarding space can be clarified.

- Draw a map – a floor plan of your dance. Include the inhabited spots, high and low space, and the 'facings' (directions in which your body faces).

There are two sets of questions to ask now: the first is related to you and your process of creating the dance. The second is related to the character's emotional journey. The first set of questions will be found through looking at the particulars of your floor plan.

- If your dance occurs mostly in one side of the space, does this relate to a cramped space in which you have been practising such as your bedroom? Or, might it be because you favour one side of your body or are you uncomfortable with part of it?

- If you have avoided the centre of the space, is this because the centre of the space makes 'you' feel vulnerable?

- If you are at the back of the space is this because 'you' are trying to hide, or be near an exit, a reassuring friend, or a prop? If you are facing the back, might this be for some of the same reasons?

- Do these choices belong to you or your character?

The second set of questions is about your body in the landscape and involves the floor plan and the imagined space. Be meticulous, clear and precise in answering the following type of questions:

- If you have favoured one side of the space, is this part of the character's dilemma within the journey? If so, how are you utilizing the whole of the space to tell the story of this 'no-go' area?

- If you are on the floor, what is the volume of space above you?

- Are you ever dominant in the space, or engulfed by it?

- What surface are you on? Is it hard or soft? Is it spongy? Is it like paper or cloud? And so on.

IN CONTEXT: WORKING WITHIN BLOCKING

You can draw a map or floor plan of your character's moves in the play. Ask if this tells you anything about the character. Spatial blocking is necessary and can become fixed quite early on, so differentiate (a) when it is of your character and 'fits', and (b) when it is of the world to which he has to conform. For example, you have to cross the stage and exit through a particular door as the geography of the play dictates it. Without necessarily changing the existing blocking, as you discover more about your character he can 'bend the rules' – just as a person does in life, he can cross the space in his own particular way. The bending and pushing against structures can add to the definition of your character. This can be useful when blocking has already been put in place (that is, for inherited or understudy parts). You still have to find the ways that allow you to embody the given spatial patterns as that character.

Practical Section: Stage Four

One Found Moment Can Be Replicated

One moment in the dance may help you to find something new in yourself. If you understand this in one moment, the same learning can then be applied to all the moments in the dance.

If, for example, you had an awareness that you carry tension in the upper chest but have found an openness across the chest through the intention of one moment:

- Look for all other similar moments and realize them in your body in the same way.

Check through the following pointers (they are not unusual forms of tension to occur in the actor; you may find them occurring in your body as you work on your dance). When you experience held energy:

- Check that the moments that are held are meant to be and release any that should not be.

- Refine the movement.

- Remember that lines through the space speak if you release the energy out into the space beyond the body and its extremities.

- Find the moment before the tension takes over.

- Find out where there are appropriate times to hold the breath and when it should not be held.

- Notice if you are curling or tucking up the fingertips – the extremities. This may be a physical habit. However, within the context of the dance, releasing the joints and straightening out the fingers means that the hands will be in contact with the world, offering you sensory experience of it. You will be touching, or 'in touch with', and receiving the world.

- Perceive your toes, fingertips and the top of your head as simply the extremities of the open channels of the limbs and the spine.

Revisit Your Relationship with the Music

- Enliven your response to the music again, as if it is another actor with you in the space. Let the relationship with the music dominate again. Has it become a wash of background sound for you? Are there times when you are cutting it out or ignoring it?

- With your music on (not through headphones), lie on the floor in the middle of a large room and see your dance in your mind's eye. Experience and feel the journey.

- Now experience a relationship with a different choice of music. Do your dance with this other music, but don't change it to fit. Understand the dance in this new relationship; its mismatches may reveal or clarify parts of the journey for you.

- You can take anything you discover back to your relationship with your original music.

- The audience will understand the music better through you and will understand you better through the music. The audience is always free to choose between watching and listening, which is as it should be.

Permitting Style

▶ An Example of an Extract from a Novel.

Don't fight the style, the period, the use of language, vocabulary, terms, expressions and terminology of the novel.

- Take one moment in your dance and think about the feature that makes the movement particular to the style of writing, novel and author with which you are working and characterizes the dynamic and architecture of your dance. Think, for example, of the difference in writing style between Dickens and Austen and what the imprint of each might be in a dance.

- Choose an excerpt from your book that in some way involves your character's emotional journey.

- Read the excerpt from the book out loud, clear enough for an audience to hear.

- Imagine that any other actors are listening as though they were eavesdropping. Sit in the way you sit when reading silently alone. This is not about performing or presenting the excerpt.

- Is there an echo of the style of writing in the choices you have made in your dance?

- If there is, you can now trust your instinct.

IN CONTEXT: PERMITTING STYLE

Reading out loud is a usual first activity when in rehearsal for a play. Physical choices are not generally explored here. Yet, much can be discovered through the process of the read-through. There can be obstacles such as you dealing with introducing, 'selling' yourself to a new group, but try to avoid imposing your own style by staying open. You can then experience the writer's particular style in the writing, use of language and the style of the time in which it was written as well as of the playwright's created world. The rhythm of your character might be hinted at in the length of the sentences; or the quantity of vowels or consonants may offer a physical emotional map. This is one of the many times when doing less offers more. (See Chapter 3: *Outer Stillness on Text*.)

Step into the Material as the Actor

If there are sticking points, gaps, or self-conscious moments as actor:

- Cleanly hand them back to yourself as choreographer and allow yourself to deal with them in that role.
- Be the actor, then be the choreographer.
- Switch cleanly between the two roles.
- There can now be a dialogue between the two of you.
- Hand the dance back and forth many times.
- Allow the dance to take control.
- You, the actor, can then simply commit to the emotional journey.
- You can start to grapple with, and even attempt to frustrate, the now identified dynamic feelings in the movements that you as the choreographer created.

Performance Space

For you to learn the most from the moment of performance, the chosen space should offer four distinct things. It should:

1   be a designated and defined performing space;

2   be an actor's space;

3   expose the actor to the audience;

4   allow the audience to exist separately but in close proximity to the actor as he performs.

The ideal space for this project, then, is a black-box space (dark-walled or curtained theatre performance space), with audience in front and no lighting design as such, but rather a general lighting state. It is worth noting that this project would be better placed in a space that meets the above criteria even if it had an unsuitable floor rather than in a dance space.

8

EXPLORING WAYS OF BEING: EFFORTS AND OTHER CODES

OVERVIEW

Part One: Laban's Efforts of Action Drive
This is a process for the actor to acquire a deep physical understanding of Laban's Eight Efforts of Action Drive. One Effort is examined in detail as a template for how the other seven Efforts might also be examined and understood.

Part Two: Being in the World – Physical Codes and their Keys
This is an advanced technique in physical observation and translation. This work enables the actor to identify and work on a character from the text through a process that leads to unique and exacting choices.

Part One: Laban Efforts of Action Drive

Rudolf Laban (1879–1958) was an artist, scientist, architect, choreographer, philosopher and movement educator. Born in Bratislava, he lived in Germany during the Bauhaus and Expressionist periods.[1] He analysed movement through the study of dance and developed the first comprehensive system for recording human movement. The application of particular elements of

---

[1] For an overview of Laban and his work, see K. Bradley, *Rudolf Laban, Routledge Performance Practitioners*, London: Routledge, 2009.

Laban's work has informed and transformed movement processes for actors worldwide.[2]

Working within Laban's theoretical framework can be an extremely powerful, and in some cases life-changing, experience. The approach described here keeps the focus on the actor's process.[3] It is designed specifically for the actor who wants a direct and accessible route to existing in someone else's reality while developing his own imagination and instinct. Through observation and investigation, an actor can break down personal qualities and characteristics; over time he can develop skills in movement analysis that expand his physical and emotional range and equip him to work physically as a character.

Laban believed that the actor 'derives a certain inspiration from descriptions of movement that awaken his imagination'.[4] This understanding and control of language can lead to an actor making active choices for a character. Even better, it can foster the instinct to create a full range of dynamic and contrasting characters.

Looking More Specifically at Your Own Movement

We believe we are very complex, yet, everyday we get up and essentially move the same way we did the day before. If you didn't move the same way everyday, you wouldn't be 'you'. It would be noticed. There is a limited range of driving movement within each of us.

Laban's work demonstrates that all human movement can be expressed through a combination of eight basics 'Efforts'. The Efforts of Action Drive identified by Laban are:

* *Gliding*
* *Floating*
* *Flicking*
* *Dabbing*

* *Wringing*
* *Pressing*
* *Thrusting*
* *Slashing*[5]

---

[2]J. Newlove, *Laban for Actors and Dancers: Putting Laban's Movement Theory into Practice, a Step-by-Step Guide*, London: Nick Hern Books, 1993. Also J. Newlove, *Laban for All,* London: Nick Hern Books, 2004

[3]Ewan's process of work with the actors. New material or specific ways of thinking are second generation Laban and supplementary to Laban's insightful work. The intention is solely to serve the actor.

[4]R. Laban, *Mastery of Movement*, Tavistock: Northcote House, 1988, 21.

[5] Ibid., 69.

Laban's elegant system offers detailed and comprehensive information about the whole vast range of human movement. Individuals understand each other, ultimately, because of this simple shared palette. What can be perceived as 'personality' is a matter of some Efforts being more dominant than others.

A Laban process and a Stanislavski process can be used in tandem, creating a fertile dialogue between the craft of acting and the craft of movement.

Motion Factors

See Practical: *Building the Efforts from WTS* (p. 216)

Weight, Time and Space (WTS) were introduced in Chapter 4 as 'Observation Prompts'. These are now considered within Laban's particular terms of reference. Each is one of three 'Motion Factors', and defined by opposing Elements:

1　Weight is either *light* or *strong*.

2　Time is either *sudden* or *sustained*.

3　Space is either *direct* or *indirect*.

A combination of one Element from each of these three Motion Factors (WTS) creates each 'Effort of Action Drive'. So, for example, the 'Effort' of *floating* is made up of three of the Motion Elements: *light* (Weight), *sustained* (Time) and *indirect* (Space). This means that the actor embodying *floating* moves *indirectly* in the space (i.e. in curves), with a *sustained* quality in terms of timing, and with constant and extreme *lightness*.

The Eight Efforts of Action Drive with their Motion Factors are:

- **Gliding** *direct sustained light*
- **Floating** *indirect sustained light*
- **Flicking** *indirect sudden light*
- **Dabbing** *direct sudden light*
- **Wringing** *indirect sustained strong*
- **Pressing** *direct sustained strong*
- **Thrusting** *direct sudden strong*
- **Slashing** *indirect sudden strong*

Using Laban's vocabulary and analysis of WTS, all the possibilities of expression that have been encountered in this book thus far could also be reframed, rearticulated and worked with in terms of the Efforts. For example, within an animal study a bird's head movement could now be identified as a '*Dab*' (that is, *light, sudden* and *direct*).

Personal Effort Map

Each actor – each person – has affinities with certain Efforts. Exploring each Effort provides clues which, when added up, reveal the actor's personal expressive map. Discovering his own 'Effort Map' allows him to identify gaps in his habitual movement expression. These insights enable him to use the Efforts to create other 'physical' ways of being' (i.e. other characters) by working in Efforts which do not occur so naturally or easily within his body. It is particularly important to this process that he works to inhabit, love and understand each Effort equally; it becomes clear that a person dependent on one 'way of being' is necessarily neglecting other ways and is incapable of a broad movement palette, of total transformation.

The Efforts will be expressed by the actor with varying degrees of ease. Each actor will therefore assume that some Efforts communicate more clearly than others, depending on which he personally finds easiest or hardest to embody. Insight and practice should be able to shift this belief so that the actor expands his expressive vocabulary to embody every Effort fully.

Action Drive

The full title 'Efforts of Action Drive' is long and so, for practical reasons, is abbreviated to 'Efforts'. However, the words 'Action Drive' are worth keeping in mind, as they remind the actor what the work explores. Laban identifies an action as a functional human movement which takes muscular energy or force and has a distinct effect in (and thus relationship with) space and time. 'Drive' means that each human action has purpose. Nothing is purposeless, even if it appears so, and no action is ever fully devoid of expression.

Translator of Experience

The actor is a translator of all experience, a torch-bearer for revealing more of what it is to be human. As has been explored in previous chapters, he uses a process of observation and translation to 'collect' people. This is not done in a self-centred or judgemental way, but in order to access different ways of doing, thinking and feeling. These modes of being can now be analysed through the Efforts. (See Chapters 5 and 6.)

Laban as a Language

It is important for the actor to take on Laban as a language and not as a technique. Once the actor takes on and owns the language, he finds independence from both Laban and the tutor. When reflecting on the work 10 or 15 years later, he may even have taken on the language to such an extent that he feels he has always known it.

Embodying the Motion Factors

When working with the Efforts, the actor's first challenge is to understand each of the Elements of WTS.

Weight as Motion Factor

Weight is divided into two clear Elements: *strong* and *light*.

Strong is to do with activating force and power. It can have a sensation of *heavy weight*, which means the actor allows personal body weight to exist within the movement: giving in to the intention of the movement and committing to the emotional weight or impact of it.

Light is active in its defiance of gravity. There is also the sensation of *light* weight: a *lightness* of being that creates minimum impact in terms of physical weight in the space.

There is a gravitational link between *light* and high space, and *heavy* weight and low space. The actor can execute the quality of *strong* both when it feels like a natural match between movement and sensation (as in lowering his body downwards into low space) and when it may not (as in moving upwards). Likewise, *lightness* should be experienced both when moving upwards towards high space, and also in low space.

The quality of *light* weight (the sensation of soft, feather-like lightness of touch) is transferred to the actor's entire being. It is possible to recreate this in any place in the body, including the mind. The term 'lightweight' is used as a way of disparaging something – dismissing its worth. It is important for the actor to acknowledge and remove this linguistic connection, which may affect the actor's perception of the value of working with *light*.

In a rehearsal context, if the actor is told to 'find weight', this is probably a note to find one of its two aspects – either *strong* weight (force), or *heavy* weight (gravity; gravitas). It is unlikely that he is being asked to find *light* weight. This note to 'find weight' doesn't mean putting in a step that represents *strong* weight (e.g. a stamp). It asks the actor to examine and find the nature of the weight, and how it is present and embodied in the movement's expression.

How *light* and *strong* exist together in a body or a moment is an individual thing. The actor might, for example, have a muscular understanding of *strong* weight but an emotional understanding of *lightness*. *Light* and *strong* are both of equal importance.

Time as a Motion Factor

Laban divides time into two clear elements: *sudden* and *sustained*. *Sudden* might be broken action or many actions which are 'momentary' in time. *Sustained* might be joined up action or one continual action.

The process here, conceived with the actor in mind, imagines *sudden* and *sustained* in relation to any given action: *sudden* is the beginning and the end of the action with no middle; *sustained* is the middle of the action without end or beginning.

When developing an understanding of *sustained*, the actor finds the middle part of the journey in a ceaseless movement that is constantly experienced as the present moment. *Sustained* can relate to 'eternal' – a quality of hopes and dreams – without start or finish.

When developing an understanding of *sudden*, the actor finds the beginning and end of an action without the middle part; he starts and stops only to start and stop again.

Sudden does not mean manic. Nor does *sustained* necessarily imply slow motion, although slow is related to *sustain*: it is naturally easier to *sustain* a slower physical action and it will always possess some sense of that to the objective eye – a measured, long, drawn-out quality. The actor's endeavour is to *sustain* the movement rather than working in 'slow motion'. It may be helpful to think of the sustained natures of both snow falling and a tornado (as long as the imagined tornado is constant).

Space as a Motion Factor

Laban's division of movement in space as *direct* or *indirect*[6] can be simplified to start with as straight lines (*direct*) and curves (*indirect*).

Being *direct* (as with all the Motion Factor Elements) can be manifested with the whole being, not just the gaze. Being *direct* can be understood as being focused and means attention is given to where the person initiating the movement is intending to go. Potentially this could be as far as the edge of the

---

[6]The usual word is *flexible* – this accurately describes the movement of the body itself; while *indirect* describes the pathways. However, as *flexible* has connotations with being limber and with fitness, or with dance, as well as its strong associations with 'stretchy', it is unhelpful in this process.

universe, but whatever the distance there is a destination. He might perhaps think of it like an intensely focused, narrow, laser-sharp beam of light.

Being *indirect* is unfocused: the actor coming at things circuitously without ever arriving. The journey is without end or boundary and so potentially infinite. The body can indulge in *indirect* to take on 'everywhereness'.

The Eight Efforts of Action Drive

See Practical: *Exploring One Effort in Isolation* (p. 218)

Laban's titles for the Efforts are unambiguous and evocative; they are words that can stimulate an immediate physical response. Once acquired, they will also have personal associations for the actor that can help him immediately access a particular Effort in his body. In order to reach this stage, each Effort must first be worked with independently of the others over a period of time and through a variety of stages. In this way, the actor fully explores the possibilities of each Effort within himself in an embodied process. Human physical expression is always multifaceted. Isolating each Effort and working equally on each allows clarity of vision.

Resisting the need to change

The actor may feel that he has embodied the Effort at an early stage. At this point he needs to check that he is not navigating by his own 'Effort map'[7] with the attempted Effort merely overlaid.

When the actor is discovering the potential of the Effort, the action is carried through for the whole duration of the exploration of that Effort.

It is an unusual experience for the body to work solely on one movement quality for a length of time (staying with one Effort of Action Drive). The body has an inherent need to move after a certain time in order to shift muscular responsibility. It can be exciting to discover that the body also has an in-built boredom threshold. It craves new movement patterns. When the actor's body tells him it needs to change, it also tells him what it needs to change to. It may be craving an opposite Effort, or to make a lesser adjustment by switching an Element. He needs to know that resisting any change and fully committing to the Effort worked on will ultimately reward him with a versatile vocabulary.

---

[7] This refers to the Efforts he is most attuned to; the Efforts he uses habitually – called here 'his default setting'.

Default Setting

The intruding movement (other Effort) – the shift the actor craves – tells him about an idiosyncratic part of his expressive map. It tells him which Effort his body would rather be working in, that is, his habitual place of comfort in terms of Efforts. If he allows it to pervade his movement at this point, he denies the Effort on which he is working. This will stall his development of an ability to embody it. If he switches away from it to his habitual movement (Effort) – one of the ones to which he has a natural affinity – he will miss the opportunity to find a different, but equally clear, expressive manifestation with the Effort he had undertaken to explore. So, instead, the actor should allow a short pause to acknowledge the move he is aching to do. Each actor is different and yet the strength of his experience in response to this internal question may lead him to assume that everyone else has this same need. He may believe, for example, that, like him, everyone is longing to release into *Gliding* when undertaking *Dabbing* for an extended period. A different actor, however, may feel compelled to throw it away into *indirect* thereby releasing from *Dabbing* into *Flicking*.

When the actor connects with an Effort, the body consistently moves in one particular manner. This is not the norm for 'usual' human movement. Its embodiment may, therefore, look like madness; like a person who is not functioning well in the world. The actor raised on political correctness may therefore try to 'clean up' his movement. Rather than run away from this experience, the actor should explore and expand all his responses, no matter how 'mad' or unusual the resultant movement appears.

Clean Slate

It is part of the process that the body moving in certain ways provokes emotions and thoughts. However, each Effort should be approached openly, and an understanding of it developed through experience in the body rather than through labelling or assumption. If a label is pre-attached to an Effort, for instance, *Thrusting* as 'aggressive', it's potential is restricted. Each Effort for an actor can be a vehicle for any emotion or thought.

A Journey of One Effort of Action Drive

See Practical: *The Exploration of One Effort as an Example* (p. 220)

In order to follow the Effort journey, one Effort had to be chosen. *Floating* is the example selected simply because for those who engage in the Practicals, it is an Effort that is not too exhausting or muscularly challenging for most people to embody. Also, its *indirect* use of space constantly offers new places in which to be and so it is agreeable to explore continual *Floating* over an extended period of time. As a first Effort, *Floating* allows the actor to take as much time as he requires to fully embody each element combined.

Floating: Indirect/Light/Sustained

The more muscular Efforts are responded to favourably in a fast-paced, fact-dominated daily reality. The *light* ungraspable quality of *Floating* can, therefore, end up being viewed as belonging solely to the domain of the drug-induced state. In fact, the actor may find *Floating*, with its particular quality and potential within the human movement scape, even more surprising than other Efforts.

See Practical: *Using Stimuli* (p. 222)
See Practical: *Making Links* (p. 223)
See Practical: *Exploring Details and Choices* (p. 223)

The power that *Floating* possesses is not in force or push. It is in its endless mobility and ability to keep changing, as well as its immaculate perception of delicacy and sensuality.

   Relating examples and images to his exploration of the Effort may inspire the actor imaginatively and provoke a different experience. He may thereby gain a deeper understanding of his movement response as he embodies the Effort. For example, there is no fixed centre of gravity in *Floating*. The sequential travelling of the energy through the body, as well as the body through the space, never allows the weight to get fixed. The movement of a slow loris might be described as a voyage of lightness, and the creature itself as a specialist at shifting its centre of gravity. Referring to this observation, and other such examples, the actor can see them in the mind's eye when exploring different Efforts.

Floating Continuously Shifts

See Practical: *'The Knot'* (p. 223)

Floating moves on constantly, without breaking the journey up into bite size pieces. It never undoes a move as there is only ever one constant movement. To not move on would not be *Floating*, but would instead be 'wafting' or 'waving'. If the actor were to waft or wave, the movement ceases, and *Floating* would need to be reinstated.

   Indirectness perpetuates an ongoing motion that results in never doing the same movement twice. This adds to the sense of the continuum, of the *sustain*.

Once the actor starts moving in *Floating*, there can only be one movement forever. It might be useful to envisage *sustain* as a continuous golden thread. *Sustain* produces one ceaseless existence through the length of the action (which in this case is also the length of the exploration). *Sustain*, felt as one move 'for the rest of his life', does not end or offer new beginnings. The actor can register his desire to stop or start, but should try and retain the ambition to keep developing the 'foreverness' which is the movement's essence.

No Plan

See Practical: *Understanding the Place of Control* (p. 224)
See Practical: *Making a Sound* (p. 224)

If *Floating* feels unsafe, to an actor, it is not because it is physically dangerous but because it doesn't have a plan: it has no gravitational pull and has a loss of focus. *Floating*, when fully discovered and embodied, makes a persuasive argument for the potential exquisiteness of *sustain*: it creates a positive imperative to keep going continually, to endlessly persevere. In this grouping, *indirect and lightness*, like incompetent allies, are unable to help with the eternal nature of *Floating*, so *sustain* is left to take the responsibility – to be the solo expert. Therefore, through extended exploration of *Floating*, specialism in this Element (*sustain*) becomes an immutable part of the actor's language, as each of the other Elements will also become when the entire scope of the Efforts has been embodied.

Quality of Lightness

For *Floating*, the *light* weightedness is what holds the way of being. The body has natural weight, but imagination can deny this. The actor controls the quality of *lightness* and, therefore, his natural body weight. The actor achieves total *Floating* when every part of his body, including his voice, is held within this *lightness* and he does not allow an interplay of Efforts to occur. If the actor, even momentarily, tries to hold onto the feeling of the *Float* because it is pleasurable, the quality 'dips' into an almost imperceptible *stronger* weightedness – changing the quality to a 'chewiness' of movement. A 'knowing' *Float* is no longer *Floating*, but has changed with the *strong* weight to become a *light Wring*. He has moved from total *Floating* to an interplay of Efforts. In this case the interplay created is recognizable as an expression of flirtation – an easier physical communication to achieve than *Floating*. True *Floating* has the potential to offer an audience the empathetic experience of the sensual.

A Survivor

See Practical: *Continued Existence in One Effort* (p. 224)

Daily life on the planet demands use of spatial *directness* and *strong* weight. Yet *Floating* can also be seen as a successful way of surviving. The *Floating* archetype is a survivor within the human condition: a survivor with continuous mobility for whom life just happens. He shifts and changes without the need for plans. Being able to move his way through the space (life) in this way enables the character to succeed.

    Floating is not a lazy Effort (as can be the perception). The continual movement and ongoing control of the *sustain* required for *Floating* means that the actor is fully occupied when embodying the Effort. True *Floating* takes great commitment, ongoing attention and energy, just like all the other Efforts.

Emotional range

The actor can challenge his range with an exploration of emotions that wouldn't usually be associated with a particular Effort quality: for example, he might choose anger with *Floating*. To do this, the actor has to commit himself fully to both the anger and the Effort of *Floating*. As he does this, he may discover potential vehicles for his anger in both the 'never endingness' of the *sustain*, and the 'all over the place' sense of the spatial indirectness. Of course, he has to work to keep *strong* weight away. However, his *lightness* means he must depend on the *sustain* and the *indirect* to carry his anger. Anger in *Floating* is not stable: it spirals and moves constantly; it is off-centre and it has the potential to be everywhere. Anger expressed in *Floating* infects the space around the actor. Every single part of his body and every particle of the room are affected. He and the anger are trapped in *sustain* and *lightness*. It is both captivating and exciting to watch – and also surprisingly real for such an extreme combination. This is a useful exploration because it means that *sustain* and *indirect* have to be taken seriously and the actor finds a way to use them and trust their capacity to deliver meaning.

Existing in the Effort

Once the actor is secure in his understanding of the Effort, he is able to take on the challenge of the physical, mental and imaginative constancy of wholly being that one Effort. This can either produce feelings of great comfort or entrapment. It is worth acknowledging that these opposing states can be experienced in the same vehicle (in this case, the same Effort) – this is, of course, the nature of the human condition. So, the *Floating* archetype may, for example, experience indulging in space and time; never wanting it to end (and it doesn't). Yet, equally, he may yearn for a new beginning; he may desire to stop (but, of course, he cannot).

The *Floating* archetype could find those who are *direct* absurd and full of restriction. He may see those who keep stopping and starting as utterly foolish: stopping means having to start again, and starting only to stop once more. This is madness to a specialist of the *sustain*. He might also find those who are *strong/heavy* vulgar, and so on.

Physical Orchestration

See Practical: *Doing the Process with Another Effort* (p. 225)
See Practical: *'Bottling' Exercise – Revealing an Internal Effort* (p. 225)

The Efforts offer the practice of relaying the emotional truth by allowing it to travel through different physical 'vehicles'. The task is to work on the vehicle (the Effort) whilst still retaining the truth of the emotion.

The actor needs to have understood and embodied the internal feelings and emotions that drive the surface (visible) emotions in any given situation (in the play). If anger is shown in a scene, for example, he may discover on closer examination that this anger is driven by hurt (which remains unseen). The externalized anger is necessary for the character not just to deal with the situation in the scene, but also to ensure that nobody sees the hurt that is inside; it hides it. Just as in real life, the character does not openly reveal the hurt that drives the anger. This unseen hurt, in reality, may be an internal 'mess' of *Wringing*, or perhaps even *Floating* (lost, although eloquent).

An audience is empowered by the experience of watching emotional turmoil being physically contained through the embodied Efforts the actor is playing. They clearly recognize the turmoil to be present after catching a glimpse of it in the character's action, and they understand it to be just that – a glimpse of something much greater.

If each Effort is given equal and specific investigation, the actor develops real clarity of action. He is then at liberty to play with this new language. He can combine Efforts; he can internalize them to affect his action; he can contain the Efforts within stillness whilst allowing them to colour the expression and communication of his words; he can use a journey of Efforts for both inner and outer readiness for rehearsal.

Most importantly, with its speciality in action, the Efforts of Action Drive offer a succinct, apposite and empowering mechanism for an actor to transform much of his physical 'way of being' to other characters.[8]

---

[8]For more advanced processes with the Efforts than this book has the scope to offer, see V. Ewan with K. Sagovsky, *Efforts in Action*, London: Bloomsbury Methuen Drama, forthcoming.

IN CONTEXT

An actor engaged in a long run of a play with emotional content may want to use different Efforts from those he habitually uses to communicate. He can channel the emotion differently whilst still remaining true to it, and therefore without depleting himself and his psyche over time.

Part One: Laban Efforts of Action Drive Practicals – The Efforts as a Language

Building the Efforts from WTS

When you have an understanding of the Efforts as made up of *light* or *strong* (Weight), *sudden* and *sustained* (Time) and *direct* and *indirect* (Space) – as well as the Effort names housed just vaguely in your memory – all you will ever need to work out and build the Efforts for yourself is the imprinted memory of the three words: Weight, Time and Space.

- Experience the combination of one Element from each of WTS in the body.
- Allow this physical experience to bring to mind Laban's word for the Effort in which you are engaged. For example, if you were to choose *light* (Weight), *sudden* (Time) and *direct* (Space), and your experience of this physical combination is your hand moving on and off a surface, it might be named 'tapping', 'patting' or 'knocking'. Any of these could bring to mind Laban's name for this Effort: *Dabbing*.
- Move your three chosen elements again but this time with this word in mind. Notice how it fits: the word *Dabbing* offers a clear *light*, *sudden* and *direct* physical articulation.
- To proceed to accessing each of the other seven Efforts, choose from Weight, Time or Space, and then change just one of the Elements each seach time to find a new Effort.

In the list below, the underlined element is the one which has changed in order to create a new combination, and therefore a different Effort.

light/<u>sudden</u>/direct = Dabbing   strong/<u>sudden</u>/indirect = Thrashing
light/sustained/<u>direct</u> = Gliding   strong/sustained/<u>indirect</u> = Wringing
light/<u>sustained</u>/indirect = Floating   strong/<u>sustained</u>/direct = Pressing
<u>light</u>/sudden/indirect = Flicking   <u>strong</u>/sudden/direct = Thrusting

Key point

See the Eight Efforts of Action Drive as a language and not a prescribed method of movement so that you don't remove yourself from your usual sense of 'reality'.

Exploring One Effort in Isolation

Each Effort is worked with through a series of stages. This practical offers the first two essential stages of the process.

Stage one: Working technically

Stage One is exploring, developing and collecting a movement vocabulary within the boundaries of each Effort. This provides you with the chance to work through any perceived problems with the Effort for yourself, using your own body and in your own time. You can stop and start, use a journal to log your responses and thoughts and try things out.

Experience a first encounter with the Effort, committing your whole body and self to it.

- Capture your initial personal response to the Effort and make a note of it; express your idea of the limitations that the quality has for you. Articulate both what you find 'interesting' and your felt response – it might be, perhaps, that you hated it. This will be useful information to retain and refer to as your understanding grows.

- Shift the emphasis of where the Effort movement is primarily located; let the movement travel through to different places in the body; employ isolated movements; use whole body movement, and so on.

- As soon as you can, acknowledge and understand the inherent and natural position, posture or movement that you will inevitably find yourself doing as you start to embody the Effort. This is its default 'signature'. It is important to notice this so that this signature doesn't hold you back or trap you.

- When you think you are fully engaged in physically expressing the Effort, check if you are glued to the spot or stuck on the floor. If this is the case, start to focus on how the Effort moves through the space. Keep the mindset of 'working it out'. Work on questions such as: how do you get to the floor? How do you get back to standing? How do you get to the edge of the room?

The *sustained* Efforts offer you a particular challenge as you travel across the space. In these Efforts, practise ways of travelling across the space, as much as possible without stepping; each step is a separate action so stepping, even in slow motion, is splitting the single action of crossing the space into lots of different physical actions. It is not, therefore, offering the experience of *sustain*.

- Find for yourself a reminder of the physical characteristics and/or quality of each Effort's movement. When the intensity of working on a particular Effort means you lose its quality, you can immediately recall it through that trigger. For example, if you are working on *Dabbing*, blinking provides a perfect reference to draw you back to the quality, as it is an innate movement which is always accessible.

- Try vocalizing a sound which replicates the Effort quality you are embodying. This is a way of you hearing your own movement. It also means that you will be able to hear when you stray away from that specific quality. If you are exploring a *light* Effort and the sound gets *heavy*, it means your movement has also become *heavy*. Through creating the sound, you can also be particularly aware of your breath choices within the quality.

Key point

Stay within the scope of the human condition: keep the mess of real life in your consciousness and simply be the living breathing organism that you are.

Stage two: Amoebic

▶ Floating Amoeba Obstacle Course.

- Imagine you are a single-celled living organism: you simply exist; you just 'are'. Have a sense of the amoeba existing successfully in its simple way of being and pre-dating and potentially outliving the human being.

- In this stage you exist continually in the Effort: you 'are' the Effort made up of three Motion Elements of WTS. You cannot come back to yourself as human to create a new phrase of action. The single-celled organism adheres only to the rules of its form, in this case the Effort.

- Preset an obstacle course – 'a world' for your amoeba – with sturdy tables and chairs (no sharp bits or hard corners). Discover how the amoeba as Effort moves in this extreme landscape. You will find it can go over/under/around/on top of/against/in and out of these obstacles.

- Allow yourself to vocalize the Effort you are embodying as you move through the world.

Key points

In undertaking this work you are embarking on a process of physical transformation – you will not look like 'you' as you express the Effort and you mustn't try to hold onto 'you'. You've got to find out what each Effort gives you and you can't predict what that is going to be. Existing in the Effort will give you the answer.

The Rules of Engagement are:

- The whole body gets to experience the Effort – every molecule. Feel a connection between the toes and the fingertips. Be aware of the outer extremities of your kinesphere.
- You attempt one action for the duration of the exploration.
- You must become the Effort.
- Ensure that you are not a victim of a state associated with the Effort, for example *Floating* as though you were drunk.
- You move across the world; you are never stuck on the spot. You are continually shifting. Your survival is tied up in how far you can travel. Holding this understanding as you work ensures that the Effort is productive, not static.

The Exploration of One Effort as an Example

 Floating.

Floating (light/sustained/indirect)

- Find a spot in the room.
- Focus on being still.
- Begin to shift the body into *indirect* slowly and carefully, and *sustain* this one movement.
- As there is only *light* weight in F*loat*, there is no influence of gravity. You may or may not remain upright; you can make the surface of a wall or the ceiling the same as the surface of the floor – it is possible to *Float* against them. Know that every surface has the same level of resistance to the weight of your body as you defy any sense of downwards gravitational pull.

Finding a way in: Imagining

- First, imagine there is no gravitational force. Then notice how this means there is no difference between up or down. Third, be aware of being in continuous movement. Don't imagine yourself as an astronaut though; it is important to fully invest just in the Effort alone. Combining these three imagined facts in your body as you move, let your movement inform you how you get to the floor and get up off it again (remembering always that the wall can be the same as the floor and vice versa).

Finding a way in: The eyes

- First, *Float* the eyes: keep the eyes open – you don't need to defocus but don't land your gaze on anything – just keep the eyes travelling. They are *light, sustained* and *indirect*. Allow the face to *Float* too, so that the expression is not fixed. Check that nothing in your face is reacting through tension, such as your eyebrows or your jaw. Keep these released. They don't need to participate at this stage (remember: roll the eyes, loosen the tongue and jaw).

- Now add the neck: *Float* the neck. This breaks the upright, direct channel from the skull/head to the mid- and lower spine. In tandem with the continuous movement of the eyes, it offers an immediate experience of *Floating*. Whilst doing this, try making a list or a plan. Notice how hard it is to think directly or plan. Reinstate the 'straight' line up through the spine. Notice how this instantaneously takes *Floating* away and returns directed thought.

- Allow the existence of responses triggered by the movement: feelings, sensations, wants, desires, difficulties or struggles. However, stay in the present tense (and thus within the *Float*). This means not stopping to react to your own experience or any of your responses.

- There is no plan to the journey as there is no movement in any particular direction. The body is off-centre. It is asymmetrical.

- Deal with the shifts you make to move through the *Float* in order to be always at a point of balance, or holding your balance. You move through these because in *sustain* you are always moving. There is nowhere to stop; there is no arrival.

- There may be a feeling of falling, but landing would involve *strong* weight, which is not an option in the *Float*. The *sustain* enables a continuum of falling: falling without landing. You need the feel of the *lightness* to counteract the inevitable and continual overbalancing that is happening to you through the actual force of gravity.

- Identify the default position for *Floating*. Note how *Floating* tends towards use of the mid-area of the space around you; how it is spacious, allowing peripheral movement but without the capacity for full stretch of the limbs.

- Also, note any particular movement related to other Efforts that is trying to intrude on the Effort you are doing (but don't let it). Ask yourself which particular Effort quality it is. Allow this discovery a moment of analysis before it is lost: you will never again have this new experience of identifying the Effort into which you are longing to relax with so compelling and clear a result. It can inform you about your affinity to particular Efforts – creating your personal Effort map.

Experiencing an Effort: *Floating*

Using stimuli

- Music
  You can use particular types of music as a stimulus for *Floating* (and other types for the other Efforts). Much choral music has a quality of *Float*, and certain sound effects may also evoke the Effort for you. Notice the sounds that provoke the varying sensations of each of the Factors. Stop using the music once you are en route to the quality of the Effort. This will not take long and you will be able to retain the sounds that help you connect to *Floating*. When other textures and qualities in the music start to invade your consciousness it is no longer useful.

- Images
  Create any imagined landscape that offers you what you need. For *Floating*, for example, you can imagine a landscape of visible air. Begin to move through the air without disturbing it. There is sensitivity within the *lightness* that comes when there is an acknowledgement of your influence on the space. Find how, when *Floating*, moving even a little this way or that affects and disperses a lot of air, creating draughts. Move among them. Think of clouds and how they move.

- Imagine moving through a cloud – but without reshaping, scattering or destroying it. You cannot move the particles of the cloud violently, or you will create a storm, which would be a different Effort quality. You are neither being 'you' or 'air'; you are being *'Floating'*.

Making Links

There will be certain exercises which you have previously encountered to which you can connect this work. These exercises may help you to locate a particular Effort, Motion Factor, or Element of a Motion Factor. In order to deepen your understanding of the *indirect* of *Floating*, for example, you might chose to connect this to exercises you have experienced that explored sequential movement or that allowed your body to spiral or track through space. (See Chapter 2, Practical: *Rolling,* Appendices: *Finding Flow from the Head; Contact Improvisation: Rolling Points.*)

Exploring Details and Choices

To work on particular ways or details of expressing an Effort quality you can find imaginative scenarios (or real-life examples) to aid you. For example, for *Floating* you might choose to work on experiencing an up-tempo *sustain* which can be a challenge:

- To work on this you could watch a wasp close up as it flies (being careful not to get stung). Follow it ceaselessly with your eyes and you will start to embody *sustain* at pace.

'The Knot'

This exercise is for the individual within the group. (Note: you have to be warm for this exercise.)

- The whole group joins hands to form a chain, which is then closed to form a circle. The whole group is now connected.

- The group begins to move in a slow *sustained* way, following the impulses of the entire group. Surrender your sense of direction and allow yourself to be moved in an *indirect* way. You must respond to the movement and direction, and not impose your own pathway.

- The group does not let go of each other's hands. The aim is to interweave yourself with the members of the group into a knot, whilst maintaining the control of *light* and *sustain*. You must hold your weight and balance as a fall would be a *sudden* move. Likewise, if the group goes too fast, the movement will become *sudden*.

- Let the movement continue until there is a natural stillness. At this moment the group can then begin to unwind the knot, as easily and softly as possible,

- Through being a part of this experience find out how spirals, together with turns and curves, solve the problem of undoing. Find how the body responds to the *indirect* movement as the knot unravels back out into the circle.

Understanding the Place of Control

If you feel as though the movement is 'out of control', this may be due to a cultural understanding that 'control' is spatial and inherently *direct*. This is the widespread and predictable understanding of control belonging to one particular Motion Factor (Space) and its Element (*direct*). However, being *indirect* does not necessarily equate to being out of control. In fact, there is no instruction regarding control (or lack of control) within the inherent structure of *Floating*.

- You can be a 'control freak' with *Floating* – the expression of control is simply placed somewhere other than in the Space Element. It can be placed in the *lightness*; it can be placed in the *sustain*.

- As you are *Floating*, the *sustain* becomes impossible to break up; *lightness* is all there is, and *indirect* becomes the 'thing' to play. Let yourself have real freedom in the space where the same moment is never experienced twice. Secure in the constancy of both the *lightness* and the *sustain*, begin to understand their potential to create for you a trapped place, or a place of great comfort, or both.

Making a Sound

- Keep experimenting with vocalizing a sound which replicates the Effort quality.

- Hear what your body is doing echoed in your voice. For *Floating* there may only be a sense of sound coming from inside your body, but still make the quality of your movement audible to you even though the sound might be so light it is inaudible to anyone else.

- Regulate it: it will allow you to detect, for example, any stops in the *sustain* or any *heaviness/strength* in the weight.

Continued Existence in One Effort

Continue to explore embodying the one Effort. As you do this, carry on experimenting. For example, in *Floating*, try to:

- Place the attention in different body parts to make the Effort easier.

There is no reason why your feet can't be as *light* as your hands or fingers; even if this is physically difficult, use your imagination to make this possible.

- Bring your attention to the *sustain*. Because its nature is eternal, you have lots of time to solve the problem of keeping in *sustain*; there is nothing therefore to stop your exploration of it or your continuing focus on maintaining the *sustain*.

- Gradually come to stillness and stand. Internalize the feeling of the movement and acknowledge where it resides in your body. Is it in your head? Perhaps it is in your thoughts? Is it changing locations? How does the movement actually make you feel?

Doing the Process with Another Effort

Once you have done one journey, in this case *Floating*, you know the mass of information that it can offer you. You are aware of its ways, modes and challenges and how your body can meet these and work safely with them.

- Go back to the list of the Efforts to choose one to work with by deciding which one Element you may want to shift. Or, you might wish to change all three Elements: in this case you would explore all the opposite elements to those in *Floating* (*strong/sudden/direct = Thrusting*).

- Give yourself time to go back to *Exploring One Effort in Isolation,* and begin work on the first stage (*working technically*), knowing that there is a second stage (*amoebic*) also provided.

- From your physical experience of the different stages in the example of *Floating*, develop your own journey, framework and inspiration for any of the other Efforts with which you chose to work. This work is an embodied exploration, so each Effort requires two particular commodities: commitment and time.

The following is an example of an exercise using the Efforts once you have explored all eight individually and fully.

'Bottling' Exercise – Revealing an Internal Effort

This text-based exercise is designed to be used as a pre-rehearsal warm-up. However, it is worth doing out of context so that you can understand how to use it for yourself. It lets you uncover the internal reality (the unseen) that drives the outer expression. You put in place a physical memory of the character's emotional Effort map that may come to surface within the play; or may just fuel a need for the outer movement to be stronger in order to suppress the emotion that is trying to surface.

Caution is required here to stop you going up a blind alley:

A note on frustration as expression

'Frustration' as expression, can demand substantial energy and feel tangible, powerful and overwhelming to an actor. You might therefore think of it and treat it as an emotion. However, frustration is not an emotion: frustration is the barrier between emotions and the world. It is the interface between the inner self and outer circumstances. It is an imposed action that simultaneously blocks, thwarts and upsets.[9] Frustration can only exist for you as the actor if you know what it is that you are frustrating – what it is that is being blocked or thwarted. It needs to be looked behind, beneath or inside in order to perceive it doing its job of holding back feelings. In other words, frustration should neither be perceived nor 'done' as a feeling in itself. Once the feelings have been discovered, there is then something to frustrate.

The *Bottling Exercise* is so-called as it is concerned with a character's 'bottled' emotions: the feelings which exist inside himself.

- Place yourself in the space with the idea of an imaginary audience, so that you have a front (a public space) and a back (a private space).

- When you are facing the front, be your character and do all that your character does: you are in the world of the play and communicating with text.

It is important to note that the character's personality and habitual movement are not the focus of this exercise, so don't focus on this when you are facing front. Instead, think back and connect to the exercise on stilling the outer body (see Chapter 3, Practical: *Outer Stillness on Text*).

- If it helps, to begin with you can use *Glide* as the character's allowed external Effort when facing front – this choice can be justified as the Effort the character aspires to be.

- When you are facing the back, imagine yourself as invisible and that your character's raw emotion, which is usually kept bottled, is allowed out to play.

---

[9] For further definition or thesaurus, see Oxford Dictionary Thesaurus and Wordpower Guide, Oxford University Press, 2001, p. 514.

- Choose a speech that has an emotional journey and in which the motivation and intention for the speech are clear. (Shakespearean text offers natural rhythms or patterns of human behaviour as governed by both thought and emotion, so is dependably good for this exercise).

- Identify the possible internal emotions/feelings present in the speech from the clues offered by the text.

- Choose one of these on which to work.

- Identify the moment when this inner emotion starts telling you it is there: it is quite often mid-sentence, just before its overt appearance in the text. Mark this point in the text with the emotion/feeling. Commit to a choice even if you are uncertain of where it begins. You will only know if it is the right choice after you have committed yourself to it: if it feels wrong in action, change to another starting point (and so on repeatedly) until you arrive at the point that feels 'right'.

- Select an Effort for this emotion/feeling.

- Move into the working space.

- Start your text; be clear, committed and loud.

- When you get to the moment that you marked in the text, turn to face the back. When you are facing the back, there is no outer person (character persona) to hide your emotion. Embody the Effort fully with sound; you can use words as long as they are disconnected from sense – no sentences; you are in a fully amoebic emotional state. Let the Effort of the internal emotion reveal its power in you. Make sure your body is liberated from any reminders of being the character – do not take any postures or positions that are habitual for your character. You can be on the floor, upside down – all over the place – as long as you don't ever face the front.

- Once you have fully embodied this inner-emotion Effort state, 'bottle it': hide it inside you as you turn round to the front, without either indulging in this moment or rushing. If it helps, physicalize the bottling: imagine the movement rushing in through the top of your head and down into your belly.

- Straight away – with no hesitation – grapple with the scene, using your permitted externalized Effort (visible emotion). While the exercise is new to you, use *Gliding* or attempt stillness to prevent the inner Effort (hidden emotion) from emerging. Let the words channel the full effect of the inner–outer Effort conflict, rather than playing your interpretation of them. Let the words do their job of working to civilize and make sense of what you are feeling inside.

- You may want to do the exercise again, but be aware that there will be a point when it is embedded in the map of this text and that you can trust it to your body memory.
- Do the process again, choosing a different point in the text to explore and map in another inner emotion/Effort, and so on.

Key points

This exercise may mean that some emotions present within the text are not explored – and that is okay. The text will then do its work and – if it is a good text – tiny moments of the chosen Effort will surface when that feeling is experienced. These are unworked moments that reveal glimmers of the suppressed interior.

Give yourself this opportunity not to demonstrate these emotions, but to work with the words of the text; to invest in them and understand why the character chooses these particular words.

- In order for you to realize that you are not tied to your personal Effort map on emotion, try the exercise with a different Effort on the same inner emotion.

IN CONTEXT: BOTTLING EXERCISE

The bottling exercise can offer dynamic potential, particularly to long emotional passages of text. It reveals movement that, in the play, is seen only as the tip of an iceberg. The facing-the-back part of this exercise is your private experience as much as it is the character's. What is revealed to the front is the aspect that is ultimately worked on and consolidated in the rehearsal with the director.

Part Two: Advanced Practice – Physical Codes and their Keys[10]

The terms 'Code' and 'Key' are used in this context to denote specific aspects of physical behaviour. The work is developed in the studio to enable the actor

---

[10] Ewan's process of work in the studio with the actors. The examples are drawn from Ewan's work as specialist movement coach.

to make confident and appropriate physical choices for his character. It should be an enjoyable process: when it becomes a chore, it's time to stop for a while.

'Live' Research Equals 'Live' Imagination

It is becoming ever easier to access visual information via the internet. The actor may therefore be tempted to make this his only source of research, prioritizing it over other sources that seem less familiar and less accessible. In doing this, however, the actor risks losing practice at – and therefore confidence in obtaining and working with live observation. Keeping sizeable portions of the research 'live' engages the actor's 'live' imagination. It is also an effective way of harnessing subconscious information for translation into character.

What is a Code?

Codes can be taken to mean 'states of being' that are instantly communicated through physical expression, such as the code of 'old age', the code of 'being drunk', the code of 'female' or the code of 'male'. Big codes can be broken down into smaller ones (the code of 'old age, walking', the code of 'old age, eating', etc.). The code is apparent, even when the character is at rest.

What is a Key?

Keys access codes. For example, a key to access the code of 'old age' might be '*bound* energy' or 'doing one thing at a time', or 'maintaining the centre of gravity'.

When the character is at rest, a key might be hidden; it becomes apparent in action. The actor may be given the keys to each code in advance, or he may work them out for himself through trial and error.

The same key may apply to different codes. For example, the code of 'old age' and the code of 'illness' can both be accessed by the key of '*bound* energy'.

Two Types of Code to Consider

Social codes

A social code refers to etiquette or manners specific to a given cultural and historical period; these place the character in 'the world of the play'. For example, an actor in a 1950s' drawing room comedy might decide his character would always stand up when a woman enters the room. The actor understands that if he is in a period drama, he must observe the social code.

Physical codes

Physical codes ('old age'; 'health'; 'under the influence of drugs/alcohol/spells/ curses', and so on) are not generally worked on in as much detail as period-specific social codes, yet they also require expert navigation. This chapter, therefore, focuses on the distinct physical codes of 'old age' (just one part of the age spectrum) and of 'being drunk' (a stage of 'drunkenness') and their realization as examples of physical codes. From working with these examples, the actor can then try out the process for any other code he may be working on later including social codes.

Let's say a 23-year-old actor-in-training is working on the character of Firs, from Chekhov's play *The Cherry Orchard*. Firs is Russian, a servant, he is 87 years old and was born in the 1800s. The actor who takes on this character is faced with at least six codes of: culture, class, age, period, etiquette and health. There is, however, a way through this complexity.

Deciding Which Codes: Initial Decisions

See Practical: *Identifying and Working on the Codes for your Character* (p. 235)

Period, culture and class are all social codes. They belong to 'the world of the play' and a lot of information regarding them will be embedded in the text. The actor can also look to the art, literature, music and dance of the period as sources for his own research. Particular aspects of a social code (such as how to bow in the manner of a serf-turned-servant; the etiquette of the samovar, and so on) are likely to be worked on in rehearsal by a specialist movement coach together with the director because they belong so strongly to the world of the play.

The physical codes although informed by, do not belong to history or the world of the play – they can be considered as universal. For instance, old age and ill health are the physical codes governing the character of Firs. It means that the actor's research can be taken from the world around him. He can go out armed with the relevant information supplied by the text to observe, test out his reasoning and select the keys that best reveal the codes and will allow him to embody these codes. Reasoning might supply him with old age = experience, where experience is shorthand for a full practised life and old age = deterioration a physically progressive aspect of old age.

Discovering the Keys of the Code

The actor needs to consider the following question: which keys are true, but unhelpful to the performance (for example, infirmity, resulting in an extremely shaky, quiet voice)? The actor may see someone who looks similar to how he envisages Firs. At first glance, that person offers him the idea of 'slow motion' (Aha! A key!). However, as the actor continues to watch, it doesn't take him long to realize that the most useful key is not 'slow motion'. In fact, the impression of slowness comes from the old person economizing his energy by performing only one action at a time. So the most useful key to the code of 'old age' in this instance is actually 'one thing at a time'.

Finding the Keys of a Code using BWTS

See Practical: *Observing the Code and the Keys in Action* (p. 236)

Let's say the actor is cast as Stephano, the drunken butler in Shakespeare's *The Tempest*. The actor may not have experienced drunkenness, or he may not be able to recall the experience in sufficient detail. He may hold only an image of 'being drunk' as chaotically vague. Let's say he therefore selects 'distortion' as a possible key and goes out to observe with this key in mind.

Analyse … look … analyse …

Watching a drunk man in the street, the actor wonders why passers-by are not concerned for their safety. After all, the drunk man is swearing, shouting and generally displaying a great deal of anger. The anger is real. A sober man acting in this way would pose a threat. So why is this not threatening?

He uses BWTS to investigate the key of 'distortion'. He sees there is distortion to the drunk man's breathing, an off-centred weight and a blurring of his sense of time. However, it is the drunk's distorted use of the space that offers most information. The actor realizes that the drunk does not pose a threat to anyone else because he only inhabits personal space, never general space. All the boxes have been ticked; so one key to the code of 'being drunk' is indeed 'distortion'.

Applying Each Key One by One to Actions

See Practical: *Try the Keys on Your Own Body* (p. 237)
See Practical: *Give the Keys to Your Character* (p. 237)

The actor, back in the studio, has his notes and his memories from observation. Now he needs to put his ideas to the test in the studio by physically embodying the codes on which he is working (in this case 'old age' and 'being drunk'). A key is best explored without other character information in place: if it is a universal key, then the actor can apply it with confidence to any character. Practical experience will show what is universally true and what is not.

The actor creates a simple studio set-up that reflects real life and uses this same set-up for each code. It may include, for example, a chair, a table, a pencil and paper, a jug of water and a cup. He uses common actions that can be observed happening in the real world. In this way he will notice that different codes dictate different ways of using objects. As the actor starts to explore, for instance, other codes of age with the same object, in this case, the chair, he may discover perhaps that a child explores under the chair and hardly sits on it at all, while the drunk slides off it without noticing. This sharpens the actor's understanding and he begins to develop a diverse collection of ways of being.

The Action Itself Does Not Denote the Code

The action of falling off a chair does not equate to being drunk; nor does slurred speech. There are many reasons why a sober person might fall off a chair, or have poor diction.

It is necessary to use the key to test out each action of the character. For instance, if he is dancing to show his character is drunk, the key of 'distortion' needs to be applied to the action of dancing: 'distortion of space' might be dancing with the wrong person, or with a pillar (while other aspects of the action remain normal). 'Distortion of time' could mean being just off the beat, with everything else being normal. 'Distortion of weight' might mean dancing too heavily, with everything else being normal. The actor may not need to test every aspect of 'distortion', but if he does, each should be introduced separately, one after the other, to avoid confusing the work. This creates a sharply-focused and physically specific drunk.

Trust the Key

See Practical: *Restricting the Key to a Single Body Part* (p. 238)
See Practical: *Trusting the Key (More than Your Idea of It)* (p. 239)
See Practical: *Finding and Using an Actual Experience For a Key* (p. 242)

Some keys sound exciting and others sound dull. It is often the duller sounding ones that deliver exciting results.

For the code of 'old age', for example, the actor can apply the key of 'one thing at a time' to some simple actions: sitting, getting up and standing. He can then add to this the more physically passive actions, such as thinking, looking and listening, treating them in exactly the same way. First, the actor needs to locate the place within his body for each activity: for example, for thinking, the plan happens in the brain – concentration is on planning a move which means the muscles in the body are not yet engaged. Each action is in the present tense. Again, it sharpens up the physical choices of the actor and becomes not just recognizable but captivating: it tells us something about old age.

As he becomes more confident and understands this process better, the actor can gradually add more keys. He always explores each key individually and then chooses which to put together. Several keys operating at the same time offer rich possibilities. Too many, however, and the process becomes confusing for performer and spectator. The actor should be able to judge the difference between complexity and chaos. He must bear in mind that keys enable the codes to exist as structure for the performance – they should not become the performance.

Using the Key to See More

Asking questions about the code that is being observed refines the eye's ability to look for physical detail.

In exploring 'experience' as a key of 'old age', for example, the actor might observe that sitting on a chair as an old person is just sitting on a chair: the old person, working with his particular body, is an expert at sitting efficiently. His way of sitting demonstrates the realization, gained from a 'lifetime's experience', that all shifting about on the seat leads to nothing. He knows how to get into a comfortable position and moves only when he has to. By observing through the framing lens of the key of 'experience', the actor may also discover for instance that the character does not use his legs once he is sitting down; his legs and feet are not occupied – they are empty.

Figure 7.1 Detail of mature couple sitting on sofa wearing slippers © Vladimir Godnik/Getty Images.

It takes courage for an actor to do nothing, but this is truthful and again can be captivating to watch.

Using Contradictory Keys in the Same Code

See Practical: *Using a Scale* (p. 239)

By identifying two contradictory keys, the actor creates a natural dynamic tension between each as they fight to co-exist. The actor might decide that the code of 'old age' contains the key of 'experience' and also the key of 'deterioration'. How do these keys contradict each other? It may be, for example, that the old man knows how to sit economically, but his left hip doesn't work properly, so he ends up sitting down in what is an efficient yet roundabout way. The tension between what 'experience' would like to do and what 'deterioration' dictates must be done provides rich material for understanding the character and his attitude to the world.

Conflict is Good

See Practical: *Opposing a Key* (p. 241)

It may be that evidence from the text shows a ready-made contradiction. For example, an old character may be relatively immobile but have a bubbly personality and a youthful outlook. The actor might therefore choose physically to articulate the key of 'deterioration' using 'fixed points' and then work simultaneously with 'experience' as his other key. 'Experience' means that the old person is highly adept at handling such 'fixed points', allowing the 'experience' (long-standing habit) of happiness to be expressed in a great range of movement in all the areas that are not fixed. This means the actor can simultaneously express a youthful personality without losing the expression of a body affected by old age. What seems contradictory in fact works in tandem.

An Actor Often Has to Think Laterally

Once a code is unpicked and the actor fully understands its meaning, he can use it more imaginatively. If the actor is cast as a young yet battle-worn soldier, for example, he may find that keys governing 'old age' help him in playing someone who has accumulated a lot of hard experiences in a short timespan. This character's body may therefore follow the code of someone significantly older. The actor is embodying the powerful idea of 'an old man in a young man's body'.

Back to Codes

In the same way that an actor can have contradictory keys, he can also utilize contradictory or conflicting codes. Again, it is a positive advantage to locate the conflict: the conflict is often the clarifying factor in expressing character accurately and specifically. For example, an actor playing a 1950s English male who is governed by '1950s etiquette' (social code) would stand up every time a female enters the room. He might then have to add in 'being drunk' (physical code). He is extremely drunk but still bound by the expected etiquette of standing for a woman. His ability to do so is now affected. Rather than one code eradicating the other, the two codes exist together, one code fights with and challenges the drunk's ability to abide by the other. As many times as the actor has to stand up, he does so working with his chosen keys to 'being drunk' ('distortion', and so on). He simultaneously embodies both codes, giving physical 'texture' and specificity to the character.

If the actor has made a mistake in his choices of keys or combination of codes, he will discover this when exploring actions. He should give himself time to experiment and shift his choices until he finds the arrangement that is most helpful to his embodiment of his character.

An actor could give a performance that holds sublime and exquisite observation, but it means nothing if he doesn't place it in his body and obey it as a rule. If it slips for even a moment, an audience picks it up and can lose trust and belief in his whole performance.

Keys and codes may appear to come and go according to the given circumstances but they are always present. Before the storm, Shakespeare's King Lear may feel and act 'young', but the circumstances of the storm – the force of nature pummeling his body – suddenly reveal his true age. The keys of the 'old age' code which were in place at the beginning of the play (however subtly) suddenly become more apparent to the audience.

Setting Tasks for the Character

Once the actor has determined which keys and codes serve his character most effectively, he can give himself time in rehearsal to take his character into different situations. This gives him time to discover, for example, his rhythm or how certain character traits live in his body. He carries the character within him. Use of improvisation, perhaps related to the situations in the play, helps to generate material. The actor might also choose to do one or two of his own daily tasks in character (combing his hair, cooking a meal, and so on).

Part Two: Advanced Practice – Physical Codes and Their Keys: Practicals

Identifying and Working on the Codes for Your Character

- Work out why your character is that character and how he serves the play.

- Check through who, what, where, why and when? (See Chapter 6.)

- Translate negatives: the playwright's language may hold within it a personal viewpoint, which is unhelpful, for example 'disgusting drunk'. You cannot play a negative. Translate it or disregard it.

- Decide which codes you are going to work on: the codes your character is influenced by that clearly offer something to your ability truthfully to embody the part.

- Have you included looking at the social codes of culture: morals, behaviour, style or religious practice; and at professional, class, or gender relationships, and so on?

- Have you included looking at physical codes of age, disability, illness, gender, strength, being under the influence of drugs, alcohol, curses or spells, and so on?

You should still make a note of any codes that are assumed to be within your own personal physical make-up, even if they are the reason you were cast in a part. You may still want to sharpen these up for yourself. If, for example, you are a fresh-out-of-college actor playing a teenager, recognize that 'teenager' is as strong an age-code as 'old'. It should, therefore, be identified, examined and played with (or against) as part of the character's make-up, in just the same way as if you were playing an old person who is decades away from you in terms of age.

- From the character description and text, interrogate any words that offer you something about the nature and the logic of the code. Include words related to the code that come into your mind after reading the script.

- From this, work out the uncompromising aspects of the code within this context and from this, decide on a key, or keys, that fits the code. Keep it simple.

- Research the code: create a bank of facts and artistic impressions as a resource – pictures, sketches, quotes, voice-recordings, bits of conversation, character profiles, and so on.

Observing the Code and the Keys in Action

- Go into the real world and find someone of this code engaged in a common action who you can observe.

- Observe this person and look in his action for any key/s with which you have decided to work.

- Break down what you are looking at: look at part of the action, or a section of the body.

- Build a picture of what you are seeing using the observation questions you have accumulated: questions on the world of the play; on interrelationships with other characters, including gaze, touch, breath; on the application of WTS; and on BBWSWRB, and so on. (See Chapter 4, 'Observation and Translation'.)

- Go back to looking with your key in mind and if necessary refine your key through what you have discovered through this observation.

- You may discover other keys. You will always know instinctively when the key is 'right' – either when you do it or see it – because your body understands innately. Let it share its knowledge with you.

Try the Keys on Your Own Body

- Back in the studio, create a landscape in which to play, using, for example, some upturned chairs or a low table to climb over, a chair to sit on, some objects to pick up such as a cup and saucer, pen and paper, and so on. Now play using the key(s).

- Take care not to add too many keys or codes to your actions, especially early in your rehearsal. You will have to exercise your artistic judgement – if you feel a single movement has so many keys attached to it that you don't know how to move, then you have added too many!

- Go out in the real world again and observe the keys in other people to make sure you have made the right decision.

Give the Keys to Your Character

- Trust and give them to your character to deal with. Your body memory will have retained the exploration you have done, meaning that your character has a created physicality with its codes and keys embedded within it.

Key points

You always need to know and work on the character's physical traits (rhythm, backbone, body parts leading, and so on) in addition to the relevant code/s. Do not fall into the trap of simply making the code the character, unless he is meant to be the archetype of the code, for example 'the Drunk', 'the Hero', and so on.

Experiencing Some Keys for Yourself

The following keys are offered as examples for you to try and test out, so that you can develop trust in the process. Several keys are offered for each code so that you can experience how the method works. The process will work equally well for any other code.

When testing the keys and trying them out physically, do not add any additional acting.

Restricting the Key to a Single Body Part

This is an example of locating the key in one single area or even a single body part.

Code: Being Drunk.
Key: 'Distortion' – Distortion of Information in a Single Body Part (everything else is normal).

Choose one part of the body that doesn't do as it is told. As an example:

- Walk.
- Imagine that the brain cannot reach one of your legs, creating an 'emptier' body part.
- So, the left leg walks normally but when the right leg walks forward it lands a tiny amount to the right (toes facing forward). It keeps doing this on every step.
- Keep walking with the right leg veering to the right. The brain meanwhile thinks it is walking straight forward.
- Keep it subtle.
- Arrive further over to the right of the room than you were aiming.
- Do not be aware of that until you arrive, because as you concentrate on your destination it is just your right leg that is distorting the action.
- Look for this key next time you observe people who are very drunk.

Trusting the Key in the Body (More than Your Idea of It)

This exploration involves the thought-process and so can quickly be lost in a wash of 'acting drunk'. It is essential therefore to keep the key in charge.

Code: Being Drunk.
Key: 'Distortion' – Distortion of Focus and Concentration (everything else is normal).

Note that 'distortion' does not mean diminishment; it can be a magnification, as in this example in which concentration and focus are distorted by becoming excessively heightened.

- Take a cigarette out of a packet.
- You do not manage it, because focus and concentration are distorted.
- See if you can carry this action through to completion – no matter how long it takes – with delicacy, care and excessive attention.

Another example

- Peel a cardboard beer mat with an extreme (distorted) amount of focus and concentration, as though it is a normal thing to do in public. You have not regressed in age, or lost your intelligence. It is just an exaggeration of focus and concentration; a mismatch of the level required of these and the action.
- Now distort – overwork – a personality trait, such as placing the beer mat down being overly proud of doing so, or carrying out the action overly professionally.
- Look for this key ('distortion') next time you observe people who are very drunk.

Using a Scale

Work here with Flow as a scale: child with *free* energy through to old person with *bound* energy.

Code: Old Age (65–110 years).
Key: 'Experience' and 'Deterioration' – *Bound* energy

In the world

- Observe one end of the scale: *free* energy in children as an unrestricted flow of energy.

- Observe the other end of the scale: *bound* energy in older people – as a restricted flow of energy. Look particularly at active old people so that you can differentiate between the potentially slow *tempo* of the movement and *bound* energy. In order for you to be able to translate and embody this, you will need to have identified a wide spectrum of movement.

Back in the studio

Bound energy: imagine this to be contained experience and conservation of energy. Don't muddle it with restricted or small movement; it is just the energy that is *bound* or constrained. The movement can be expansive, but it is as though cellophane is wrapped around the energy flow, gently binding the action. It is not the same thing as tension. Physically try both of the following:

- Do a warm-up swing as you would do it normally.

- Now do it with *free* energy: imagine the skin all over your body is a water sprinkler and, as you move, your 'energy' is sprayed everywhere.

- Now do it again but with *bound* energy: imagine cellophane all over your body gently preventing the energy from escaping.

- Check: have you tensed up? Have you restricted your movement vocabulary? Are you pulling faces? Have you slowed down? Have you adopted strange 'old-person' idiosyncrasies?

Bound energy, with regard to age, has to do with the ageing of a body part (it can also develop from previous stress to a body part). In old age, you can't avoid *bound* energy:

- Practise doing a wide range of simple actions whilst maintaining *bound* energy. Include your face but try not to add other 'old' affectations; lip-smacking, or humming an old war tune, for instance, are not going to help you.

- Find out about what *bound* energy gives you.

IN CONTEXT: PRE-PERFORMANCE PREPARATION

If you can see *bound* and *free* as qualities, you can better observe your own expressive use of them. As you get older and *bound* energy inevitably starts to be part of your physical make-up, you can incorporate something of *free* energy into your performance preparation to ensure that your own 'performance energy' can reach the audience.

Opposing a Key

This is an example of identifying physicality that can exist in opposition to the key. Here, you put the key in place knowing it is to be strictly maintained, so that it works against the something you have identified as being in opposition. In this example your key opposes the personality which by the same token defines it.

Code: Old Age (65–110 years).
Key: 'Experience and Deterioration' – Fixed points with youthful movement

In the real world

- Observe several old people. Look for fixed points in their postures and in their movement. Choose those that appeal to you. Keep the choice very precise. It is not 'his back' or 'his leg' which is fixed and restricts his action but one specific vertebra or one joint or muscle.

- A 'fixed point' is not necessarily a part that physiologically doesn't move, but a point that the person never moves or moves rarely. Take on a fixed point that is an expression of both 'experience' and 'deterioration'.

- Decide for yourself the why; the reason this part of the body has become a fixed point. It doesn't have to be the reason you identified in the person you observed.

- Make this point in the body fused and completely immobile.

IN CONTEXT: USE OF BODY MEMORY

In connection with this particular example of fixed points, if you have had an injury in the past, you might easily recall your reluctance to move that joint or muscle. Memory of what this felt like can enable you to use this as a location of a fixed point if you are ever doing a character that has aged or has an injury or physical disability.

In the studio

This exercise cannot be hurried. Embodied fixed points create a complex living posture. The fixed points enable you to work on the character who is dealing with living in this body. By fighting to move with fixed points rather than playing what you might think of as 'old age' and displaying the fixed points, the actor achieves realistic embodiment of the old age code.

- Find a clear space in which to work.

- Remember: embody chosen fixed points one at a time, only adding a new one when you have mastered the previous one.

- So, starting with just one: put a piece of sticky tape there – it will help you locate and feel it. Work against it as you execute a variety of actions and transitions, such as running, getting down to sit on the floor, getting up from the floor, opening a door, carrying something, and so on. Include abstract movement. Move enough so that you can trust the fixed point to be there without thinking about it.

- Then add another fixed point and repeat the above exploration until you can move without needing to think of either fixed point in order to maintain it.

- Keep adding fixed points until the age required is reached. Increase the number of fixed points with increasing age.

- Now try both the keys offered here: fixed points and *bound* energy together.

- Look for these keys in action next time you observe old people.

Finding and Using an Actual Experience for a Key

This is part of a deep-sea diving ear test and offers a sense of distorted balance:

Code: 'Being Drunk'.
Key: 'Distortion' – Distortion of balance (everything else is normal).

- Put one foot in front of the other (in line) and slightly bend your knees. Close your eyes. Concentrate on being still. Be aware that what you are doing involves high concentration on a small task. What someone sees when watching this is not the wobble but the controlling of the wobble.

- Now try recreating this sensation for yourself without your feet in line or your eyes closed. Adjust your weight slightly to create a problem for yourself and then work against this. Do not think about wobbling – focus on working against the wobble; hiding the wobble.

- Understand this exercise now as a key of 'distortion of balance' and try translating it to and experiencing it in other body parts. Identify where to put the experience in different postures: sitting, standing, and so on.

- Look for this key in action next time you observe people who are very drunk.

Making Codes and Keys Work for You

Continue to practice observing and finding codes and keys within real people's movement. Keep formulating then verbalising what the codes and their associated keys which you are observing might be called. You don't need to have a reason to do this. The more you are accustomed to observing, articulating, translating and embodying in this way, the greater your capacity will be to unlock transformative physical expression when you are undertaking a specific character.

- Try returning to all the exercises above but work with a different set of codes and keys.

9
PERSONAL SAFETY IN MOVEMENT

OVERVIEW

Personal safety in movement is about the actor's relationship with his body in class, rehearsal and production, and extends beyond purely physical concerns to ethical attitudes and behaviour. Clear boundaries and roles are therefore essential. Reckless spontaneity, being under prepared and failure to 'think through' in both practical and ethical terms can lead to irreversible damage.

The Body as Instrument

'Working from self' is a potentially confusing term that crops up all the time. It is (mis)used within the industry as a rationale for casting-to-type. But which one of any number of selves does this enigmatic phrase refer to? For Stanislavski, 'playing from self'[1] meant the engagement of an actor's subconscious mind as a means of breathing life into a performance. Knowing himself can help the actor access and shape what 'belongs' to him. This knowledge can then be conveyed by the body-as-instrument and put to its most expressive use.

The actor's body cannot be seen solely as an instrument, but it is a common and helpful simile for understanding the relationship with self. The musician's relationship with his instrument is straightforward: it is separate from him – he can put it in a box for safe-keeping at the end of the working day; he learns its individual nuances and specialisms; he is able to appreciate and nurture the

---

[1] See C. Stanislavski, *An Actor Prepares*, London: Methuen Drama, 2008.

instrument's particular sounds and to develop its qualities openly. The musician speaks positively about his instrument.

The actor may or may not speak positively about his body, but it is nonetheless his means of expression.

Creating Your Own Warm-ups

See Practical: *Warm-up Principles* (p. 252)

There is no such thing as a single warm-up for all situations and all actors so each warm-up must be tailored to the situation and the individual.

The actor may invest in his own warm-up for audition, meeting, rehearsal or performance. He will have learned over time how best to warm up. In training as an actor he can maximize the opportunity of collecting the exercises that work for him and to practise the skills they offer so that he knows he can achieve a state of readiness. A warm-up can take place anywhere with any number of creative stimuli – it has no boundaries.

The body warms up again very quickly from any physical activity that has happened within that day. The more the actor can do at home, therefore, the better. When he enters into the pressure (or even chaos) of the rehearsal or audition environment, he will feel more in control as he reconnects with what he has calmly prepared elsewhere. There are situations that he will find himself in that demand a level of physical commitment.

The warm-up also reconnects him to himself as an actor[2] – essential if he is spending his time between jobs working, for example, as a waiter. Even ten minutes of taking himself seriously as a practising actor and preparing professionally will have a positive effect.

Fitness for Purpose

Keeping physically agile and fit for acting is an individually tailored, lifelong programme, which can only be done by the actor himself. Designing this from his creative response to the movement work that he has encountered, he may build in some ongoing tasks. For instance, in the same way that he learns a certain number of lines every week to keep in practice, he might revisit movement tasks and take on a new animal study, or go out and observe or play with a code in action.

He might include gentle exercise in the gym, swimming, jogging, hiking or cycling. There is a tendency to 'yo-yo': periods of high-work demands,

---

[2]See Wangh, S. *An Acrobat of the Heart,* Vintage Books, 2000 for an inspiring chapter on this topic.

followed by not having work. If as an actor he has experienced some form of body conditioning, for example, circuit training, either under supervision or on his own terms, he will have an understanding of his body as an actor's body and, therefore, will be in a place of control *vis-à-vis* his body. This is particularly important if, at some stage in his career, he is faced with a body coach or the demands of body sculpture.

Specific Safety Considerations in Actor Movement

An actor who has an increased awareness and an objective approach to dealing with the physical demands and the ethical[3] dilemmas these may sometimes produce, will understand that he must develop his own strategies for navigating the ethical pitfalls of his working environment.

Spotting an Unsafe Situation

Acting in a play, TV show or film often involves moments of physical risk, violence and intimacy: physical risk from falling about or chasing across obstacles; violence from a playful shove, tussle or shake, shouting aggressively in someone's face, a slap or a full-on fight; and intimacy ranging from the familiar touch of a friend, sibling or spouse to erotic touching, embracing, kissing, undressing, having sex or being raped. In each case there is a fine line between acting and reality (there is, for instance, a crucial difference between staged intimacy and actual intimacy). Staying on the right side of this line demands clarity, maturity and skill. Even a playful shove can become unsafe when fuelled with personal tension or the pressure and adrenalin of performance.

In drama schools, work is mainly actor-centred. In the professional arena, however, the process is almost always director-centred (the director requires the actor to serve his vision), or commercially-centred (the producer requires the actor to serve the market). There should be no presumption – by actor, movement coach or producer – that the director or producer will have a clear and effective code of ethical practice.

---

[3] 'Ethical' is used here to mean being principled, morally correct and honourable; in other words, 'doing the right thing' by yourself and others.

Staying Focused

See Practical: *Staying Focused*

There is a difference between exposing the body and revealing it. Locating the specific emphasis of intimacy or violence in a scene offers something to work with and adds depth to any physical action. Issues of sex or violence need not overwhelm the actor if he stays focused on the acting tasks; one of the first acting tasks is research.

Working within Scenes Containing Intimacy and Violence

See Practical: *Listening to Your Instinctive Feelings*

The most difficult movement task for the professional actor is likely to be the sex scene. These occur rarely in theatre but very frequently in screened media where exposure – in every sense – is likely to be greater. As society moves towards ever-higher expectation of sexual openness, the pressures on the actor increase. Physical intimacy, even when acted, can trigger very deep emotional reactions in performers. It should also be recognized that when acted intimacy or violence has not been worked through in a safe process, trauma may surface long after the event.

There are methods to tackle these difficulties. Some are to do with the way the rehearsal or performance environment is managed and, in the absence of industry guidelines,[4] they require commitment from the company or production team. Even though an actor may appear secure and happy with a situation, external boundaries and structures are still necessary to provide an agreed framework in which the work can exist and the actor is protected.

Looking to Fight Guidelines as a Parallel

See Practical: *Looking to Fight Guidelines* (p. 248)

Whilst general choreographic rules might be employed to create the actual choreography of a sexual or violent scene, these do not necessarily take into account the safety of the actor. Most actors have learned or will learn stage combat. When working with other actors on a fight scene there are clear

---

[4]The British union Equity sets out rules for auditions, but there seems to be little advice for a stage actor on dealing with these matters once employed.

boundaries. The tutor is qualified. There are agreed rules of safety in contact combat. This can be a useful template for negotiating moments of acted intimacy or aggression.

Say it in Words

See Practical: *Say it in Words* (p. 258)

The actor needs to be able to put into words requests and actions of a sensitive nature. As soon as he has done this once, he discovers how easy it is to bring these areas into the work, sharing the problem frankly and pragmatically within it. And he can then approach heightened moments by breaking down the action and verbalizing it.

Being Spontaneous, Creative *and* Safe

The actor may have to engage with many fleeting but extreme moments of action, which are nonetheless considered too minor to necessitate a fight director. Slapping someone or being slapped across the face is a common example; many actors have done this 'for real' or have allowed someone to do it to them 'for real'. It may be that the actor is left to prepare and craft these moments by himself; he is concerned that not doing it for real will spoil the spontaneity of the scene. It is, after all, 'only a slap' – it doesn't really hurt. Similarly the actor might give or receive a real shove across the room. Unguarded and unplanned, these seemingly simple moments of action can, however, lead to damage. Taking time with a fellow actor (and/or movement director) to establish boundaries around areas of concern not only allows greater control but in fact secures greater freedom and spontaneity of expression.

Trying out ideas that involve the actor throwing himself about requires thoughtful preparation. An actor need not silently put up with continual bruising. If the costume department is made aware of the situation, the problem may easily be solved with hidden padding. The moves can be changed, mats can be provided. There is always a creative solution.

It is Not about Body Parts

Imagine a female actor is cast as Franchesina in *The Dutch Courtesan* by John Marston. Her character is described in the following speech:

I will shew thee my creature: a pretty nimble eyd Dutch Tanakin; An honest soft-harted impropriation, a soft plupe, round cheekt froe, that has beauty inough for her vertue, vertue inough for a woman, and woman enough for any reasonable man in my knowledge.

The actor is to play a role written by a seventeenth-century male playwright in a twenty-first-century production. The director is a man of a generation whose idea of 'sexy' in this genre equates with the stock figure of the 'buxom wench'. However, the body shape of the actor in question is not 'buxom'. She cannot, therefore, externally fulfil the director's idea of her character being a 'buxom wench'. She is lost. Sticking to and searching for this image leads her to attempts at 'acting' buxom, but you cannot act a body part. She has not worked on this character the way she would on others because the body part is the focus. She must investigate such a character with the same rationale as she does other characters, focusing on movement and motivation. Trying to pursue the external stereotype in this situation can only lead to padding (offensive) or surgery (ludicrous).

So the challenge for the actor in playing Franchesina is to see through the layers of context and to investigate all facets of the character. Of course there is no need for padding or surgery; she can effectively manifest the Courtesan's powerful, tantalizing sexuality through her use of space and body language.

Open, Not Vulnerable[5]

The 'open body' is already a commonly used term and the ultimate goal in movement. Willingness, utter conviction and openness are amongst the main targets of actor training. Being available to discovery does not mean being sexually open, or open to unnecessary criticism or manipulation. The actor should be confident that he is able to be open without being made unduly vulnerable.

Transforming the Character and Not You

The acting profession is considerably affected, even compromised, by the fashions of the prevailing culture. The industry can demand of men and women a certain 'look': for example, an appearance of youth, muscular

---

[5]What is 'being open'? Allowing access, passage, or view; not closed, fastened, or restricted; exposed to view or attack; not covered or protected; frank and communicative; not finally settled; still admitting of debate; accessible, receptive, or available; admitting of; making possible; vulnerable or subject to. Thesaurus: candid, honest, forthcoming, forthright, direct, unreserved, plain-spoken, outspoken, free-spoken, up front. Vulnerable: susceptible, liable, exposed, and easy target for, at risk of. *Oxford Dictionary Thesaurus and Word Power Guide*, Oxford: Oxford University Press, 2001.

build, or extreme thinness. This pressure may be increased when taking on a lead role or aiming for high-profile roles within the industry and can lead to mental illness and body disorders. The industry is not pure; it is practical. The actor must accept that the industry is compromised. The level of personal compromise in response to industry pressures and expectations is, however, up to him. Some male actors take steroids to make themselves stronger, and some female actors starve themselves (and vice versa). Yet, how many are fully aware of the consequences? If body-shaping is taken to an extreme, it becomes apparent that a body and mind wracked by an eating disorder achieves shape change, but that the grip of the disorder is such that it prevents further transformation.

Is Starving Acting?

The choices an actor makes are always individual: he is self-employed and he does not set out to be a role model when he chooses to take on a part; he just gets on and does anything he thinks is right to meet the demands of expressing the character. There are respected actors who go to great physical extremes for a role: Hugh Jackman, for example, went on a dehydration diet to play the prisoner Valjean in *Les Misérables*; Christian Bale starved himself to play Reznik in *The Machinist*, and so on. The media, another deeply compromised industry, often hold up these actors as truly dedicated individuals and revel in the 'before-and-after' pictures. It is necessary for the actor to be alert to the way in which the media operates and the smoky glass through which it portrays reality. Such examples are presented as the actor's choice, and a strong one at that. Yet, who is to say whether this is a weakness or strength in his craft? It is also possible that it could be due to manipulation, or that extreme shape change is in fact being used as a substitute for acting. It may also be that the marketing departments have deliberately exaggerated the suffering of the actor in order to gain press coverage. Hollywood stars can afford specialist advice (although this does not always mean they take it). The situation, however, is not the same for a young, inexperienced actor who may feel pressurized to make similar sacrifices for a break-through part. No one should tell the actor what to eat or how he should eat.

Nudity

See Practical: *Nudity Guidelines for Film* (p. 258)

An actor can consider all of the above in relation to taking on a role that contains nudity. Careful research and preparation by the actor can help 'frame' in his mind any nudity that is required. He may be the only person in the company affected by this issue and, with, little to guide him, perspective is easily lost. It may help to imagine nudity as a character costume: costumes are not commonly used throughout the rehearsal process as they may get damaged. Damage to the actor should be equally unacceptable. There is rarely need for nudity in rehearsals; in fact it can get in the way of crafting a performance. There is, on film sets, a commonly used protocol (use of closed sets, clothed technical walkthrough, and so on) which can be transferred to theatre.

Personal Safety in Movement: Practicals[6]

Warm-up Principles

Take the play or film you are working on, or the meeting, or audition you are preparing for.

- Plan the amount of time you want to spend on this and find a space to work in.
- Pick out the general demands.
- Identify what you can explore, warm-up and make ready. For instance, if it is a physically creative and active situation you are going into then you might prepare so that you – and your body – are stretched and prepared to launch into fully committed physicality. However, in this situation a physical warm-up is probably going to be offered. If, on the other hand, you are going into an inactive situation (this includes interviews) you may feel that a physical warm-up is not required. In fact, the opposite is true. In this situation it is highly unlikely that a warm-up will be offered. So it comes down to you. Your preparation can be high-energy, physically explorative and expressive in order to enable you to inhabit your stillness with confidence and possibility.

In warming up your imaginative and physical connection to the world of the play and the character do something that:

- awakens the senses and evokes the feel of an environment:
- even something as simple as, for instance, taking a short walk through a tree lined avenue for Congreve's *Way of the World*.

---

[6]Ewan's process with the actors.

There are practicals and exercises offered throughout this book that involve and warm up the expression of the physical being. For instance, in relation to your character the following might work for you: Effort Weave, Solo Dance or an Animal Study. For working in relationship with others the following might be productive: Contact Improvisation, Explorations of the Space and so on.

- Reflect on and draw from the exercises you have gathered over your career to date.

A warm-up:

- connects you to breath and imagination;

- awakens all your muscles, including those of your face;

- makes your reach within your kinesphere available – particularly the side space for your arms and the space above your head;

- loosens up your spine and opens up your posture, particularly the area around the clavicle and the back of the neck;

- makes a range of energy available and gets your heart racing even if only for a short time;

- reminds you of your expressive range: gravity and lightness, power and softness, sudden and sustained and so on.

- As you gather new approaches to work, update the exercises that you use.

- As you take classes, continue to build a repertoire:
  when in a class if an exercise feels good for you, as a one-off,
  allow yourself to mentally shift from the class context as you do the
  exercise so that you can 'physically bank it' in your personal warm-up
  collection.

Working with Clothing, Set and Props

- Check for belt buckles, jewellery, things in pockets, sharp objects on you, the set or props, that could cause yourself or others injury.

- Know how revealing the costume is going to be.

- Understand how the clothing moves; how it may be exposing.

- Any clothes that have to be removed should be the clothes used in rehearsal whilst wearing a body suit underneath. This allows you to familiarize yourself with buttons, zips, and so on.

- Focus on the action and the quality of the movement.

- For falls or contact with props or set, consider padding underneath your costume from wardrobe. If out of the sightline, or if it can be disguised, the part of set or prop you make contact with can be padded.

- Consider the effect of a long run on yourself.

Staying Focused

You are working on a scene that involves violence or/and sex.

Research social context

- Research the gender discourse in the following areas: clothing, etiquette, social codes, family structure, work, dance, sport, eating, rituals, superstition and religion.

- What were the norms?

- What were the prevailing gender expectations at the time?

You can then question:

- Why is this part written as a female/male?

- How does gender affect her/his role in the piece?

- Does the character deviate from the expected roles of the time?

- What are the expected gender-based social responsibilities?

- What are the communication codes of flirting, relationships, fighting, emotion and linguistic patterning?

Locate the balance of power

There are countless motivations for sex or violence. This exploration is about finding the humanity in the intimacy or aggression. You can question:

- Who is in control? Find the political agenda of the depicted sex.

- What is the scene for? What does it express in the larger picture of the play?

- Where are the power shifts? How are they shifted?

- Are you evoking a given and particular image or are you reminded of one? Shift from self as much as possible.

- Take inspiration from other forms of art, such as paintings and sculpture.

- Use different 'Efforts' from your own. Offer yourself more freedom through utilizing a different way of moving, making it less exposing, less confusing and more empowering.

Listening to Your Instinctive Feelings

With work that is potentially unsafe:

- Listen to yourself. You can force yourself and shut down your feelings only to have them emerge later.

- You need to be open and in control.

- Become aware of your mindset before, your mindset during, and your mindset afterwards.

- What are you gearing up for? How secure are you feeling with this?

- Check whether this is 'to please the director', or to get it over with because you think it will make it easier next time.

- How much are you actually comfortable with?

- Can you identify when you feel comfortable? In other words, can you identify if you will still feel comfortable about this scene at a later date?

Looking to Fight Guidelines

If you have learnt stage combat, or are in the process of learning it, you may find it helpful when working on a sex scene to think about the guidelines that are applied to working on a fight scene (these apply equally to heightened moments of physical response, spontaneous physical outbursts, or violence).

Please note that the fight guidelines are offered here purely as a template, not as fight instruction.[7]

---

[7] Fight information supplied by Bret Yount.

Comparison with Fight Rules and their Translation where possible into Choreography Guidelines for Scenes containing Sex, or Violence[8]

A fight director is a legal requirement.[9] A qualified fight director is employed. He costs money. This calls into question the necessity of the fight within the play and accordingly its purpose is clarified and sharpened. Budgeting for a fight promotes deeper thought and the 'how far they will go' issue is examined and resolved.

Unlike a fight director, a movement coach is not a legal requirement. There is therefore no budget dilemma to throw the scene into question or to determine 'how far the actors will go'. While a movement coach should be employed, his qualifications are not specific, and sex or violence choreography may not be his field. So it may be that you have to look at the necessity of the nudity, sex, or violence. It is you as the actor who can clarify and sharpen their purpose by taking relevant and thought-provoking questions to the director for discussion before you take on the role.

Basic guidelines of fight choreography

If for some reason there is no fight director, the fight or stunt and its necessity to the production are reconsidered. If the storyline demands it, it is choreographed and structured in a way which renders it completely safe (for example, stylized, slow motion, and so on).

Working on a sex or violent scene

The option with a sex or violent scene like an unsupervised fight scene is to use stylized choreography – acting under bedclothes, slow-motion violence, symbolic referencing or imaginative representation – lighting design including use of shadow, sounds for association, and so on, and these can all sharpen the scene's meaning.

Set provisos early on

Agree limits of contact for both rehearsal and performance. The earlier you do this the better, as it will give you the confidence and security to get on and do your job – acting. Work out the timing of when the sex and nudity or violence is incorporated into the scene, including the technical and practical details of, for example, designating a crew member or stage manager for tasks such as holding a dressing gown ready at the side of the performance space.

Sightlines

The fight director checks sightlines, making himself aware of the angles that offer the appearance of contact without actual physical contact always having to be made.

Check sightlines

Have an awareness of the audience view of yourself. Have someone you trust check the sightlines from the audience for you so that you can feel secure in the knowledge of exactly what the audience can and can't see.

---

[8]There are no strict universal guidelines. These are to be understood only as helpful guidance to be considered and used as a prompt for defining your own context-specific code of conduct.
[9]Equity keeps a Register of Fight Directors who have been assessed to be safe and competent. There are others who may also be in training for the register who may also be considered safe and competent.

Economy of action

The action may be broken down into small units. Fight choreography is a physical dialogue which requires the same acting homework as verbal dialogue: backstory, acting beats, intentions, objectives of each beat, and so on. Story boarding the action as a series of stills might also be considered.

The actors are instructed to mark the distances for safety, ensuring that the distance is great enough that moves and actions cannot reach the partner unless specifically choreographed to do so. Knowing how far a punch reaches, for example, gives confidence that it is safe.

Halting the Action

The fight director puts in a strategy to halt the action. A simple, practical, non-emotional word is chosen. Normally a person who is concerned shouts a key word unconnected with the character so that it is clear it is outside of the action. A dry run is performed using it to stop the action so its use and effect are clear.

Victim Control

Fight choreography uses several different concepts to achieve safe yet dynamic fight action: this includes victim control, reversal of energy, non-contact strikes to the head region, contact strikes to the torso, and counter-balancing for falls.

'No Acting'

The actors do a 'No Acting' technical walk-through.

Intentions and Reactions

The actors focus on intentions and reactions, particularly highlighting pre- and post-action moments to heighten dynamics without compromising the safety of the action sequence.

Economy of action

A potentially emotional situation can be avoided if priority is given to technical rigour. The key points in the scene need establishing. Work the action without gratuitous, ornamental movements so that structure and basic storyline is clearly laid out. Use a heightened acting process: break down the action into small units, acting beats, intentions, objectives of each beat, and so on.

Mark violent moments through until you feel ready to start incorporating a level of emotion.

Halting the Action

Put in a strategy to halt the action. Never forget that you have the power to stop, even in rehearsal. Just knowing you can stop at any point without feeling bound to continue can offer you a sense of liberation and, most importantly, a sense of control.

Victim Control

From fight technique, transfer the principle that the person who is acting as if out of control is actually the actor in control of the physical interaction. Identify the weight placement, hold or manipulation in, for example, a manoeuvre onto a bed. The person controlling the move may not be the person who appears to be, for example, the one pushing the other onto the bed. In fact, the control can rest with the actor who looks like he is being pushed.

'No Acting'

Have a 'No Acting' technical walk-through with clothed surface-contact only or just mark violent moves.

Intentions and Reactions

Focus on the intentions and reactions. Particularly highlight pre- and post-action moments to allow the focus to be on the acting rather than relying heavily on the physical contact to tell the story.

Any part of the scene involving a high level of violence, such as in a rape scene, should in part be treated as a fight scene. The fight director is involved in the moves considered to be 'fight' and will bring a technical tone to the rehearsal that you can maintain on the sections in which he is not necessarily involved. The fight director should not be involved in the intimate contact side of a scene. This aspect involves expressive movement to tell the character's story. This should be choreographed by someone who has this area of physical expression as his specialism or, if there is no movement coach, by yourself or the director.

Say it in Words

- Have words and phrases ready, even rehearsed, so that you can articulate a request or an action or stop something happening whenever you want to.

- Avoid, as much as is possible, using colloquial names for body parts/sex acts both within the work and when you are discussing the work.

- When working on a scene using the process of breaking each moment into physical actions and movement qualities, ensure you say the words out loud, for example, 'I place my hand firmly on his left shoulder, then I kiss his neck slowly', and so on. This provides a safe, objective, professional structure while still seeming authentic to the 'outside eye'.

Nudity Guidelines for Film

The following is a checklist:[8]

1 The level of nudity must be agreed contractually before the shoot.

2 Scenes should be fully rehearsed prior to the shoot. Both the actor and the director should have the opportunity to change or finesse the approach and both should understand exactly how the scene will eventually play. This reassures the actor that the nudity is not gratuitous.

3 A certain amount of cover can be devised for vital areas. This may be managed with tape or with flesh-coloured underwear. The actor should have a chance to try out the arrangement before the shoot.

4 On the day of the shoot, the call sheet and stage entrances should be clearly marked with the term 'Closed Set'. This means no one will be allowed on set without permission from the director or assistant director.

[8]Checklist kindly supplied by Richard Whelan, a first assistant film director with extensive experience in major motion pictures.

5   The director and assistant director should decide exactly who needs to be on set during the filming process. A minimal 'closed set' crew would, for example, include director, director of photography, camera operator, focus puller, assistant director and script supervisor.

6   Robes should be worn until the camera rolls and put back on the moment the camera cuts. This allows the crew to make necessary adjustments without breaching established trust.

7   All viewing monitors (with the exception of the director's monitor) should be removed from the set.

8   Nude scenes are demanding, emotionally and technically, for everyone involved. Music or lighting can help maintain a relaxed atmosphere.

APPENDICES

Exercises[1]

The following are examples of the types of exercises that can be done in relation to other work for the actor, such as developing the sense of play through improvisation, devising, physical storytelling, explorations of body language, and so on.

Basic Exercises – Some Examples

Acknowledging Your Own Physical Past (p. 263)
Alignment of Feet: Neutral Stance (p. 264)
Rolling down the Spine (p. 265)
Rolling down the Spine: Straight Legs (p. 266)
Finding a Visceral Language (p. 267)
Partner Assisted Deep Stretches – Using a Partner's Relaxed Weight, No Hands (p. 267)
Jumping off the Wall (p. 268)
All Fours to Walking (p. 269)
Partner Assisted: All Fours to Walking (p. 269)
Partner Assisted: Rolling (p. 270)
Finding Flow from the Head (p. 271)
Isolations (p. 272)
Duo Work (p. 273)
Body Parts Leading (p. 273)
Creating a Fixed Point in the Space (p. 274)
Leg Slide with Sound (p. 275)
Jumps, Sounding the Breath on Landing (p. 275)
Curl-up (p. 276)
Rising and Rocking (p. 277)
Speed Skipping (p. 278)

---

[1] It is possible to pick out certain heritages for some of the exercises offered as they were originally encountered and learnt by the authors in their own backgrounds, but as to their actual origins, they are in most circumstances from interwoven sources. Some are of the authors' own devising.

Basic Partner Work – Some Examples

Swings – Some Examples

Hybrid Exercise – An Example

Trust/Risk – Some Examples

Space Exercises – Some Examples

Basic Exercises – Some Examples

Acknowledging Your Own Physical Past

Looking at your past relationship with a skill or practice
Start lightly with chatty type questions. You are not being asked to enter into therapy; keep the questions about the movement. The answer is in the way you see the movement technique you chose. This is maybe easier to do with a friend prompting you.

- Why as a child did you stay with a particular skill?
- What was it that enticed you to take it up in the first place? For instance, you might have wanted to do karate because you saw the film *Karate Kid.*
- What did you love about the skill?
- If you got stuck or gave up, what was it that got you stuck at a certain point?
- What didn't you like about the skill?
- What didn't you respond to?

The next stage of questions is geared to your present day relationship with that skill or practice. Ask yourself:

- What are the obstacles it presents to your acting?
- What is its effect on the way you breathe?
- What is its effect on your posture?
- What is the mindset/consciousness in the form?

Looking at a relationship with a skill or practice:

You can ask of any practice:

- What is useful to you as an actor?
- What is the essence of the work for you as an actor?
- How might it best be learnt by you as an actor?
- What are the difficulties/stumbling blocks both in the philosophy and in the application?

Self versus actor:

- Are you (unknowingly perhaps) in a battle with yourself and holding onto what you had, for example a particular regime for fitness?

- How much are you sacrificing of 'your thing' because of acting?

Escapism

- Is the practice, in fact, offering you an escape from acting?

- Is the practice offering you an escape from routine or from the responsibility of making decisions? Does it encourage you to switch off? Does it mean disassociating from your personal rhythm or from your personality?

- Are you forcing yourself to do it? Do you feel duty-bound to do it?

Ask whether you have chosen the practice with a view to 'improving yourself'. For instance, have you chosen yoga because it makes you feel calm, as well as fit?

Alignment of Feet: Neutral Stance

Stand with your legs straight and feet hip-width apart and in parallel so that the knees and ankles are underneath the hip-bones. This is neutral stance.

- Locate the hip-bones and then put 'bones over bones', stacking hips over knees over ankles.

- Use the inside line of the feet to find the straight direction of each foot and its parallel relationship to the other foot (the outside of the foot has a sloping row of toes that can be confusing to line up).

A simple test:

- Shut your eyes.

- Move into the 'neutral stance'.

- Try to sense exactly where the legs and feet are when standing hip-width apart.

Rolling down the Spine

▶ Partner Assisted Rolling down the Spine.

- Stand in neutral stance. Don't 'get in position' – the only things that are organized are your feet. Allow the rest of you to just be there. Breathe and engage with your own rhythm as it is today.

- Drop the head and roll down through the spine. Simply allow the weight of the head to do the work for you as it leads you down.

- Allow your breathing to happen through the whole body, helping you to experience a sense of your weight as you roll down.

- Allow your knees to bend, as the body folds the way it wants to.

- The chest ends on the thighs.

- Bring the overhanging shape of your body forward in space, by transferring your weight onto your knuckles through a gentle falling motion.

- Allow the heels to come off the floor as the weight transfers. Don't reach forward; just shift the weight onto the hands where they are. You are now on all fours with the weight on your knuckles letting your head hang free and almost making an inward roll with your body.

- Transfer – rock – the weight back onto the feet and roll back through the spine to upright. As you roll back up, feel the connection between the forehead and the pelvis as they realign in the vertical and balance themselves out. Don't let the ribcage flare open.

Key points

No stretching of muscles. Let gravity do the work. Be careful not to let the knees fall inward towards each other.

Rolling down the Spine: Straight Legs

▶ Rolling down the Spine with Straight Legs.

When doing a spine roll with bent legs, the whole body is working in a unified way with the legs being part of the expression of the whole body. In the following exercise, the legs take on the role of support distinct from the rest of the body. With practice, this muscular support is developed and consequently the upper body is liberated from any attempt to support the body, which may be its habit, and can take on the role of expression.

- Stand in neutral stance. Put your hands behind your head, lightly clasped, with your elbows out.

- Without pushing the ribcage out, allow the breath to move through the whole body.

On the first 16 counts:

- Bring the elbows in towards each other and let the weight of the hands on the back of the head pull you down.

- Keeping the legs straight throughout, exhale as you roll down; the hands remain lightly clasped behind the head throughout.

- The legs work to maintain the same position throughout, without swaying, pulling backwards, bending the knees or turning in.

- As you hang right over on the last counts, gently open the elbows again, taking a breath.

On the second 16 counts:

- Roll back up.

- Allow the elbows to open up softly as the upper part of your spine uncurls, arriving with an open chest and open gaze.

It is important that you make sure that the pelvis and legs are not shifting into back space. To do this you will find that you have to rotate the upper part of the leg to counteract the knees wanting to fall in towards each other. If you are maintaining the leg placement, you will see that the arches in the feet do not change, and you are able to maintain the position of the feet, with a triangle under the feet.

- Repeat another set: two sets of 16 counts.

- Repeat: four sets on eight counts.

- Repeat: four sets on four counts.

- Leave the arms hanging at the bottom on the last set of four counts.

- Repeat: eight sets on two counts, arms hanging loose for these.

- Repeat: eight sets on one count, arms hanging loose for these.

Doing the exercise on two- and one-counts acts as a test to feel and reveal to yourself at speed what you are actually doing on the slower movement sets. This fast movement should be no different from the 16-count part of the exercise. (A note of caution: work at this speed requires a developed physical awareness.)

- Finally, arrive and rise onto your toes and balance there, then lower the heels while still feeling the rise in the spine.

You can try this exercise with your back to a wall, the feet a couple of centimetres from the wall, to check whether your pelvis is moving backwards.

Finding a Visceral Language

When working though the body, a language relating to movement experience – a visceral language – starts to emerge and then become familiar. This practical is ongoing through your learning.

- Take a moment to acknowledge as many anatomical words as you know that conjure something real for you to work with.
- Find trigger words and images to connect to quality: fluid, liquid, pliable, empty, soft and elastic; sharp, firm, translucent are just some that may work for you – there are any number.
- Note down as many definitions of the words that get used as you can, for example rising and sinking (to do with weight) – what does sinking actually mean to you? Going downwards, going lower and lower, being pulled downwards, inevitably going down, going down under the surface, slowly dropping down, and so on?

Key point

If you don't relate to one word, there is another to which you will.

Partner Assisted Deep Stretches – Using a Partner's Relaxed Weight, No Hands

▶ Partner Assisted Deep Stretches.

It is very important to keep these stretches safe physically. The main safety rule is that the person giving weight never uses his hands. The person being stretched (see Partner A below) is always in charge. Keep any speaking to a minimum, so that the breathing can be heard, experienced.

Partner A

- Sit down, bringing the soles of the feel together, knees outward; make sure you are sitting firmly on the sit-bones. Curve your back over; allow stretch through relaxation on the outbreath.

Partner B

- Place yourself behind A, and, without using contact through the hands, establish a position against A that offers the right amount of your body weight for stretching A over his hips.

Adjust the amount of weight you offer by taking more or less weight through your hands placed on the floor.

You might, for example, be kneeling on one knee in line with person A's spine, or kneeling on both knees, torso squarely across partner A's back. You should be relaxed, using body weight and not strength or push or any sense of working.

Remind A to breathe and breathe with him.

Partner A

- Respond to B's body weight to stretch you in your posture – forward over your hips and on the out-breath release further into the stretch.

- Repeat with the same principles with your legs easily outstretched in front of you and then astride (not too wide).

- As a safety check at some point, without warning, sit up, gently throwing B off. This strategy is there to reassure you as you are being stretched that you are not trapped and are in charge, and that both of your bodies are listening to each other.

Key points

In the advanced alternative version, B can lie backwards over A, so that both receive a stretch. The focus is still on A.

Working with a partner over time, you discover whether more focus is needed on the upper or lower back, and so on, and you adjust the position to suit the stretch.

Jumping off the Wall

- Lie on your back on the floor with the feet parallel and flat on the wall and knees bent.

- Push into the wall with the feet and knees and use this to push away from the wall.

- Let the push propel you backwards, torpedo-like across the floor towards the centre of the room, and lift your arms up and back behind your head in the direction of sliding.

- Feel the sensation of the pull up though the front of the thighs, up across the front of the hips and into the torso.

- Feel the work that is going on with the feet and toes in the extremity of the push away from the wall.

Key points

Really engage with the pelvic tilt, the pull-up of thighs into the body. The movement is a muscular suspension through the lower body. The response is a muscular impulse and lengthening of the feet and powerful extension of the legs. Find the relationship of this exercise to *Rising and Rocking* and *Curl-up*.

All Fours to Walking[2]

On all fours:

- Swing the right leg forward, knee towards the chest, and notice the curve of the lower back.

- Swing the leg back freely – height is irrelevant – and then forwards again, but this time replace the right hand with the right foot, stepping onto this into upright.

- Take a step onto the left foot, transferring the weight sufficiently so that the ball of the right foot is on the floor poised to lift off it as though to walk, but arrest it at that point. Maintain this walk position to feel the residual sensation of both the impetus and the scoop movement of the pelvis that has powered you through, up and forward.

Partner Assisted: All Fours to Walking

See Practical: *All Fours to Walking* (above)

Work as partners A and B. Partner A stands by the side of B. Partner B is on all fours. Partner A is going to use the hand nearest B to do this exercise.

Partner A

- Keep one of your hands hovering over B's lumbar spine.

- Catch the momentum with your hand on B's lower back of B's second swing forward through to the step-through that brings him upright. It is as if your hand joins in with the scoop of the pelvis as the leg swings through in order to land the foot to walk. Try to have your fingers pointing downwards to the tail bone.

---

[2]See Bartenieff Fundamentals in I. Bartenieff and D. Lewis, *Body Movement – Coping with the Environment*, Philadelphia: Gordon and Breach, 1980.

- Try again if you 'missed' the moment. You will know when you have caught it, as will B. Momentum or propulsion from the base of the body is highlighted when caught accurately by the hand in contact with the back.
- Follow the momentum and breath and 'propel/push' your partner into the space.

Partner B

- Do the exercise as outlined above.
- Feel when the catch of the momentum is accurate – you will know when it is as you will be propelled forward by A's hand when you are upright.
- Follow the momentum from the hand as you move onto your feet and forward into the space. Let yourself experience being pushed into the space.

Partner Assisted: Rolling

This is a partner assisted exercise involving rolling down the length of the room – like a log (See Chapter 2, 'Practical: *Rolling*').

Partner A

- Start supine, arms above your shoulders on the floor.
- Initiate the rolling.
- Respond to B's hands as they guide either your hips when you are on your back or your shoulders when you are on your front.

Partner B

- Start kneeling close to A. Guide the initial arcing movement of the hip nearest to you and its landing on the floor on the other side with your hand, making sure then that once A is on his front, you grasp the shoulder nearest you as it lifts so that you capture the impetus of the shoulder circling over to the floor to the other side as A rolls on to his back, and so on as A's torso twists and moves sequentially during the continual rolling.
- Keep responding to A's movement. You might have to wait for the body to release into the twist and gently but firmly hold back either the hip or

the shoulder if either is anticipating the move rather than allowing the movement to be sequential, or initiating the movement when it is the role of the other to initiate.

- Stay close to A as he rolls so that you are not straining your shoulders. You need to work from your centre.

Finding Flow from the Head

This is a partner exercise (A and B) to release into free flow. Alternate roles.

Partner A

- As with 'Sticking' (see Chapter 2, Practical), listen and stay with – even be able to anticipate – the contact of B's hands that are always on your head and remain in contact as he moves through the space.

- Let your spine follow your head wherever it goes. Allow a pause to release and give the weight of your head to B's hands.

- Make sure that your legs, ankles and feet are released and pliable – that they are not shuffling or that you are falling into them.

- Let your body work as easily as it can – it may need to be very muscular at points, but keep that sense of free flow all the time.

Partner B

- Touch/hold A's head in stillness and then start moving your hand keeping in contact. The head is the whole head so contact with it can include the face.

- Move through the space together so that A is dancing with his body following the movement of his head and your hands.

- Change hands whenever you need to. You are not holding onto A's full weight otherwise the exercise would be inert. It is give and take between you but without you losing hold/contact. Make sure now and then to let the back of A's skull absolutely rest in your hands, waiting until B allows his head right back in your hands, and that you keep yourself released and grounded and breathing – particularly release your ankles so you can move fluidly in the space.

- Continue this for a while.

- Let A know that you are going to release his head with a clear physical signal and let go of his head.

Partner A

- Acknowledge B's removal of his hands and begin to move solo. Imagine strands emerging from your head and touching the walls, ceiling, floor, and so on, and however quickly you move your head, the crown of it always has attachments to a surface of support via these imaginary strands. You might think of this as the fast-paced orienteering version of 'braid to rafters', which is the image you have used earlier.

- Physically surrender and follow the head to realize off balance and balance.

Isolations

This exercise is a sequence of small movements for specific body parts, emphasising one side of the body, so can be repeated on the other side.

- Stand in neutral stance, facing front, with arms naturally hanging by your sides for the sequence.

- Incline your head to the right and return to vertical – imagine the vertical mid-line down the centre of your face and body, and then another separate vertical line just down the centre of your face. When the head is inclined towards the shoulder with the mask/face to the front, the mid-line of the face creates a clean angle with the mid-line of the whole body, and when the head returns to vertical the two lines coalesce. Find the timing of the inclination as you make the movement precise.

- Jut the chin forward and then back.

- Raise the left shoulder; lower the left shoulder.

- Rotate the right shoulder up and back and then up and forward. Return to neutral.

- Lift the sternum (chest) up and forwards and then back again cleanly, unbound though muscular.

- Twitch the right elbow outward to the side as though in reflex – as if nudging someone, 'Hey' – with the short arrival moment of the bent elbow creating a triangle with the sharp joint pointing to the side, before returning to the arm hanging by your side. The hand remains where it was when the arm was hanging normally, close to the thigh, as the elbow arcs forward.

- Bend your knees.

- Move your hips to the side (right), back, side (left), front, back, centre.
- Straighten your right knee; bend it again.
- Straighten both knees.
- Turn your left leg and foot out, keeping the hips to the front; return to parallel.
- Rise onto the balls of your feet, then lower your heels.
- Raise both shoulders, then lower.
- Raise the eyebrows, then lower.
- Nod your head and return to centre.

Key points

Remember that precision does not equal muscular tension.
Maintain alive stillness in the rest of the body; work for accuracy of the movement.

Duo Work

- Stand opposite a partner and go through this form, working as though each of you is the reflection of the other, and so working on opposite sides of the body.
- Alternate the sides of the body.
- Make sure you have an effective little loosening up exercise to do every now and then.

Body Parts Leading

In partners A and B. This is a crossing the floor exercise. One of you leads, one of you follows.

- Stand facing each other at one end of a room. A has his back to the space.

A (The Leader)

- Connect to a part of B's body by an imaginary thread about a metre long.
- Lead B around the space by this thread. Don't move so quickly that it prevents B finding some fluidity.

- Keep the thread long and make sure he can always see you.

- After a time, drop this thread and create another connected to another body part and so on.

- Have as much fun as possible (eg. taking B to the ground, or in circles, by the elbow, by the groin, by the ear) while B should remember it is A's turn next!

B (The Follower)

- Find, no matter what body part is leading, a fluidity and a natural way of moving as if this is the way you always move.

This exercise can also be done by responding to someone calling out different body parts for you to lead with as you cross the space.

Creating a Fixed Point in the Space

Use a wall to establish a fixed point.

- Stand far enough away from the wall to place a flat hand on it with an extended arm.

- Keep the flat of your hand against the wall.

- Take one step towards your hand and then step back to your original place.

- Repeat several times.

- Take note of the mechanics. What moves first? In what order do other parts move and how much?

- Now leave a 10cm gap between your hand and the wall.

- Repeat the move, maintaining the hand in space as a fixed point.

- Have someone watching, or film it.

- Note any movement in the fixed point or changes to the movement of the arm or stepping.

- Whenever you need to, go back to doing it with the wall.

- When you have mastered this movement maintaining the fixed point, repeat the process through a range of movements: rising up on your toes or even jumping and bending down; rotating your body towards the fixed arm and back out again, and so on.

Now repeat the whole exercise with a completely different part of the body that is fixed in the space.

Leg Slide with Sound

This is an exercise for integrating movement with the breath.

Part A

- Lie in supine.
- Breathe out and slide one heel on the floor back towards the sitting-bone.
- Breathe in, resting the leg in the posture it has arrived at.
- On the next out-breath, let the heel retrace the journey along the floor to extend the leg back out again; let the heel lead, but keep the foot relaxed.
- Rest in supine on the in-breath.
- On the out-breath, repeat the same pattern but with the other leg.
- Continue with alternate legs.
- Pay attention to the response of movement in the pelvis during the exercise.

Part B

- Now *sound* a 'sss' on each out-breath as you also move the leg. Marry the sound to the full length of the slide in towards the sitting-bone and out again.
- Repeat with the other leg.
- Pay attention to the sound of the breath's journey: you may arrive at the end of a leg-slide but with the out-breath still going on; or, conversely, run out of breath with the movement still going on.
- Make the sound, breath and movement one simultaneous experience.

Jumps, Sounding the Breath on Landing

- Move in the pattern: run, run, jump, land; run, run, jump, land…
- Make the jump as another step: so, take off from one leg and land on the other.
- Accept that as you land, you let out a sound, sort of punched out as you give in to gravity.
- Observe this in animal behaviour. This can of course include any pets you come across: a cat's landing from a high jump, or a dog when it jumps up to greet the owner often grunts upon landing.

Curl-up

- Lie supine with the legs and ankles together and straight, the feet relaxed and hands clasped behind your head with the elbows outward.

- Breathe out, consciously softening the chest; feel as though the sternum is sinking and hollowing; lengthen the back of the neck as you bring your chin towards your chest, keeping the shoulders down and calm.

- Let the elbows move toward each other at the same time as the chin comes towards the chest, all in response to the movement of the breath and the sternum. The elbows are not how you lift your head off the floor or move yourself into the curl-up of the upper body – they move simply and subtly on the wind of your breath. The curl-up is just to the shoulder blades which remain in the floor.

- At the same time, tilt the pelvis forward: scoop the tail bone towards your navel, and point the toes. Feel the abdomen as it becomes taut along with the thighs and the feet as the pelvis tilts.

- Breathe in, lower your head back down to the floor and lower your elbows towards the floor back to the start position. Find a moment of rest before the out-breath moves you into the next curl-up.

- Continue for up to ten repetitions.

Key points

The out-breath allows time to feel the power of the straight leg and the full stretch of feet. Think about how this can be transferred to work on your feet. (See Appendices: *Jumping off the Wall*; *Rising and Rocking*.)

Rising and Rocking[3]

This exercise uses heightened awareness of internal muscular engagement of the abdominal muscles and the corresponding subtle forward-tilt of the pelvis, which supports the balance. This can be felt even more clearly when the out-breath is sounded.

- Stand, keeping your legs straight in neutral stance throughout, with arms hanging down by your sides.

- Breathe out and rise onto the balls of your feet as high as you can.

---

[3] Derived from Dragon Stamping, from T'ai Chi warm-up work

At the same time, lengthen the fingers and thumb down towards the ground as though being gently pulled by somebody from below.

- Allow a 'ssss' sound to be strongly emitted as you rise up on the feet throughout the exhalation; feel the expiratory action assisted by the rectus abdominis muscle (all the abdominal muscles are recruited, but this is the easiest to feel).[4]

- Soften the lower front ribs gently down to the navel; let go of any tension in the chest – any muscular lifting. At the same time, widen your upper-middle back.

- Feel the sensation of the pressing/squeezing of the abdominal muscles towards the spine, downwards and deep into the pelvic region of the body.

- Allow yourself to listen to the feeling of muscularity which subtly tilts the pelvis forward as the out-breath continues. Draw from your experience of this in floor work; it is a transferable sensation (see Appendices: *Curl-up*).

- Come into balance.

- There is a sense of inner lift and of poise, as well as muscular strength and inner support, as you recruit the abs and pelvis at the height of the rise. The increased abdominal muscularity that occurs when supporting the end of your out-breath can be exploited as you balance in this rise.

- Feel the lengthening of your spine and breadth of your back as you balance (use 'braid to rafters' if this helps).

- Feel your in-breath begin its seamless takeover from the out-breath.

- As you continue to breathe in, lower your heels to the floor, keeping your height in your mind's eye.

- Allow the back of the ribs to widen and fill as you rock backwards on your heels.

- Balance on them, keeping yourself in an upright unit as you do so.

- On the out-breath, rock forward and rise onto the balls of your feet, and so on.

- Continue for a while, with and without sound.

- On the last rise, stay up on your toes and stay there breathing normally.

---

[4] The most familiar abdominal muscle: the long flat muscle that extends vertically between the pubis and fifth, sixth and seventh ribs divided lengthwise down the middle and horizontally by tendinous sheaths.

- Perhaps imagine yourself hanging as if from a clothes hanger, thereby allowing the weight of the body to drop down whilst knowing that you also possess height.

- Lower the heels and remain standing with a sense of your full height.

Key points

Note the intense physical experience of the pelvic tilt forward on the rise and the feeling of the abs working right to the end of the out-breath. These sensations and the extension of the thighs up into the torso, the lengthening of the legs and the stretching of the front of the ankles and metatarsals on the out-breath can all be related to the *Curl-up* and *Jumping off the Wall* exercises and vice versa.

Speed Skipping

Speed skipping is usually associated with the way a boxer skips. This can be a useful reference. You cannot learn to speed skip intensively. It requires steady and progressive practice over time.

- Locate an appropriate space to practise skipping for three-minute sessions. (With a short warm-up and stretch you are looking at six minutes in total.)

Preparation

- Adjust your rope to make it the right length for your height. It should be taut when you stand on the rope with both feet and hold the handles at hip height.
- Wear running trainers.
- Before each session, walk on your heels, pulling your toes up, and then on both sides of your feet, for at least two minutes. Although this is strangely ungainly, it is an effective preparation and guards against shin splints.
- Try to use your wrists and not your arms to turn the rope.
- Aim to skip from one foot to the other alternately at speed. Do not jump too high: the rope is only about 1cm thick.
- As a learning process, you can start two feet together for several jumps, going to hopping a few times on one foot before changing to the other, building to alternate feet at a fast yet comfortable speed.

- When you have mastered basic speed skipping from one foot to another, you can start playing with combinations of two feet to one foot, several on one foot and then on the other, two footed jumps with a double spin of the rope, crossing and uncrossing the rope while skipping without breaking the rhythm, travelling skipping and skipping in someone else's rope with them.

- If you trip the rope, don't stop the rhythm. Try to keep your feet going and get the rope turning on either side of you, holding both ends in one hand, and then simply get back into the rope.

- When you can skip, try to open up to the space, letting go of any sense of 'working' the action of skipping. Keep it relaxed, even at high tempo.

- Start building your stamina by playing with different rhythms and speeds.

- A three-minute timing sequence to help build stamina is:

  1 First minute: Normal tempo for 50 seconds and a ten-second sprint.

  2 Second minute: Normal tempo for 50 seconds and a ten-second sprint.

  3 Third minute: Normal tempo for 30 seconds, 20 seconds up tempo, and finish on a ten-second sprint.

- Try out different music to find what works for you. Lightness in the music can be an advantage.

- Conclude with some simple stretches: calf and hamstring.

It is important to note that it is better for the rope if you hang it up as often as possible, but it is best for you to have it with you as much as possible.

Key points

Ensure the legs are under you or in the front space – so not kicking up at the back. Stay close to the ground on the jump; don't think of it as jumping upwards but just keeping the footwork light and easy. Bend your knees only as much as you need to. Avoid bouncing between each jump.

Basic Partner Work – Some Examples

Back-to-Back Breathing

This is a partner exercise.

- Sit back-to-back with your partner, with legs bent up or outstretched, making sure your lower backs are together.

- Ensure you are comfortable; ask yourself what is needed to be more comfortable. For instance, is there too much weight against your back, making you lean forward over your legs? Do you need to assert more weight to find the particular balance for that partnership? Be like bookends.

- The aim is to sit and feel the support of your partner's back. Can you feel your partner's breath through your back? It may be that your height is similar, so that you also can lean the back of your heads together.

- As the exercise continues, allow yourself to follow the impulses of even the slightest movement through the contact with your partner's back/ spine, whilst sitting.

- Continue for up to ten minutes.

- Then take your time to separate from your partner.

- Thank your partner.

Key point

Work without expectation.

Stroking up the Spine

This exercise is done using a simple roll down the spine in partners A and B. It heightens your sensation of the two-way 'upness' and 'downness' of your standing posture.

Partner A

- Stand in neutral and bend your knees. Fold over at the waist to hang over your hips, the crown of the head dropping towards the floor. Make sure you are letting the head hang and the shoulders be calm in this posture. As you hang there, pay attention to your feet, making sure they are released and spreading; that they are really supporting you.

Partner B

- Stand behind A.
- Move your hands with long, easy strokes down A's spine from midway between the ears to the tip of the tail bone.
- Encourage A to slowly unroll the spine with the long strokes until A is standing upright.

Partner A

- 'Stack' the vertebrae up one-by-one from bottom to top, in response to B's touch.
- Find the sensation of 'pouring' yourself into your feet and sinking your weight downwards at the same time as rolling upwards through your spine.
- Respond to the strokes of B's hands to bring you to upright and let the knees straighten as you bring your head onto your neck.

Partner B

- Use little downwards strokes on the back of A's head and neck to encourage A into a final upright position.

Partner A

- Imagine the back of the head and neck being pulled upwards by a long plait of hair, as well as a sense of hanging downwards from its attachment to the ceiling, giving you a sense of rising up, while your feet are still rooted in the floor ('braid to rafters').
- Think about your feet and how your body weight is distributed – you want to make sure that you are standing perpendicular to the floor and ceiling with two-thirds of the weight at the front of your feet between the little and big toe joints and a third in the heel.

Partner B

- Give A the sense of upness-and-downness by stroking simultaneously in the two directions with each hand: upwards from the mid-shoulder blades to the top of the head and continuing the stroke above the head with one hand (you can enhance this sensation by pulling A's hair up on the way too) and downwards from the mid-back down to the lumbar spine and tail bone.

- Find your own way to finish this assisted roll-up; for instance, stroke down from the shoulders and finally gently pull the fingers down towards the floor, stroking right off the ends of the fingers.

- Leave A in the space and move to the side of the room to observe.

Partner A

- Stay in the upright position.

- Pay attention to what is happening in your body.

- Take yourself into a walk and notice how you are and if anything feels different.

Key points

Make sure the feet are absolutely rooted into the ground during uncurling to standing upright; pay attention to the spine and its alignment; listen to the sensation of up-and-down as guided by the hands stroking your back.

Container and Fluid

This exercise involves partner work and can run for up to five minutes per role. It works with and without music. Partner A (Fluid) sits in between the legs of Partner B (Container). Use a cushion/pillow between you for added support and to take away some of the intimacy of sitting in another person's lap or having another person in your lap.

Partner A

- Sit with your legs easily outstretched and astride or cross-legged, in B's legs.

- Let go of the top half of the body and head.

Partner B

- Sit with your legs astride and, unless flexible and strong enough to be unsupported in the centre of the room, with back against the wall for support.

- Support A with your arms, legs and body.

- Push and support and nudge and sway A by holding/squeezing his arms with your upper arms, or use your hands or legs or torso and body weight to manoeuvre him; involve your whole body in the role even though sitting down.

Partner A

- As you move imagine that you fill up the whole of the space of the container you are sitting in, flowing into any interstices. Find moments of draping your body over B's supporting body – arm, shoulder or leg – in surrender, lying back with throat exposed, with that sense of continual pouring happening in every movement and even in stillness.

Key points

Fluid needs to keep upright on the pelvis, and renegotiate the position if sliding onto the tail bone and therefore half lying backwards against Container. Container is involved with total listening to Fluid's movement and momentum from body weight and its release, as well as 'playing' the manoeuvring from personal movement resource and impulse. It is important to note that intimate contact can provoke embarrassment, discomfort and even fear.

Counterweight Exercise: Smelling the Rose

Variation one

The in-breath within the work of suspension – the rising in preparation for falling – is no gasp of breath but an elastic, malleable, prolonged inflation of the inside of your body that expands you from the inside out and creates space and mobility. To feel the in-breath as inhalation takes conscious practice – breathing in per se requires none, as it is a reflex.

- Experience the in-breath as a soft inflation or expansion of your upper-middle back and back of the ribs that circle round to the front.
- Notice the breath radiating out from the sternum along the curves of each clavicle to the shoulders, filling your armpits and then suspending and prolonging itself.

Stand opposite a partner and using one arm cross-link wrists.

- Pull away and then use the impetus to come upright on the in-breath and release each other's wrist.
- Circle this arm above your head and backwards, inhaling as if trying

to squeeze out the last trace of scent from something as lovely as a perfumed rose.

- Breathe out and let the other arm come from underneath, from down by the hip, up to horizontal and your partner's wrist.

- Grasp it just at the point when if you did not to do so, you would fall backwards. Let your body weight drop back into the first counterweighted posture. Find the physical give and yield and elasticity rather than tense muscular holding.

- Continue rising and falling, listening to the breath pattern between you.

Variation two

Partner A

- Walk towards B as you control his descent to sitting and lying, keeping hold of his wrist so that you can pull him up again and you become the partner who sits and lies down.

- Walk alongside B as B lies down, the same side as B's lifted arm, and release the arm for a beat and then recapture it, as you go back past and move into counterweight movement so that B can take you to the floor.

- Release the arm and walk forwards and around B's head as he lies down, and then backwards down B's other side, and gather/take up the other arm with your opposite arm, and go into counterweight with the other arm.

- Use the rise, suspension and fall of your breath in the walking next to or round B.

- Improvise on all these: seesawing; counterweight work; suspension and fall.

Partner B

- Proceed as above.

Key points

This is tiring to do for any length of time as it is heavy thigh work. Its look belies it, as it seems lightweight to the viewer.

50/50

This is an exercise involving a partner.

- Create a point of contact with your partner (back to back, shoulder to shoulder, head to head, leg to back – the options are endless).
- Give weight equally to each other, and then create a movement dialogue, making sure that the weight exchange is 50/50.
- What the dialogue is depends on the manner of the touch/contact and the weight exchange between the two partners and the relationship with the floor as the third partner.

Key points

Here are three rules that can be set/be useful for Contact Improvisation work: respect yourself and your partner; take responsibility for the self; listen – to yourself, each other and what you are being asked to do.

Full-bodied Weight

This is an exercise involving partners: A and B. Start by facing each other with both hands up and press the flats of your hands together so that you are in hand-to-hand contact and allow yourself to move into an A frame shape together so that you can:

- Explore working with full-bodied weight in partnership.
- Play around with that full-bodied experience of hand-to-hand contact which may take you into leaning against your partner's hands until you reach 'deadlock' or weight stalemate of 50/50 with your bodies in that diagonal of an A frame. Allow this strong weighted contact to move your whole body through the space. Do this for a while.
- Submit to the full weight you have available and, therefore, use the energy and power/force that this body weight gives you when you commit to it.
- Ask yourself if you are allowing your personal full weightedness; are you utilizing it?

You can now work with hand to body. (Do this in stages with A as 'hand' and B as support for several balances. Swap over, alternate being hand then support on each balance and then move into an improvisation). Dare to fall onto the support. The next stage is body to body.

- Notice to whom you feel you can give your whole weight and others to whom you feel you cannot.

- Negotiate strong weighted push with your partner and with whomever you're working with next, and so on.

- Are you offering support, as well as softening into and using the support?

Experiencing Light Touch

This is an exercise involving a partner. Maintaining contact throughout, stand opposite your partner and bring the flats of your hands together.

- Use a 'light touch', with your fingertips hardly touching. Allow yourself to move from the impulses and shifts of the fingers and hand-to-hand contact and move through the space with the quality of the touch between your hands moving you through the space.

Light and strong

- Create an interplay of strong-weighted and light-weighted contact, and mirror the quality of the touch of your hands through your whole body as you move with your partner through the working space.

Contact Improvisation: Rolling Points

This is an exercise involving partners: A and B.

- Start with your heads back to back.

- Gently roll your heads side to side, exploring the rolling points of the contact between your heads – the point of contact around which you roll.

- Continue in an improvisation.

Next:

- Start back to back.

- Find the rolling points of the contact between your shoulder girdles.

- Improvise.

Next:

- Start back to back.
- Find the rolling points of the contact between your pelvises.
- Improvise.

Next:

- Then improvise with the combination of the rolling points: head, shoulder girdle and hip girdle.

Swings – Some Examples

Building a Swing

- Stand in a relaxed position, maybe even with weight into one hip.
- Start from 'nothing'. Simply connect to a personal memory of the sensation of a swing. Register this in one arm.
- Take the time it takes for you to recall the feeling of the drop, the swing, the suspension.
- Allow a very small movement in an arm or a hand, evoking and, therefore, allowing you to experience, quietly to yourself, the remembered sensation.
- Which bit of the swing do you enjoy most?
- What part of it do you immediately connect to: the drop, the swing or the suspension?
- When you find yourself connecting to the movement, expand to a full swing.
- Feel the breath becoming part of the movement and let it take over.
- There will be a point when you feel ready to take it into a fuller swing.
- Without interrupting the flow, gently shift into neutral stance so that you let the legs join in and power the swing.

Swings (Wheel Plane)

- Stand in neutral.
- Raise your arms up in front of you in a soft line of high diagonal forward, from your ankles to beyond your fingertips, but not lifting the shoulders

out of their sockets (this is not a 'shaped' position, just a place to move from).

- Follow the line into the space with your gaze.

- From here, let your weight fall down: release the breath, let your torso and head drop and your arms swing right down and behind you, allowing your fingertips to brush the floor in the swing.

- Use the momentum to go up again, but before that enjoy the miniscule moment of suspense here as your body changes direction; the momentum and out-breath.

- Swing your back upright.

- The legs bend and straighten on the way down, and bend and straighten again on the way up, so each journey has a small lift, a rebound, in the legs.

- Don't 'place' your body or hold it at any point; let the movement happen as a consequence of dropping the weight, dropping the hips, like a live pendulum (with a hiccup).

Paddle-Swings

▶ Swings.

- Stand in parallel, feet slightly wider than normal. The arms are raised above and to the right of the head, both palms facing outward, gaze directed at the back of the hands.

- Keep the arms straight; drop the weight of the arms, letting them fall down to the diagonal in parallel.

- You are beginning to create a figure of eight with your arms made of two parallel circles, one at either side of the body.

- Place your arms straight in front of you, parallel to each other.

- From here, begin by sweeping both arms backwards to the left side of the head, then let them fall forward in a circle and swing up in a circle on the right side of the body. Continue the swing: experience the rhythm – up–down–up – as you swing your arms in parallel.

- You are drawing two parallel circles, like wheels on either side of you whose edges just touch at the centre-line of the body. It is almost a sense of paddling.

- You are scything through the air, slicing circles. Allow the corresponding breath to happen, and allow the knees to soften as the breath escapes and the weight drops.

- After a while the rhythm of the swing shifts the whole body, so that as the swing sweeps forward and down, you move the leg backwards out of the way of the swing.

- You will begin to hear the rhythm of the swing being punctuated by the sweep of the foot moving backwards and the beat of the heel landing down.

Key points

In this exercise the upper body twists as a consequence of the swings, but the hips remain parallel and in the centre line.

Oppositional Arm Swings

▶ Swings.

- Start in a low ski-sit position, legs parallel, spine horizontal to the floor in table plane, one arm forward and one arm back. The face and eyes look forward, and that gaze is maintained throughout.

- The movement starts in the pelvis: drop the pelvis, let the knees bend and the arms drop, allowing the arms to swing to the opposite position.

- As they arrive at their opposite positions, the momentum lifts you and your feet are almost elevated.

- You may even jump here, but this should only happen as a consequence of doing the exercise, through the use of weight and dropping the pelvis in the exercise.

- Drop in this way on six counts. During the seventh swing, allow the arms to continue the journey of a full circle all the way over the top, straightening out the knees and torso; complete a second full circle as the eighth swing starts and arrive from there at the beginning position to start again, reversing the direction of the arms.

In relation to rhythm, the accent is on the down-beat, when your pelvis drops and your breath releases.

Windmill Arms

▶ Windmill Arms.

- Stand in parallel in a low skiing position, hips tilted, strong legs, knees pointing forward and aligned over the toes, arms hanging loose.

- Begin by moving the hips in a loose figure of eight. Allow this to be a bit messy, like a child having a tantrum, feeling your arms move and swing as a consequence of the movement in the lower spine.

- Now let the arms move in a forward windmill motion, keeping them extended (but not stretched) right through the fingers and allowing them to take up their full length. The arms are moving not from the shoulders but deep from the base of the back; allow them to 'speak' from the kidney, the gut, the heart and lungs. The movement is initiated in the hips so that it runs through the whole body; the arms are more or less thrown forward by the movement of the rest of the body.

- Keep the rhythm of the windmill uneven, as otherwise the legs pump the rhythm and the arms join in/follow suit – allow the hips to dictate an uneven (jazz) rhythm. Let the feet push into the floor as though they are in wet cement.

- The general shape is of the back making a high diagonal forward, your neck in line with your back. Your gaze falls down and forward out of this in a low diagonal.

Lunge Swing

This is an additional swing exercise drawn from T'ai Chi warm-up practice. It is for the individual and the individual within a group.

- Stand in a lunge position with the left leg forward with toes pointing straight forward and the right leg behind, hip-width distance apart from the left, with the toes turned out to not more than one o'clock on a clockface. (This is called the bow and arrow position and perhaps you can think of it as a warrior stance.) Knees are bent throughout and aligned over the middle of the feet in the still, starting posture with two-thirds of the weight in the front (left) leg. The belly may want to face slightly to the diagonal because of the turned out back leg, so endeavour to keep your hips square to the front. Your intention is forward, through the belly and front knee and middle of the foot. You are in a position of real turn out or openness of the hips.

- Keep upright as you transfer the weight from the front foot to the back foot. Perhaps think of this rocking forward and back as swinging under the floor in an arc from under the back foot to under the front foot.

- Let the arms swing forwards and backwards with the momentum of the rocking. Let the arms feel long and loose.

- The movement is triggered from the centre of your belly; the tail bone is dropped down. Feel as though you are hanging down from the ceiling even while you are powering the rocking from the belly and correspondingly from your feet maintaining the triangles under both the front and particularly the back foot.

- Imagine you have a huge beacon of light at your belly which is shining way out into the distance and would be what was seen should there be anyone on the horizon looking in your direction.

- Really have a sense of the width of your belly, the width of the inner thighs and groin, making sure that your buttocks and ankles are released, so that your pelvis can keep dropping down, between and at the centre of your legs, so you are really in balance – perhaps thinking of the tail bone as a thick reptilian tail dropping downward and then behind you might help. Having the pelvis – sacrum and tail bone – at the centre of your legs may sound so obvious anatomically, but knowing that the work has come from self-defence may make the instruction make more sense – you need to be ready to move anywhere at the drop of a hat and leaving your pelvis behind you will slow you down, pull you back, or make you stumble forward out of balance.

- Because of the repetition of the movement in this stable posture, take the opportunity to explore the sense of rootedness in your feet. Explore the work going on in them to shift or even bounce the weight from front to back foot as you keep the intention in your belly.

- Keep your upper body relaxed: chest, shoulders, neck and jaw, for instance.

- Continue for up to five minutes at a steady rhythm, or you can accelerate and let your body adapt to the fast tempo then decelerate and make the appropriate adaptations in your embodiment of this slowed down version. Ask yourself what you need to do physically in either of these extremes of tempo. Finish at a regular tempo.

- Stop on a swing forward and rhythmically step the front leg (at this point, the left leg) back to five to one on the clockface, with the feet, that is the heels, together, toes turned out slightly. Get ready to transfer

into it and empty the right leg, and step into the forward lunge position
and begin transferring the weight between your feet once more.

Low Lunge Swings on the Diagonal

▶ Swings.

- Start in a deep lunge to the diagonal, right leg forward, placing your
  right hand on the bend of the leg.

- To begin with, just bend the front leg all the way into the lunge and
  straighten all the way back up, to get a sense of that motion. The back
  leg remains straight. The free arm drops and swings forward every time
  the leg bends into the lunge, with the fingertips brushing the ground.

- During this, the hip over the bent leg is facing in the direction of
  the throw while the back leg is open/turned out (not a position that
  stretches the calf).

- Repeat this four times as a preparation for the 'throw', building the
  commitment, psyching up to throw, becoming familiar with the diagonal
  line through space that you are going to throw into or along.

- After four times, this drop of the arm turns into a proper throwing
  motion, which then makes a full circle over the top of the shoulder: the
  lunge becomes really deep, allowing the torso to lie horizontal to the
  ground, all the way down on the thigh in the front, and then to shift
  back past the centre line as the arm moves to the top of the overarm
  circle and back.

- The arm that is throwing remains extended and the fingers open; the
  gaze follows the ball of energy which you are throwing along an endless
  expanse of floor.

- The breath is expelled with every 'throw'; the throw is a very powerful,
  energetic movement. Let the movement move you. Again, there is no
  'shaping' in this motion: allow yourself to be moved by the momentum.
  Don't be tempted to 'dance' this by turning it into an 'arabesque' or
  indulging in 'épaulement'.

- Repeat the throw eight times; on the eighth, pull in the front leg and
  drop the arm to arrive upright with the feet together, then drop down
  into the lunge with the other leg to start again.

Leg Swings

This is a role reversal of legs and upper body. The upper body is strong and open, the torso and core are in charge and are the support, and the moving leg is free.

- Stretch the arms out to the side, hands open and palms facing forward, feeling the line from your fingers connecting you through the space and right through the walls of the room.

- In preparation, take one leg slightly back. From here you swing/throw your loose leg forward as high as it will go without collapsing in the upper body. Then let the leg fall and swing through to the back, brushing the ground, free to swing all the way to the back as high as it will go without the torso tipping forward. As you swing the leg, it should be only slightly turned out, and the supporting leg remains straight.

- Swing seven times, and advance one step on eight. The upper body commits to this shift, advancing your whole presence forward.

- Repeat on the other side.

- The legs are free to swing, and should be a challenge for your upper body; almost throw your legs, destabilizing your torso. It is great to make visible the chaos in this, the conflict between the control on top and the revolution below.

- As you move forward in the door plane, experience the space in front and behind. Perhaps imagine that the space in front of you is one colour and the space behind you is another; as you advance you are bringing a different colour across the full width with you; you are bringing the sea in with you as you push the air forward; if in a group, you are an army and are an advancing wall, and so on. You may want to imagine you are wearing a tall hat, or are attached by strands to the ceiling, to help you extend into the space above your head as well as widthways.

Swing, Stab, Release

▶ Swing, Stab, Release.

- Stand in neutral stance.

- Raise your arms up in front of you, so that they are extended in a high forward diagonal. There is a soft line from ankles to wrists. Follow the line with your gaze beyond the wrists into space. Your shoulders should not be lifted. This is not a 'shaped' position; it is an active place in itself.

- Swing: release the breath as you fall forward in one piece from the hips. Fall as much as you can risk falling, and then save yourself by the interruption of a full swing: by your knees bending; the head dropping; the body following the curve; the hands brushing past the floor; and the arms swinging right behind you, with your chest to your thighs. Don't worry if you involuntarily shift forward in a small jump in order to allow the experience of the fall to happen.

- Use the momentum to swing you back up to the first position – the high diagonal forward. Enjoy the miniscule moment of suspense in the swing as your body changes direction. The legs bend on the way down and straighten at the back of the swing, and bend and straighten again on the way up, so each journey has a small lift and rebound in the legs.

- Stab: you have arrived back at the high diagonal where you started. From there, with a rush of exhaled breath, you contract – tucking the pelvis under, bending the knees, the head tucking onto the chest and arms brought in. The elbows are pulled in to the stomach, the hands are in fists. The shoulders are over the hips, creating a strong enclosed position. Your weight is in the centre, going down through the ground.

- Release this punctuated movement. The body unfurls; the arms uncurl as though there is no gravity, extending until you reach and return to the first high diagonal again.

- All parts of the body, including the eye focus, are in unison with the release upwards and outwards.

- From here you can start again.

Key points

Really allow yourself to fall; the swing – stab – release exercise is done to 4/4 tempo, which means it has a specific time form in which it fits.

Hybrid Exercise – An Example

Side Stretch Hybrid

▶ Side Stretch Breakdown.

- Stand in a wide position with the feet astride and turned out; legs deeply bent so that the thighs are parallel to the ground and the pelvis is dropped. The knees must stay over the toes through a combination of rotating the upper legs back in the hips and the positioning of the feet. The torso sits easily between the legs; the body is open; and the arms reach out to the sides at shoulder height with the palms of the hands facing forwards.

- Lunge and reach to the right side and maintain the low and open position facing the front. The face turns towards the direction you are lunging in. The legs drive the lunge to the side, the torso taking it that little extra bit further, with the arms remaining at shoulder height.

- Shift, lunge and reach in one movement over to the left side. This is motivated as though reaching for something which is out of reach.

- Do this eight times in total.

- On the eighth lunge (which will be towards the left), realign the head with the spine to face the front. Stay in the lunge, now in the door plane. Adjust the torso to the side diagonal high. The right arm drops while the left arm rises onto the diagonal line of the right leg.

- Lift the right arm as well, so that both arms are above the head, parallel to one another on the diagonal. Create a small shift to let the torso become the extended diagonal line of the right leg.

- Drop the left arm down in front of the left knee and foot, placing the hand on the ground, shifting the extended leg into a deeper lunge, creating a new diagonal from the right foot through the hip, along the ribcage and the fingertips of the right hand. The left arm can maintain the open positioning of the leg by gently pushing against the knee.

- Lift the left arm back up, using your core to lift yourself back to the diagonal extension where the torso and arms in parallel are in line with the right leg.

- Turn your hips towards the left, ensuring you realign the back foot. Maintain the lunge on the left leg as you do this, reaching both arms upwards to keep the high diagonal. The eyeline is a low diagonal.

- Launch into the table plane: transfer the weight fully onto the left leg, lifting the right leg upwards so that arms, spine, head and leg are in line.

- Rotate 360 degrees in four counts by pivoting on the foot. (The experience of this is an echo of life: the wobbles and off-balances that occur are the embodied sensations of the drama of life. There should be no embarrassment at this.)

- Lower your back leg all the way back down, resulting in a deep lunge stretch. Lower your arms to place both hands on the ground parallel with the inside of the front foot (or, for a deeper stretch, place the lower arms onto the ground). The back leg is straight, and the upper back curves so that the head tucks in to look at your back foot. (This is the first curve in the spine in this exercise.) Stay here for a stretch.

- From here, in one shift of the whole body over four counts:

- Straighten out the head, extend the arms, taking weight into the hands, and simultaneously move the left foot out to join the right foot so that both legs are extended and you are in a 'push-up' ('plank') position.

- Do a four-count press-up; the nose touches the floor. If you can't do a full press-up, slowly lower yourself all the way to the ground (instead of pushing back up), putting the hips on the floor, bring the knees sideways through sitting and then put the legs back out into the press-up position.

- After one press-up, extend your left arm across your body underneath you as you begin to lower. Let this take you into a roll: soften the left shoulder-blade into the ground, and then release both shoulder-blades into the floor, allowing the head to release onto the ground, so that you end up on your back.

- On your back, move into 'the foetus position': bring your bent legs up above your hips at 90 degrees, crossing the ankles, and your arms above your shoulders also at 90 degrees, keeping them soft. Lift the head between the arms, curving the upper back off the floor. Use your abdominal muscles, but stay soft through the rest of the body. There may be a slight tremor that you feel shouldn't be there. Keep the shaking soft; practise letting it be there and accepting it as a quality.

- The legs and arms very slowly extend from here and then open length-wise towards the floor, opening like a flower. Aim for your hands to touch the floor above the head and your feet to touch the floor at the length of the legs at exactly the same time.

- Engage your core muscles, and the right leg and the right shoulder now tip you over to roll onto your front, arms bent, hands under your shoulders; imagine lying under the sand in a vast desert.

- The crown of the head comes up as you breathe in for four counts. Imagine the warm sand running down the back of the head and spine, as the arms and hands organize themselves to push up into a 'sphinx'. Keep the back of the neck connected to the spine. The elbows stay bent so that the shoulders remain open and don't get pushed up into the ears. The gaze extends far into the distance, taking in the periphery as well.

- Turn the head from facing the front to look over the shoulder on an out-breath for four counts, and then once more back towards the front for four counts on an in-breath. Repeat to the other side and back to centre. The eyes stay in the head, looking long distance without blinking.

- Lower back down to the ground on an out-breath.

- On four counts, come back up into the sphinx, do a 'Cheshire-cat' wide-mouthed grin, and expel breath with a threatening hiss, which extends evenly over four counts without a crescendo, pressing equally both in front and behind. Then lower the back down to the ground.

- Like a little caterpillar, lift the pelvis backwards out of the floor with a tiny 'eeh' sound. Try to experience the lightest movement you can imagine while moving the largest muscle in the body.

- Fold your pelvis backwards onto the heels, arms extended in front, and forehead resting into the ground. (This is similar to the 'folding leaf' for those who do yoga.)

- Initiate this movement from the base of the spine. The base of the spine draws you back. The arms turn outward with the back of the hands curved naturally onto the floor as you move back to sit on your heels, shoulders over the hips, hands resting on your knees, palms facing upwards, and the head dropped forward so that you are sitting in a curved shape – in the wheel plane.

- Feel the dynamic of the invisible wheel that your body is making – you can make the movement of a forward turning wheel with your arms. Once you have the sensation of that motion, you shift the weight onto the hands on the floor in front of you momentarily, and then back onto the feet (which find parallel). Leaving the head dropped, you proceed to uncurl through the spine to upright standing.

- Stand. Feel the space; all 360 degrees of your kinesphere; the space all around you. Extend all of your senses into the space, and wait.

- The tutor or another actor shouts 'Ha!' (or, you can imagine it). This is an outcome of being ready, alert and in the now. Your response to the sound is reflexive; you would be ready to go at any moment. 'Alive stillness.'

- Respond immediately with your own voiced 'Ha!' This is a jump with a quarter or half turn into a deep, wide open, low position: legs facing outwards, knees bent, arms wide. Then bring the arms in as if to cuddle a baby. This is an expansive, warm, loud, strong, open movement, holding no tension, but with the urgency and softness of catching a falling baby.

- From here, you repeat the whole series to the other side.

Key points

Rather than thinking of left and right, where possible establish a front and make your choice of direction in relation to that. The general rule is to move away from any audience first so that you 'return' to the audience later in the form. Try it: position your body in profile to the audience and experience turning both directions. Which one offers the movement to the audience and which one takes it away?

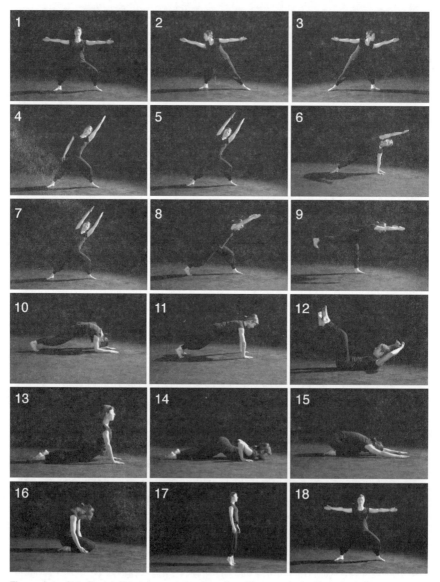

Figure A.1 Side Stretch Breakdown. Actor: Nina Fog. Photographs by Todd Padwick.

Trust/Risk – Some Examples

Preparation for Falling

This is a sideways knee roll – as an example (see also Chapter 2, Practical: *Rolling*). You are practising, in this simple roll, landing on the firm and soft parts of your body, not the bones. There should be no sound of crashing or banging the bones.

- Start kneeling, sitting on your heels.
- Lower your torso over your knees and bring your upper left arm and elbow across the front of the body and curl your body over to the left, taking your outer upper arm and side of your thigh to the floor.
- Roll across your back and onto your knees, keeping your buttocks close to your feet, making sure you release your neck and head.
- Roll to the other side.
- Now, stay on your knees but come right up on them so you are high with the thighs vertical and fall downward from here buttock to heels and roll over your side and back as before.
- Let your neck release, with the back of the head free to roll on the floor.
- Unfold to upright once you are back on your knees and build up through the spine with your head, arriving last on the top of your spine.
- Continue rolling and find the breath of the fall, the rise and the suspension before the next fall.

Partner Falling

With a partner:

- Stand close to a partner.
- Work together, with one of you falling into the other's body to be caught and supported.

Key points

This experience is intimate and particular to each partnership. It enables confidence in working with body weight as preparation for further free-form Contact Improvisation (CI) work.

Falling in a Group of Three

This is a commonly practised exercise, but one that endlessly offers valuable experience if committed to.

- Three of you form a line, with the two end people, the Catchers, facing into the middle person, the Faller, and all equidistant.
- The middle person falls forwards or backwards to start, focusing on keeping yourself in one unit, keeping tension as much as possible out of the ankles as you sway and fall forwards and backwards.
- As the end person, you catch the Faller when he is falling towards you and push him towards the Catcher opposite.
- Your focus as Catcher is to allow and receive the fall, to rescue the Faller, taking the weight of the falling middle person into your body and gently, using this momentum, push him forwards (from your perspective) into the hands and the body of the Catcher at the opposite end of the line.
- Find the breath of the arc of the suspension/rise and falling. Keep listening to the rhythm you are creating between you.
- The pushing and receiving continues between you.
- You change roles after an agreed length of time, and each take it in turn to become the Faller to experience the fall.

Key points

The Faller maintains vertical alignment: the distance apart need only be small, but it is important to allow the Faller to truly fall and not be guided or controlled into the Catcher's hands. The rhythm is particular to the group when listening to each other is the focus.

Trust/Risk for Group of Four: Throw Head Backwards

Identify a Diver, a Catcher and two Holders: the Catcher stands behind to catch the back of the head of the Diver and the Holders stand on either side and a little to the front of the Diver to hold the Diver's wrists.

The Diver

- Stand in place, with the others positioned around you.
- Throw and arc the top of your head back, as if diving backwards off a

diving board, with a real sense of jumping upwards and backwards like a whale throwing itself out of the sea, keeping your feet on the ground in a wide position with arms outwards and forwards and firmly held by the Holders.

- As you dive backwards, keep your pelvis lifted as in limbo dancing, knees bent.
- Have about four dives.

Catcher

- Catch the Diver's head in the palm of your hands, and then softly, elastically, push it and the Diver upright once more.
- Make sure that you do allow the Diver's head to fall into your hands.
- Gauge how near or far from the floor your hands can be for catching by really tuning in to the Diver.

All

- Swap roles.

Key points

This demands group attention and is an exercise that offers a bit of fear, with adrenalin flowing. Also note the quality of suspension and fall.

The Catcher and Holders need to allow the Diver to fall.

Space Exercises – Some Examples

Marking the Kinesphere

▶ Marking the Kinesphere.

- Start in parallel.
- Start with only the arms; the feet stay planted in a wide parallel. The knees stay pliant, and the torso follows the arms.
- With one arm at a time, reach to a point in space.
- Then reach to another point.
- Then, to another.
- Be specific. Take your whole attention to the one point.

- Test out how far you can reach into your kinesphere as you touch these pinpoints in the space.

- Use the whole space, 360 degrees, low and high, diagonal, front, back, sides, and above you, including crossing the body.

- Leave one foot at your fixed centre-point and lunge into the space with the free leg to enable you to reach further out in the space with your hand.

- Return to centre between every extension into the space.

- Now using the legs instead of the arms, do the same thing, and use the arms and the movement in the supporting leg to help you maintain your balance adding support as needed with a hand on the ground.

- Let your body solve the problems and counterbalance, or maybe even revolve out a potential or real fall. Include high and low levels.

Additional to the Dimensional Scale

Explore the planes within your kinesphere.

- Start the scale with both arms and whichever leg you like.

- Stop when you are in that vertical line.

- Envisage it as a plane in space that you are in, the space on either side of your height.

- Think of this plane as the door plane and just let yourself be in this plane.

- Explore the 'door' whilst maintaining the geometry – you as/in one plane – its corners high and deep. You can sweep through the plane with your arms or point out points on it.

- Lie down and explore the door plane.

- Bring yourself back onto your feet and continue with a door-plane shape exploration.

- Move yourself and the shapes in the general space in the door plane.

- Continue with the scale.

- Repeat with lateral/horizontal as the table plane, remembering that you can rotate around yourself here too and irrespective of the height level.

- Continue with the scale.

- Repeat with sagittal as the wheel plane.

Additional to the Diagonal Scale

Work in partners: exchanging the roles of Catcher and Faller the diagonals can be experienced to physical extreme.

- Identify the Catcher and the Faller.

Faller

- Step into the high diagonal. Trust the catcher will catch you, so take this as far as you can and although you are going to fall downwards with gravity, keep the imagination travelling up 'alongwards' on that diagonal.
- Allow yourself to embody that high diagonal even as you are caught at the last possible moment by the Catcher.
- Step into a deep diagonal – you are falling downwards with gravity, but keep the imagination travelling down along that diagonal. Think of the lines as infinite in the space.
- Allow yourself to embody that deep diagonal even as you are caught at the last possible moment by the Catcher.
- And so on.
- Take a turn as the Catcher.

Catcher

- Find your own way to contact and catch the Faller at the last possible moment (experience of Contact Improvisation (CI) helps here).
- Take a turn as the Faller

After the Partner work

- Re-do the Diagonal Scale alone, allowing the residual sensation and memory of falling to enhance the off-balance and risk element of the scale.
- Let the experience ignite the form with danger.
- Find the full extent of the dynamic impetus of the scale.

Running Round the World

Imagine that you are circumnavigating the world:

- Run in a large circle, facing outward, your back toward the inside of the circle, leading with the inside shoulder and that side of the body.

- On the inside of the circle that you make behind your back is the world, warmth and everything that supports you. On the outside is the universe, endlessness.

Additional to Running Round the World – Bird Circling

- Begin to follow a spiral pathway inwards, until you arrive at the centre of your spiral, on one bent leg, as the rest of the body is lifted in the table plane; supported by a thermal wind or a cloud, you gaze down over the landscape, experiencing the breath and air as one. There are no rigid or placed straight lines here and the supporting leg and the other leg and arms remain pliant.

- Now lower yourself down to earth, bending your supporting leg further, and your back leg lets you into a roll on your back across the tops of the trees.

- Continue rolling, out to the edge of the space (when the space is free someone else takes over). As you are rolling it should feel as though you are taking all that air and space from the whole journey with you. Ensure that you let your head gently yield to the floor.

Linear/Circular Pathways

This is an exercise for the individual within a group.

- Walk in the space, using all the space, without stopping. Avoid walking in a circle. Walk without agenda, with no sense of improvising.

- If you are doing this in a group, resist falling into a group rhythm: stop, close your eyes and remember your own pace, step length, and so on. Open your eyes and walk again with your own dynamic.

- Now change to walking in straight lines with hard corners and take on board the feeling this gives you. Over a period of several minutes let these straight lines and hard corners become a formulated plan in your mind, for instance, 'I am going to walk to the middle of the room, turn right halfway across the room and then turn left ...'

- Now, keeping the same energy and commitment, lose the straight lines and the hard corners, keeping walking.

- Without stopping, touch the ground with parts of your body other than your feet; still with no straight lines, no hard corners.

- Go back to straight lines and hard corners for a short time.

- Then back to meandering (without straight lines and hard corners), introducing moments of crawling or rolling as part of touching the ground with parts of your body. Don't let it become a 'dance'. It is still 'walking' – just on different levels with different ways of travelling, different points of contact.

- Keep moving without straight lines and hard corners, reducing the size of the available group space and expanding the size of the group space.

- Gradually and slowly come to a stop.

Acknowledge the difference between the two ways of moving; one dependent on making plans and the other in the present tense, not planning but dealing with life as it happens.

Direct and Indirect in Conversation

This is just one example of a studio exercise. With a partner, do the exercise in each of the following pairs:

Both A and B *direct*;
A *indirect* with B *direct*;
B *indirect* with A *direct*;
Both A and B *indirect*.

- Choose a subject to talk about together that can be both everyday and weighty. For example, fish.

- Have a conversation. Keep it as intellectual transfer and non-emotional.

- Both parties must be engaged in communication throughout.

- Be as *direct* as you can be when you are *direct*. Include your eye focus' – don't even blink. Square up your body but without tensing up – keep open. Be as *indirect* as you can be when you are *indirect*. Include lack of eye focus.

- You may do this standing up or sitting down.

- Note your findings. Register the personality and status you have automatically taken on.

- Carry on with the conversation. Engage with the *direct* and *indirect* as both dominant and submissive characters, and explore what types of personality emerge.

- Note your findings.

- Register your personal reaction to *direct* and *indirect*. Identify any struggle you have with being *direct* or *indirect*.

- Keep an open mind. Two *indirects* can have a conversation.

- Observe this in people around you in everyday life.

Key points

In this exercise, whether you are *direct* or *indirect*, you must positively engage in the conversation. *Direct* easily becomes bossy, and *indirect* ineffectual. However, it is important to explore the opposite possibility as well, so play with *indirect* being the protagonist.

BIBLIOGRAPHY

Recommended Reading

Ackroyd, P. (2000). *London: A Biography*. London: Vintage.

Arbeau, T. (1967). *Orchesography.* New York: Dover Publications.

Bainbridge Cohen, B. (1993). *Sensing, Feeling and Action.* Northampton, MA: Contact Editions.

Barker, C. (2010). *Theatre Games: A New Approach to Drama Training*. London: Methuen Drama.

Bausch, P. (2012). *Le sacre du printemps* [DVD]. Tanztheater Wuppertal. Paris: L'Arche.

Berger J. (1972). *Ways of Seeing.* Harmondsworth: Penguin.

Bogart, A. and Landau, T. (2005). *The Viewpoints Book: A Practical Guide to Viewpoints and Composition.* New York: Theatre Communications Group.

Bradley, K. (2009). *Rudolf Laban*. London and New York: Routledge.

Brook, P. (2008). *The Empty Space.* London: Penguin.

Calais-Germain, B. and Lamotte, A. (2008). *Anatomy of Movement.* Seattle: Eastland Press.

Caldarone, M. and Lloyd-Williams, M. L. (2004). *Actions: The Actor's Thesaurus*. London: Nick Hern.

Chekhov, M. (2002). *To The Actor*. London: Routledge.

Cheng, M. (2008). *Cheng Tzu's Thirteen Treatises on T'ai Chi Ch'uan*. Translated by M. Hennessy. Berkeley, CA: Blue Snake Books.

Clark, A. (2002). *T'ai Chi: A Practical Approach to the Ancient Chinese Movement for Health and Well-being*. London: Harper Collins.

Damasio, A. (2000). *The Feeling of What Happens: Body, Emotion and the Making of Consciousness.* London: Vintage.

Darwin, C. (1965). *The Expression of the Emotions in Men and Animals.* Chicago: University of Chicago Press.

Dennis, A. (2002). *The Articulate Body: The Physical Training of the Actor*. London: Nick Hern.

Feldenkrais, M. (1980). *Awareness Through Movement: Health Exercises for Personal Growth*. London: Penguin.

Goethe, J. (2006). *Theory of Colours*. Mineola, NY: Dover Publications Inc.

Grant's Atlas of Anatomy (2012). Philadelphia: Lippincott Williams & Wilkins.

Hackney P. (2002). *Making Connections: Total Body Integration Through Bartenieff Fundamentals*. London and New York: Routledge.

Humphrey, D. (1959). *The Art of Making Dances*. New York: Rinehart.

Iyengar, B. K. S. (1998). *Light on Pranayama*. New York: Crossroad Publishing Co.

Jarman, D. (1995). *Chrome*. New York: Vintage.

Jenkins, R. (1988). *Acrobats of the Soul*. New York: Theatre Communications Group.

Johnstone, K. (2007). *Impro: Improvisation and the Theatre*. London: Methuen Drama.

Kemp, R. (2012). *Embodied Acting: What Neuroscience Tells Us About Acting*. London and New York: Routledge.

Laban, R. (1984). *A Vision of Dynamic Space*. Edited by L. Ullman. London: Laban archives in association with Falmer.

—(1988). *The Mastery of Movement*. Edited by L. Ullman. Plymouth: Northcote House.

Lecoq, J. (2006). *Theatre of Movement and Gesture*. Edited by D. Bradby. London and New York: Routledge.

Mamet, D. (1998). *True and False: Heresy and Common Sense for the Actor*. London: Faber.

Marshall, L. (2008). *The Body Speaks*. 2nd edn. London: Methuen Drama.

Newlove, J. (1993). *Laban for Actors and Dancers: Putting Laban's Movement Theory into Practice: A Step-by-Step Guide*. London: Nick Hern.

—(2004). *Laban For All*. London: Nick Hern.

Novack, C. J. (1990). *Sharing the Dance: Contact Improvisation and American Culture*. Madison: University of Wisconsin Press.

Olsen, A. (2004). *Body Stories: A Guide to Experiential Anatomy*. Lebanon, NH: University Press of New England.

Paxton, S. (1975).'Contact Improvisation'. *Drama Review* 19(1): 40–2.

Pepys, S. (2003). *The Diary of Samuel Pepys: A Selection*. London: Penguin.

Pisk, L. (1975). *The Actor and His Body*. London: Harrap.

Preston-Dunlop, V. and Ann-Sayers, L., eds (2010). *The Dynamic Body in Space: Exploring and Developing Rudolf Laban's Ideas for the 21st Century – (Presentations for the Laban International Conference 2008…Laban Conservatoire of Music and Dance London)*. Southwold: Dance Books Ltd.

Roth, G. (1995). *Maps to Ecstasy*. London: Thorsons.

Siler, B. and Turlington, C. (2000). *The Pilates Body*. New York: Random House.

Stanislavsky, K. (1980). *An Actor Prepares*. London: Eyre Methuen.

—(2008). *My Life in Art*. Translated by J. Benedetti. London: Routledge.

Suzuki, T. (1986). *The Way of Acting: The Theatre Writings of Tadashi Suzuki*. New York: Theatre Communications Group.

Tanizaki, J. (2001). *In Praise of Shadows*. London: Vintage Classics.

Todd, M. (1980). *The Thinking Body*. Princeton, NJ: Princeton Book Co.

Tufnell, M. and Crickmay, C. (1993). *Body, Space, Image*. London: Virago.

Van Kooten, V. (2000). *From Inside Out, Book 11 (A Yoga Notebook)*. Bristol: Ganesha Press.

Wangh, S. (2000). *An Acrobat of the Heart*. New York: Vintage.

Zinder, D. (2009). *Body, Voice, Imagination: Image Work Training and the Chekhov Technique*. 2nd edn. New York: Routledge.

Extended Reading

Johnson, M. (2007). *The Meaning of the Body*. Chicago: University of Chicago Press.

Lakoff, G. and Johnson, M. (1999). *Philosophy in the Flesh*. New York: Basic.

Ree, J. (2000). *I See a Voice: A Philosophical History of Language*. London: Flamingo.

Zarrilli, P., ed. (2002). *Acting (Re)Considered: A Theoretical and Practical Guide*. London: Routledge.

Ethics

Alexandrowicz, C. (2012). 'Pretty/sexy: impacts of the sexualisation of young women on theatre pedagogy'. *Theatre, Dance and Performance Training* 3(3): 288–301.

Cohen, R. and Calleri, J. (2009). *Acting Professionally: Raw Facts About Careers in Acting*. 7th edn, Basingstoke: Palgrave Macmillan (see nudity in auditions at 58 and 202).

Equity – on actor nudity – 1980's rules.

Seton, M. C. (2010). 'The ethics of embodiment: actor training and habitual vulnerability'. *Performing Ethos* 1(1).

LIST OF PRACTICALS

In the order they appear in the book

1st page number is of the expo each one is cited in.

(I used the expo citing the practical – and the 2nd number is from the See Practical numbers.)

LIST OF VIDEO EXERCISES

To view a particular video, please visit its URL below, or go to https://vimeo.com/channels/actormovement.

INDEX